THE INTERNET SUPPLY CHAIN

The Internet Supply Chain

Impact on Accounting and Logistics

Dimitris N. Chorafas

palgrave

First published 2001 by
PALGRAVE
Houndmills, Basingstoke, Hampshire RG21 6XS and
175 Fifth Avenue, New York, N.Y. 10010
Companies and representatives throughout the world

PALGRAVE is the new global academic imprint of
St. Martin's Press LLC Scholarly and Reference Division and
Palgrave Publishers Ltd (formerly Macmillan Press Ltd).

ISBN 0–333–94963–3

This book is printed on paper suitable for recycling and
made from fully managed and sustained forest sources.

A catalogue record for this book is available
from the British Library.

Library of Congress Cataloging-in-Publication Data
Chorafas, Dimitris N.
    The Internet supply chain: impact on accounting and logistics/
    Dimitris N. Chorafas.
        p. cm.
    Includes bibliographical references and index.
    ISBN 0–333–94963–3 (cloth)
    1. Electronic commerce.   2. Business logistics—Automation.
    3. Accounting.   I. Title.

    HF5548.32 .C478 2001
    658—dc21
                                                        2001027366

10 9 8 7 6 5 4 3 2 1
10 09 08 07 06 05 04 03 02 01

Printed and bound in Great Britain by
Antony Rowe Ltd, Chippenham, Wiltshire

This publication is designed to provide accurate and authoritative
information in regard to the subject matter covered. It is sold with the
understanding that the author and the publishers are not engaged in
rendering legal, accounting or other professional services.

Contents

List of Tables

List of Figures

Preface

The purpose of this book is to examine the issues, prospects and benefits from Internet supply chains. The second major objective is to bring to the reader's attention the impact real-time supply chain solutions have on accounting and logistics. The text offers many examples of successful Internet supply chain implementations, both through co-operative efforts and by means of a lone wolf strategy.

The book considers the challenges companies face in implementing an Internet supply chain. These relate to the fact that the rapid advancement of technology and of Internet commerce in a globalised market brought a wave of change at a rate which has been unprecedented. As a result, credit institutions, manufacturing, merchandising and service companies are finding that their traditional methods and tools for accounting and logistics no longer suffice. They must now develop more efficient processes, which are able to:

- ensure management control in real-time;
- promote transparency in accounts; and
- make possible immediate corrective action.

This is a 'need to know' book which explains, and documents, why the effective management of change is a prime responsibility of every member of the Board of Directors, of every chief executive officer (CEO), of every chief financial officer (CFO), of every controller, and of every chief technology officer (CTO), as well as of their immediate assistants, and also of many other members of the management team.

Senior executives *need to know* how to position their company against the forces of the twenty-first century. To help in this mission, this book focuses on the most significant developments taking place in the market, their impact on the accounting and finance function, and how new technology currently coming into the mainstream would change commerce. Many experts believe this will happen the way Henry Ford's assembly line radically altered manufacturing nearly a century ago. Characteristics of our epoch are:

- far-reaching supply chain issues which influence practically every firm;
- the impact of globalisation on markets, costs and the bottom line;
- new types of reliable managerial and financial reporting;
- better control over logistics through real-time accounting; and
- continuous auditing made possible through technology.

Based on an extensive research project in the USA, Britain, Germany, France, Austria, Switzerland and Sweden, this book explains what can be expected in business opportunities and in cost savings from selling and purchasing online through the Internet. It also discusses value differentiation through new technology.

The text outlines the reasons why Internet commerce must be examined from the perspective of each company's business challenges. It suggests there is a synergy between trading on the Web and dynamic business partnerships. It also underlines top management's accountability for being ahead of the curve in the major changes taking place in the first decade of the new century.

Change in the landscape of accounting can take many forms: first and foremost is adaptation to evolving reliable financial reporting. Accounting is, after all, the most basic information system of any company. But the accounting practices themselves must also become more efficient through real-time bookkeeping, faster turnaround, less paperwork, lower error rates, better information services, and a rapid visualisation of results. The need for timely and accurate management of change is the message Chapter 1 brings to the reader.

As Chapter 2 documents, professional people should adapt to the forces of Internet commerce and to online supply chain challenges. New priorities always impact on accounting procedures and standards. The text brings to the reader's attention the reasons why not just accounting and logistics, but every profession, must take advantage of technology.

Chapter 3 elaborates on the concepts underpinning restructuring of the supply chain, as old economy companies form vast partnerships to take advantage of business-to-business (B2B) deals on the Internet, and compete with new economy companies. Alert management is keen to capitalise on the forces of Internet commerce, as the GM/Ford/DaimlerChrysler/Renault-Nissan example, and so many other recent cases, document.

The goal of such partnerships is to reduce costs by 10–15 per cent through online issuance and execution of purchasing orders. To face this challenge, survivor companies will have to thoroughly revamp their policies, the structure of their accounting systems and the way they manage logistics. It is projected that by 2002 every company worth talking about will be connected to the Internet. The leaders are already there. Chapter 4 outlines the lone wolf strategy of General Electric. It also brings to the reader's attention congestion problems connected with Internet commerce and trucking service exchanges.

The subject of Chapter 5 is *selling*. I have chosen selling banking services as the main topic. Online banking presents both opportunities and risks. It also has consequences for the institution's accounting system. For any practical purpose, the business of banking is *buying and selling time*. That is what banks do when they take deposits and give loans, when they make investments, and when they engage in derivatives trading, whether for interest rates, currency exchange or for other deals.

Chapter 6 concentrates on the importance of rigorous organisational solutions. A basic fact which the Board, CEO, CFO, CTO and their assistants must appreciate is that all by itself technology will not bring to their company all the success in the world. But at the same time, failure to adapt to and adopt high technology can be fatal. To the reader, this statement should not be a surprise. The impact of technology at large on the economy, and most particularly of the Internet, is global, and so is the aftermath.

Chapter 7 presents a bird's-eye view of the reasons why globalisation poses major problems in the interface between *legislation* and *taxation*. These are augmented by cross-border networking which bypasses national legislation, regulation and taxation. Today's legal framework is fully incompatible on a global basis, and it cannot act as a system. The bits and pieces that seem to converge rest on one of more of three criteria:

- residence of the seller;
- residence of the buyer; and
- type of commerce.

Type of commerce is the most difficult to handle in an Internet sense, but this does not mean that issues connected to the residence of the seller and of the buyer are easy to define. The member states of the Organisation for Economic Co-operation and Development (OECD) have been working since 1997 on these criteria and have found them elusive. The type of commerce on the Web is steadily changing. As for residence of the seller, a crucial notion is that of a *stable establishment* (SE). The text explains the difficulties involved in defining the word 'stable' in Internet commerce.

Getting our company ready for the shifts in market power, in legislation and in taxation is not an option but a duty, as Chapter 8 explains. The senior management of companies should try to read the future, and be keen to capitalise on the relationship between technology strategy, business opportunity, competitiveness, efficiency and financial performance. What really matters most in the forward-looking management of investments is insight and foresight:

- in all business sectors, *insight* is at the heart of the rise of technological entrepreneurism;
- *foresight* makes the difference between dynamic firms poised for survival and those losing their clout.

Capitalising on these concepts, Chapter 9 provides a wealth of examples in logistics. We should be always keen to learn from the best companies in the industry. The text also includes some of the problems the larger organisations come up against when trying to master sprawling logistics problems, and it concludes with the need to establish boundary conditions. There are limits to any system, whether natural or man-made. People and companies who benefit the most from new technology are those able to:

- rethink their business;
- reinvent their strategies;
- redefine their policies;
- empower their human capital; and
- revamp their information resources.

Patterns must be developed and visualised but, as Chapter 10 brings to the reader's attention, without high speed filtering the information base will remain weak, contain lots of noise, and be neither accurate nor comprehensive. This is true in all organisations, whether civilian or military, and it poses complex software requirements including the need for analytics and for simulation studies.

The last chapter of this book addresses itself to some of the operational risks associated with Internet supply chain solutions, privacy and security being at the top of the list. As Chapter 11 points out, new legislation is coming onstream for the protection of the consumer, but technical solutions regarding security are still wanting because crooks are so inventive and, in a surprising number of cases, they are equipped with the best technology can offer.

In conclusion, nobody in any business can or should be under any illusion that the road ahead is hazard-free. This principle evidently applies to Internet commerce, supplier partnerships, management information, new accounting tools and control over logistics. Market power is one of the most basic conditions for innovation, but *if* we want to benefit, *then* we have to get ready to face the challenges which come with it. This book says not only *why* but also *how* we can get ready to benefit from business opportunities of the twenty-first century.

Valmer and Vitznau   DIMITRIS N. CHORAFAS

Acknowledgements

I am indebted to a long list of knowledgeable people, and of organisations, for their contribution to the research which made this book feasible, and also to several senior executives and experts for constructive criticism during the preparation of the manuscript. The complete list of the cognisant executives and organisations who participated to this research appears at the end of this book.

Let me take this opportunity to thank Stephen Rutt and Zelah Pengilley for suggesting this project and seeing it all the way to publication, and Keith Povey and Gail Sheffield for the editing work. To Eva-Maria Binder goes the credit for compiling the research results, typing the text, and making the camera-ready artwork and index.

*   *   *

The author and publishers are grateful to Swiss Re for permission to reproduce copyright material in the form of Figures 1.2, 1.3, 2.1 and 2.3.

List of Abbreviations

ACM   Association for Computing Machinery
AFOC   Association Force Ouvrière Consommateurs
ALM   Assets and Liabilities Management
AMA   American Management Association
ARPA   Advanced Research Projects Agency
ATMs   Automatic Teller Machines
auto-ID   automatic identification
B2B   business-to-business
B2C   business-to-consumer
B&N   Barnes & Noble
BIS   Bank for International Settlements
B/S   balance sheet
C2B   Consumer-to-Business
C2C   Consumer-to-Consumer
CA   Certification Authority
CAFE   Conditional Access for Europe
CED   California Environmental Dialogue
CEO   Chief Executive Officer
CMF   Corporate Memory Facility
CFO   Chief Financial Officer
CTO   Chief Technology Officer
EDI   Electronic Document Interchange
EFT   Electronic Funds Transfer
ePC   Electronic Product Code
ERP   Enterprise Resource Planning
FCC   Federal Communications Commission
FDIC   Federal Deposit Insurance Corporation
FFR   Fast Flow Replenishment
FTC   Federal Trade Commission
G10   Group of 10
GDP   Gross Domestic Product
GE   General Electric
GMCF   Global Mobile Commerce Forum
GUI   Graphic User Interface
HOTs   High-Occupancy Toll Lanes

HOV	High-Occupancy Vehicle
IAMIS	Internal Accounting Management Information System
I-commerce	Internet commerce
IIA	Institute of Internal Auditors
IPOs	Initial Public Offers
IRS	Internal Revenue Service
ISP	Internet Service Provider
IT	Information Technology
JAR	Java Archive
JIT	Just in Time
JND	Just Note Difference
M&A	mergers and acquisitions
MEMS	Microelectromechanical System
NASD	National Association of Securities Dealers
NIST	National Institute for Standards and Technology
OCC	Office of the Comptroller of the Currency
OECD	Organisation for Economic Co-operation and Development
OTS	Office of Thrift Supervision
P&L	Profit and Loss
PE	Price:earnings
PINs	Personal Identification Numbers
POS	Point-of-Sale
PTTs	Post Telephone and Telegraph (formerly nationalised authorities, now telcos and post offices)
QOS	Quality-of-Service
R&D	Research and Development
REITs	Real Estate Investment Trusts
RF	Radio Frequency
RFQ	Request for Quotation
ROI	Return on Investment
SE	Stable Establishment
SEC	Securities and Exchange Commission
SEMPER	Secure Electronic Marketplace for Europe
SEPP	Secure Electronic Payment Protocol
SET	Secure Electronic Transactions
SOSCARD	Secure Operating System Smart Card

STRGL	Statement of Total Recognised Gains and Losses
STT	Secure Transaction Technology
TPS	Terabit per Second
UPC	Universal Product Code
VAT	Value-Added Tax
WAP	Wireless Applications Protocol
WIM	Wireless Identification Module
WYSIWYG	What You See Is What You Get
Y2K	Year 2000

Part 1

Developments in the Global Economy which Affect our Daily Business

1 Membership of the Board of Directors is Indivisible from the Management of Change

1 INTRODUCTION

Three and a half decades ago, in the mid-1960s, I carried out a study with the American Management Association (AMA) published under the title *Developing the International Executive* (New York, 1967). Litton Industries was one of the companies participating in this research; it was a highly decentralised conglomerate whose chief executive officer (CEO) purposely kept the headquarters staff down to two dozen professionals. These were highly qualified people for whom the CEO had defined the prime mission as being *the management of change*.

In the year 2001, in the Internet age, the management of change is more important than ever. The Net destroys corporate pricing power and turns many other principles of governance on their head.

For a conscious being, and for a well-managed company, to exist is to change; to change is both to *mature* and to become *more efficient*. Life is a matter of time rather than space. In fact, as Dr Charles P. Steinmetz once said: 'Time and space exist only as far as things or events fill them.' They are forms of perception which lead dynamic entities to choose:

- change rather than position; and
- quality rather than quantity.

The New Economy is the economy of change. Under the impact of change, business life is much more than a redistribution of matter and motion; it is a flexible and fluid continuous creation. Yet change does not come easily in industrial and financial organisations because people feel comfortable with what they know. They have learned how to carry out their daily routines and prefer to keep things that way, rather than turn their beliefs and their knowledge upside down.

3

Change involves unknowns and as new situations develop people always ask: 'What is in it for me?' Leo Tolstoy made the penetrating statement that most men he knew, including those at ease with problems of the greatest complexity, can seldom accept even the simplest and most obvious truth if it is such as would oblige them to admit the falsity of conclusions which they have:

- delighted in explaining to colleagues;
- proudly taught to others; and
- woven, thread by thread, into the fabric of their lives.

But change is unavoidable. '*Ta panta ri*' (everything changes) said an ancient Greek sage. A study done by the National Association of Securities Dealers (NASD) in the early 1990s in Silicon Valley, where most of its mighty clients are located, came to the conclusion that, to survive, a high-tech company must reinvent itself every 3½ years. A decade down the line, this has become 2½ years. Other estimates indicate that the average technology (not high-tech) becomes obsolete in 5–7 years, while electronic components and advanced systems become obsolete in just 2–3 years.

The able management of change is, therefore, a prime responsibility of every member of the Board of Directors, of every CEO, every CTO, every CFO, and every controller. This is a *need to know* book which focuses on developments taking place right now because of the Internet and its supply chain, as well as their impact on accounting and logistics. To introduce the concepts underpinning these developments properly, let us return to the fundamentals.

2   THE ROLE OF SENIOR EXECUTIVES IN THE MANAGEMENT OF CHANGE

Human know-how, therefore the technology which we use in our daily business and in our life, can get out of tune. In the late 1980s a study by First Wachovia, an American bank in the mid-Atlantic states, documented that if not steadily trained a banker loses 50 per cent of his skill in 5 years. Another study which I did quite recently came to the conclusion that, without lifelong learning, professions in rapid development, like that of technologists, lose 50 per cent of their skill in less than 3 years.

Since change affects so deeply the profitability and survival of an organisation, somebody has to be in charge of its management, and that is the Board. But to manage change in an able manner, and steer the company forward, the directors must have access both to a mechanism which helps them do so in a proactive way and a reliable feedback providing intelligence on everything that moves and everything that does not move. Such feedback is part and parcel of the flexibility and adaptation which must be shown by any profession. That is why a first-class internal control system (see Chapter 6) is the cornerstone of the management of change (D.N. Chorafas, *Implementing and Auditing the Internal Control System*, Macmillan – now Palgrave, London, 2001). Basically, internal control serves as the organisation's feedback channel, and this is a steady progress. Improvements in feedback are necessary to ensure the company's arteries are not clogged.

That is where the management of change comes in. Internal control is a concept and a process whose responsibilities lie squarely on the shoulders of the chairman, the Board members and the CEO. As Figure 1.1 demonstrates, internal control, auditing, accounting and risk management have common parts, but they are also characterised by critical functions distinct from one another.

As a feedback process, internal control needs guidelines on what to look out for, as well as tools. One of the basic means at its disposal is auditing. Is the main theme of an auditing mission technology? If yes, what is the state of the art the Board, CEO, CTO, CFO and the auditors should be aiming for? (See also in Chapter 2 the developments on the Internet which should attract top management's attention; and in Part 2 breakthroughs in logistics as well as issues concerning taxation in Internet commerce.)

There are, however, some issues which cannot be audited in the classical quantitative sense because they are largely qualitative. In this case, internal control needs other, more subjective, means to distinguish reckless levels and the merely undocumented from a correct approach to product and market challenges. A good example is the role which the Board and CEO should play in managing change because of deregulation and globalisation of business activities.

Globalised markets offer greater business opportunities than those protected through national borders or regional conventions, but they also incorporate a greater amount of risk. Every entity – be it a company, an industry or a state – has its own reasons why it wants to benefit from globalisation, which is sometimes pushed upon it through exogenous factors. For instance, in connection with insurance, Swiss Re says that these can be grouped into two large categories:

- *push factors* energised by foreign insurers' motives; and
- *pull factors* originating in emerging markets.

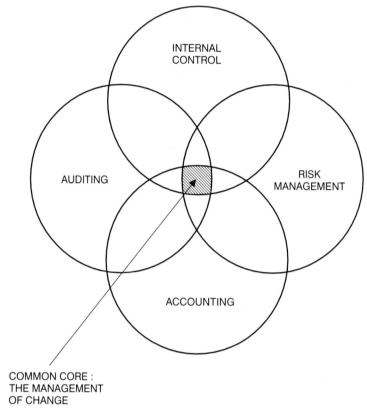

INTERNAL
CONTROL

AUDITING

RISK
MANAGEMENT

ACCOUNTING

COMMON CORE :
THE MANAGEMENT
OF CHANGE

Figure 1.1   There is a common core to the four responsibilities crucial to the proper management of any enterprise

Both promote the need for change management, as a quick look at Figure 1.2 documents. Though the references behind this figure come from the insurance industry, the careful reader will appreciate that both the push and pull factors are widely applicable, because they underpin the forces driving any industry in the Internet age anywhere in the world.

Of all the factors outlined in Figure 1.2 those characterised as 'push' are better known, and I do not need to elaborate on them. This is not necessarily true of the pull factors, particularly because protectionism has put a low ceiling on how far new entrants can go up the sales curve in a foreign market: the low ceiling applied by protectionism is slowly lifting as governments start appreciating the benefits obtained through

7

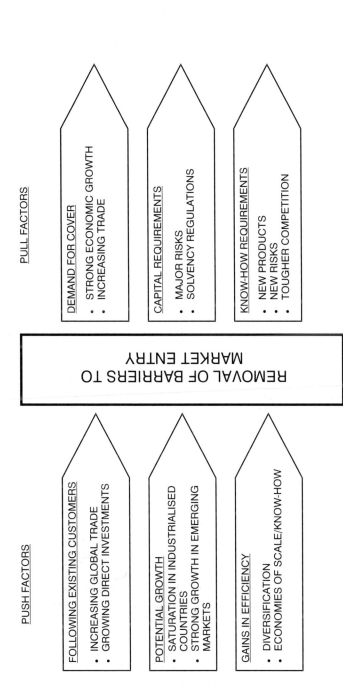

Figure 1.2 The driving forces of the insurance industry's globalisation increase the need for efficient management of change
Source: Swiss Re, *Sigma* No. 4/2000, by permission.

liberalisation, and are easing their trade barriers. Other factors, however, such as a substandard judiciary system, are still in place, ensuring that while the crust of the cake is changing, the cake itself remains the same.

Misconceptions about how deep the evolution of a given market may be are another reason why top management must be very careful about how it handles change, and how it capitalises on the benefits to be derived from liberalisation without taking undue risks. The challenge is not only that of getting change started, but of guiding it in such a way that returns are commensurate with the assumed risks.

What I am suggesting in the preceding paragraph is true of persons, companies and countries as well. The focal point of Figure 1.3 is liberalisation of insurance and the benefits this may present to emerging market economies. This is an example covering likely returns. Swiss Re has ingeniously blended the factors affecting foreign insurers with the benefits to the local economy, as a result of technology and skills transfer by the newcomers. Notice that an indirect effect of competitiveness imported by foreign insurers is that of promoting greater maturity by the local supervisory authorities. Whether or not it is appreciated, the sophistication of supervision greatly impacts upon the orderly development of financial industries.

If the local economy knows how to exploit the aftermath of foreign insurers' entry, this could well be a win–win situation. Spill-over effects will carry the rewards far and wide, while the risk that weak local companies will fail is not necessarily a big negative. They might have failed anyway, carrying the legal economy with them.

On the other hand, favourable effects for the local economy in the aftermath of entry by foreign insurers range from better dynamics of domestic savings to greater efficiency of capital allocation. Another important factor that could be added to the top box in Figure 1.3 is creation of employment and training of local workers, which turns our discussion back to the transfer of skills.

It is more or less beyond doubt that for any country and for any company an increasing effectiveness of financial markets in banking, investment and insurance becomes more important as trade changes from local and regional to crossborder (if not outright global), whether through the Internet or any other means. Removal of regulatory barriers promotes this process but also puts on the Board's shoulders the need for:

- increased vigilance for reasons of exposure;
- a higher level of technology implementation; and
- a significant upgrade of know-how for all employees.

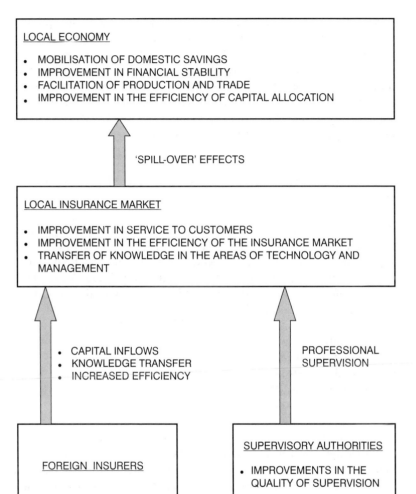

Figure 1.3   Benefits of liberalisation for emerging market economies
Source: Swiss Re, *Sigma* No. 4/2000, by permission.

The three bullets points identify milestones in the management of change. Reaching them can be helped by the push and pull factors of which we have been talking in the preceding paragraphs. They assist in deconstructing the traditional value chain, and promote value-differentiation on a new, global basis which is much more efficient than the one which used to be in place.

While the concepts underlying this section address themselves primarily to insurance, they can be applied to practically any industry aspiring to crossborder business and/or Internet commerce. Let us always keep in mind that many of what used to be special characteristics of some industries have now blended. Even the space and time framework of which we spoke in the introduction has changed, and it continues to change every couple of years or so. A couple of years is a short span, yet it can be equivalent to a lifetime on the Internet.

3   THE EVOLUTION OF CHARACTERISTIC TECHNOLOGY BEYOND THE YEAR 2000

One of the least appreciated facts in business and industry today is that, both in the short and in the longer term, professional duties and responsibilities have been influenced in a significant way by developments in technology. During the last 50 years every decade had its own *characteristic technology*. The way MIT's 'Smart World Symposium' (12–13 April 2000) defined it, the transition has been:

- computation in the 1950s/1960s;
- information, 1970s;
- knowledge, 1980s;
- communications, 1990s;
- identification, 2000+.

In this evolutionary change in core technology, internal control is acting as the electron microscope of possible failures connected to ongoing processes vital to *our* firm. Is the salient problem taxation (see Chapter 7)? How is *our* company faring in terms of optimising its tax liabilities on a global scale? Is it capitalising on local laws and regulations? On opportunities presented by Internet supply chain relationships? On discrepancies between national tax laws in regard to Internet trades? The crucial issues management must address vary with each of these queries.

As Chapter 2 will document, these are by no means academic questions. Both the Board and the CEO have to ascertain if the responsible operating departments, the finance division and legal counsel have indeed done their homework. As we saw with the insurance examples in the previous section, in a globalised, deregulated, technology-based environment this is a steady job, and it is not easy.

Since Internet companies can move their base rapidly around the globe, they can take advantage of the new, evolving concept of networked tax opportunities. If France and Germany tax Internet sales while Britain does not, stable establishments (SEs) of industrial and financial firms will move to the UK; if the UK taxes, they will go to the USA; if the USA taxes Internet sales, their next destination will be the Cayman Islands or somewhere similar. There will always be an Internet tax haven somewhere on planet Earth.

These challenges are real, and they are here to stay. Therefore, the management of change is no abstract concept, and the Board should never be satisfied by undocumented general statements such as: 'We do our best.' Factual and documented responses are mandatory. If, for instance, the auditing mission has to do with *our* company's policy regarding Internet-based business, accounting and auditing should be answering specifically whether *our* position is mainly passive, such as a 'me too' broadcast Web site, or whether it is able to seek clients and other supply-chain partners dynamically on the Internet.

Do we actively participate in auctions and reverse auctions? How do we compare to *our* competitors? Are we getting commendable results in responses from our business partners? Do we augment the reach of our employees through networked agents (see D.N. Chorafas, *Agent Technology Handbook*, McGraw-Hill, New York, 1998)? In short, what's *our* company's status versus the competition? Is it state of the art?

There are also other, more technical issues, to which the management of change should respond, because they are crucial to decisions reached by the CEO and the Board. Is our company well launched in the *everywhere Net* with nomadic computing? Are we further out in the future morphing *our* products and services to fit the requirements of different business environments?

1 Are we ahead of competition in personalising the products market?
2 Do we observe high quality standards?
3 Are we doing so at the lowest possible cost?

No organisational function escapes the obligation to answer crucial queries. If the main theme of an auditing mission is the pace of innovation and rapid time to market, then the feedback to be provided to the Board and the CEO must cover research and development (R&D) projects in the laboratory (some of which stay there forever), new products in the pipeline and their market appeal, the decay of existing products, and the decay of human skills, as well as progress in training aimed at renewing the knowledge base of managers, professionals and all other employees. Not only progress but also timetables, quality and costs are important: the Board, CEO, CTO and CFO must watch every dollar being spent like a hawk.

Cost-cutting is often associated with special projects and organisational overhaul, leading to improvements in the bottom line. The chief executives must always be ready to cut out dead wood. Carl Icahn, the CEO of TWA, tells the story of ACF, a company which he acquired, with operations in the Midwest and headquarters in New York. He asked the people in the Midwest: 'How many guys in New York do you need to support you?' and they said: 'None.' Puzzled about this sort of answer, Icahn sent his consultant to study what ACF's New York staff was doing. The consultant came back with the answer: 'I cannot find out what they do.' So Icahn fired the whole New York office.

In the case of Beatrice Foods, corporate headquarters' overheads were $220 million a year. Esmark, the company which purchased Beatrice, took a sharp knife, thoroughly restructured operations and ended by running a $6 billion company on $23 million a year of corporate overheads, or 10 per cent of the previous budget. At the root of cost control is value rather than sizzle; this value has to be investigated and kept in sight through the company's feedback channel.

Another important mission of business feedback is to analyse and report on the results of restructuring. Restructuring is always necessary when a given organisation re-invents itself and its activities. The Bank for International Settlement (BIS) offers an example. After the Second World War, the main preoccupation of BIS was with payments and monetary policy, but over the last fifteen years the emphasis has changed to:

- strengthening global financial regulation; and
- stabilising the international financial system.

Three regulators' committees at BIS work towards these goals: banking supervision; foreign exchange; payments and settlements. Among the tangible results of banking supervision have been the 1988 Capital Accord on minimum capital requirements for banks; the 1996 Market Risk Amendment (D.N. Chorafas, *The Market Risk Amendment. Understanding the Marking-to-Model and Value-at-Risk*, McGraw-Hill, Burr Ridge, IL, 1998); the 1999 New Capital Adequacy Framework;

and a score of position papers on important financial subjects. In addition, there is the drafting of international principles for bank supervisors.

BIS has also launched the Institute for Financial Stability, aimed at training bank supervisors from many different countries on the rules and secrets of regulation, and also on modern technology and more effective oversight practices. Because it represents leveraging of human capital, lifelong learning is a major step towards averting obsolescence and making the best possible use of human resources. I consider steady learning a milestone in the management of change, but like any other activity it has to be regularly audited to assure it is on target.

The same is true about technology. The milestones listed at the beginning of this section provide a vivid example of a change in emphasis over time. An entity uses technology both for strategic and for tactical reasons, as it addresses internal and external factors which influence its course. Figure 1.4 drives home this point.

Rapid response through the best, most efficient means technology can offer is so important because it is unavoidable that a company steadily interacts with its business environment by positioning its internal forces in a way which defines its chances of survival. The management of change in technology is a fundamental responsibility of the Board and the CEO. The more Board members withstand the heat of this rapid change, the higher their stock will rise.

4 OVERCOMING DISADVANTAGES OF SCALE AND ANSWERING THE NEED FOR CRITICAL SUPPORTING SERVICES

Logistics is an example of a vital management function which can be destabilised through routine. At the origin of the word *logistics* is an ancient Greek term, meaning a calculator, an accountant. Webster's dictionary defines *logistics* (noun, singular) as the branch of military science having to do with moving, supplying and quartering troops. This definition is too narrow and needs to be extended in two ways:

- in breadth to encompass not only military science but also all sectors of the economy and of industry; and
- in depth, to include prognostication, computation, planning and controlling of vital support activities.

14

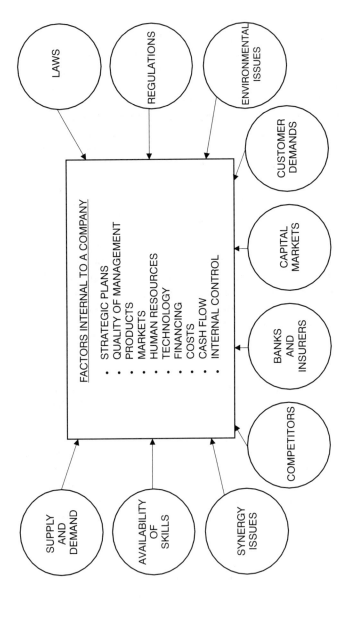

Figure 1.4   Any company feels the impact of internal and external factors which influence its course

Identification, the characteristic technology of the early part of the twenty-first century we spoke of in the previous section, has a great deal to do with logistics. To a considerable extent logistics is a complex analytical process into which enter many functions of management, from forecasting and planning to controlling. Over and above this comes the challenge of scale: large-scale logistics operations present problems of their own and require rigorous solutions. In many cases, what is supposed to be an advantage of scale ends by being a disadvantage.

As an example of the complexity large-scale logistics bring into being, Peter Drucker points out that in the Korean War the procurement and inventory policies of the American armed services were in bad shape. This did not escape the Pentagon's attention and for the next ten years there were countless studies on ways and means for improvement. Yet things got worse rather than better (see Peter Drucker, *The Effective Executive*, Heinemann, London, 1967).

Dr Robert McNamara was appointed Secretary of Defense in the Kennedy Administration, and he challenged the traditional measurement of military inventory based on total dollars and total number of items in procurement and stock management. In an application of Pareto's Law, McNamara identified those items which cost most in total procurement dollars; that was about 4 per cent of the mass of items. He also went after the few items, another 4 per cent, which accounted for 90 per cent of combat readiness. Since some of the items in these two groups belonged in both categories, the crucial list came to about 6 per cent of total military procurement measured by numbers. This 6 per cent list represented the lion's share when measured by value, and attracted McNamara's direct attention.

Having visualised the salient problem in military procurement as shown in Figure 1.5, Robert McNamara saw to it that these items were managed separately, with great care and with attention to *minute detail*. The rest, which accounted neither for the bulk of expenditure nor for essential combat readiness, he changed to *management by exception* through a system of checks and balances based on probabilities and averages.

The reason I pay so much attention to this case is that the policy Robert McNamara followed at the Defense Department applies also to supply chain management in the world of Internet commerce. It is also an excellent example of how top executives should manage change. Not only does the amount of business currently done on the Net compare up to a point to the Pentagon's procurement, but also taken together, the GM/Ford/DaimlerChrysler/Renault-Nissan type of set-up in

16

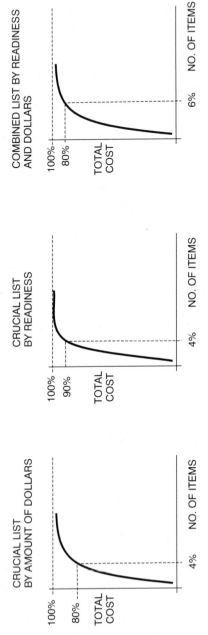

Figure 1.5   Pareto's Law can be instrumental in highlighting salient problems in procurement and inventory management

business-to-business (B2B) trades will represent the crucial part of total online procurement dollars (see Chapter 3).

At the Pentagon, McNamara's system immediately made possible highly effective decisions on procurement, and it led to the restructuring of logistics. But over the years new inefficiencies crept in. Some three decades down the line, in the aftermath of the Persian Gulf war, Desert Storm looked like a triumph of logistics. Moving 7 million tons of supplies for 550 000 troops in short order was a feat. Later, however, a little-noticed Defense Department logistics review revealed that the 1991 operation was flawed:

- half of the 40 000 containers shipped to the desert, including $2.7 billion worth of spare parts, went unused; and
- incomplete labelling saw to it that soldiers did not know what was in many of the containers they had received.

Therefore, new logistics plans were made, and they refocused on the importance of correct identification. As of 1995 the new goal of the Pentagon has been to replace a just-in-case delivery mentality with a streamlined just-in-time system aimed at shrinking inventories and speeding up deliveries. To compensate for thinner reserves, delivery from factory to foxhole has been speeded up by using bar codes, laser cards, radio tags and database mining to track supplies.

All this will dramatically change with the *automatic identification* (auto-ID) system currently under development at MIT. The concept of smart materials which is supported through very low cost micro-processors (see Chapter 2) will do away with incomplete labelling which today is a plague in many organisations: financial, industrial and military. It also promises to turn inside out the design of a variety of devices and machines in everyday use. Auto-ID can make their employment more:

- accurate;
- timely; and
- efficient.

The automotive industry provides an example of the benefits to be reaped through an effective combination of smart identification and computing power. A top of the line motor vehicle today has up to 100 processors, and this number will tend to increase. Eventually, every component and subsystem in a car will have a 10 cent microprocessor with at least 1024 bits of information on it, enriched with the ability to communicate with other smart materials. That is where the bulk of non-human intelligence might reside in the years to come.

Human-to-human communications will also become smarter. It is expected that by 2002 at least 8 per cent of individuals living anywhere in this globe will have cell phones. This will mean 500 million smart phones capable of automatic identification and any-to-any linkage, whether radio or terrestrial. Smart materials, too, will communicate with these cell phones and their owners. The processes of logistics and accounting will never be the same again.

What these examples help to demonstrate is that even the best accounting processes and logistics solutions available today wear out over time, as new supply challenges come in and the rapid advance of technology sees to it that what was state-of-the-art some years ago is now wanting. The objective of a steady upkeep of tools at the service of management planning and control, which is at the heart of any logistics system, must be to:

- provide a cost-effective and consistent quality of service;
- ensure shared usage of resources in a steady manner;
- see to it that reliable and secure services are offered on-time; and
- continuously re-invent itself so that it does not become useless.

The answer to the challenges posed by these four bullet points is no hit-and-run business but one calling for a coherent solution with a well-defined level of dependability. The logistics services model must be kept dynamic and able to leverage the basic infrastructure, providing *our* company with competitive advantages in global reach, and helping to improve its knowledge base. We will talk more about this in Chapters 2 and 3.

On the technological side, this logistics system and its smart materials will be supported by a variety of local and wide area networks that communicate effectively with each other. The solution which we adopt must be characterised by an intelligent backbone into which integrate the present status and its improvements, while it is always possible to incorporate more advanced approaches which replace those components which get obsolete and enhance the overall results. This, too, is an area to which a well-tuned system of internal control must address itself.

5 BUSINESS PRACTICES, INTERNAL CONTROL, AND THE UPKEEP OF MANAGEMENT CULTURE

As far as the banking industry is concerned, the new directives by the Basle Committee of Banking Supervision make the Board of Directors and senior management responsible for promoting high ethical values and standards of integrity, as well as for establishing a culture within the bank which emphasises the importance of internal controls. Such policies are promoted in the belief that a strong control culture is a critical element of the profitability and survival of any organisation.

Why is this issue important in a book on the Internet supply chain? Three reasons justify its inclusion, and everyone of them is mission-critical. First and foremost, the Internet is a service industry and it has many of the characteristics of banking and insurance; second, because, as Demosthenes (382–322 BC) aptly said, business is based on confidence. Internal control and ethical values promote confidence in a process which is in steady change; in addition, there is the need for a system able to keep a virtual enterprise as one integrative and functional entity.

Cognisant readers will appreciate that there is more to be said on ethical values and cultural issues. The prevailing concepts, attitudes, words and actions of the Board of Directors, the CEO and senior management affect the integrity and ethical standing of the company as a whole. It is important to appreciate ahead of events the consequences of our decisions because down to its fundamentals internal control is the responsibility of everyone in the organisation. One essential element of a strong internal control system is the recognition by every employee of the need to effectively carry out his or her responsibilities. Another essential element is the ability to communicate risks resulting from operations, instances of non-compliance and other policy violations.

This does not mean that the question of a control culture comes up for the first time in the history of banking, or that industrial organisations have been alien to it. Classically, financial institutions have used a range of control techniques but these were largely oriented towards the prevention of fraud. Examples include cross-checking, reconciliation of accounts, double signature, staff turnover and limited access. They have also instituted follow-up procedures for breaches, whether carried out individually by one party, or by many. Classically, the audit department has handled the detection of such cases.

While they are always necessary, these control policies are not sufficient all by themselves. As far as shareholders in a given firm are concerned, a new type of fraud is management's inability to be ahead of the curve, because it cheats the company of its survival opportunities and keeps its capitalisation low. By falling behind the competition, whether in the virtual world of the Internet or in old economy trades, a company loses both its credibility and its competitiveness. These are two of the most critical assets, which management after management has found difficult to recover. There is also the fact that the effectiveness of past control procedures has varied widely. Results depend on a number of factors ranging from the particular area to which 'this' or 'that' control technique is applied, to the tools being used, the type of organisation, size of the business, and how strongly the Board and the CEO stand behind the controls.

There is plenty of evidence to document that the success of management controls is indivisible from prudential policies defined by the Board and senior management in accordance with the risk-taking strategy of the institution, and the existence of a supportive information technology which permits real-time response to events. Other things being equal, the internal control effort is more successful the better managed is the company, reflecting the principle that the administration of an institution should be consistent with:

- the nature of the business; and
- the pursuit of its objectives.

Both high ethical standards and a rigorous internal control system help in putting into place what we usually consider as the operational and management structure of an entity. Because this operational structure changes with the environment in which the firm operates and the sort of relationship it establishes with its business partners, it is not surprising that over the past few years the scope of internal control functions has been subject to an evolution reflecting the development of business activities, including the wave of financial innovation and advent of derivative financial instruments. (See D.N. Chorafas, *Managing Derivatives Risk*, Irwin Professional Publishing, Burr Ridge, IL, 1996.)

Risks have become more pervasive, encompassing sophisticated types of exposure and novel forms of non-dependability, which must be carefully watched. Neither should we forget that globalisation and deregulation increase the opportunities for human error (see section 2). Human error can always occur, but at different frequencies which often reflect control measures. Combined with changes in operational conditions, human errors can partially or totally invalidate current internal controls. However, if the existence of human errors at large is unavoidable, specific mistakes *can* be edited out of the system:

- business ethics help to provide guidance;
- better organisation weeds out error-prone conditions;
- management culture assists in practising damage control; and
- new technology provides dependable identification, reducing by so much opportunities for mistakes.

All four bullet points lead to the doorstep of the Board of Directors, and engage its members in taking actions which put *our* company ahead of the competition. The only way to discharge part of this responsibility is steady auditing to assure that internal control functions are performed in a way commensurate with the risks being taken. Management controls should be flexible and able to:

- adjust themselves to evolving conditions; and
- face different sorts of irregularities in an able manner.

As Chapter 6 will explain, the establishment of rigorous internal controls which go beyond classical fraud cases should be governed by a risk assessment concept able to facilitate the identification, analysis and management of all known types of exposure. This is tantamount to an advanced control culture. The communication of internal control intelligence, enhanced by open channels and through adherence to ethical values, helps in avoiding policies that provide incentives for non-compliance with the highest standards of behaviour. Practical examples include:

- premiums and commissions skewed towards greater risks;
- unreasonably high compensation rewards and golden parachutes;
- undue emphasis on unrealistic performance targets; and
- failure to capitalise on supply chain opportunities presented by the Internet.

Few chief executive officers appreciate that they weaken their institution's control culture by promoting and rewarding traders and managers who are successful in generating short-term profits but who fail to implement limits (see D.N. Chorafas, *Setting Limits for Market Risk*, Euromoney, London, 1999), do not address risks identified by internal control, and pile up toxic waste. The most scrupulous chief executives monitor the performance of all activities under their control closely enough to notice unusual events: financial, technological, commercial, or of any other type.

Among organisational ills leading towards unwarranted risks are loopholes allowing the concealment of poor performance. Board members should appreciate that no matter how good their company's product, they are only a year away from failure, and in some cases just a couple of months. Moving ahead, too, is a matter of ethics. While having a strong ethical culture does not guarantee that an institution will not take extraordinary risks, its absence raises by so much the probability that unwanted and unwarranted exposures will be assumed (among them, that of falling behind one's competitors).

Last but not least in this list of unwanted events is the inability or unwillingness to appreciate that even the best system solution implemented today can tomorrow become inefficient or plainly obsolete. 'Predicting is very hard. Especially about the future,' Niels Bohr once commented. As the case study from the Pentagon we examined in section 4 documents, it is hard to keep a system solution efficient after operational conditions change or routine sets in.

6   THE REGULATORS' VERDICT: INTERNAL CONTROL CAN SIGNIFICANTLY STRENGTHEN THE PRACTICE OF MANAGEMENT

On 22 December 1997, the four main regulatory agencies in the USA (The Board of Governors of the Federal Reserve System, Federal Deposit Insurance Corporation, or FDIC, Office of the Comptroller of the Currency, or OCC, and Office of Thrift Supervision, or OTS) published in common the *InterAgency Policy Statement on the Internal Audit Function and its Outsourcing*. This is a document to be read by all members of the Board and of senior management, in connection with internal control, because:

• It spells out the duties and responsibilities about which they should be doubly careful; and
• for any practical purpose it applies to all industries, no matter what their specific business line.

The InterAgency Policy Statement on the Internal Audit Function and its Outsourcing is one of the best practical examples which has come to my attention on the management of change. As such, it applies at two levels: the four regulatory agencies themselves, which refocus their activities from predominantly quantitative accounting checks to both quantitative and qualitative internal controls; and the institutions under their supervision which are prompted to do the same.

Of course, the InterAgency Policy Statement addresses itself primarily to the US banking industry but this in no way diminishes its global importance. It underlines that 'effective auditing procedures are a foundation for the safe and sound operation of a credit institution'. It takes only a small step to add to this statement: 'And of any other company'. The regulators leave no doubt that members of the Board of Directors and senior managers are personally responsible for ensuring that the system of internal controls operates effectively; their responsibility cannot be delegated to others within the institution or to outside parties.

The InterAgency Policy Statement presses the point that an important element of an effective internal control system is the internal audit function. This fully applies to companies engaged in Internet commerce. The Statement also emphasises that when properly structured and conducted, internal audits provide directors and senior managers with vital information about weaknesses in the control system, so they can take prompt corrective action. For this reason, federal examiners are instructed to review an institution's internal audit function and recommend improvements.

A key issue I would highlight from the references made by all four major US bank supervision agencies during our meetings is that regulatory authorities expect the Board of Directors and senior management to ensure the observance of the aforementioned InterAgency Policy Statement clauses, and also to make sure that the importance of internal control is understood and respected throughout the institution, while the Board and senior management see to it that this happens.

Another crucial reference from these meetings is that the overall accountability of directors and senior managers cannot be delegated down the line. Top management may, however, delegate to lower-level management the design, implementation and monitoring of specific internal controls, as well as their testing and assessment. Still, members of the Board and the CEO should have reasonable assurances that the system in place prevents or at least detects:

- inaccurate, incomplete or unauthorised transactions;
- deficiencies in the safeguarding of company assets;

- unreliable or fraudulent financial and regulatory reporting; and
- deviations from laws, directives, and the company's own policies.

The steady upkeep of accounting standards, observance of tax laws (Chapter 7), thorough revamping of the logistics system to keep the company lean and mean (see Chapters 8 and 9) and implementation of automatic identification, as well as use of smart materials, are, in my judgement, integral parts of sound management of the Internet supply chain.

Computer-literate Board members appreciate that new information technology has enabled the development of more effective risk control, and has promoted the design and use of global supervisory procedures. What has been learned by the financial industry during the last 20 years, regarding the control of exposure, can be and should be applied in Internet commerce. At the same time, however, these developments have not changed the fact that nobody really controls the global market and its gyrations while, by providing more timely access to information through network globalisation, it has increased market volatility. This calls for much greater prudence than ever before. To fulfil their responsibilities, the Boards of some institutions have chosen to rely on management self-assessment, whereby business line managers and their staff evaluate the performance of internal control and practise self-criticism. The problem is that self-assessments are not always as objective or impartial as, theoretically, should be the case.

Directors and senior managers who rely too much on self-assessment reviews may not learn of control weaknesses until they have become costly problems. This is particularly true in those cases where directors are not intimately familiar with the different aspects of their company's operations and the hazards associated with them. Therefore, the US regulatory agencies strongly recommend that:

- institutions should have their internal controls tested and assessed by independent auditors and/or units without business-line respon- sibilities; and
- directors should be confident that both internal control and the internal audit function meet the demands posed by the company's current and planned activities.

Since in any and every company internal control accountability weighs heavily on the Board, the directors should assign the oversight of internal control to a senior member of management who understands the function and has no line duties in operating the business. A similar statement is valid regarding the manager of internal audit, who should be responsible for:

- internal control assessment;
- audit plans and programmes; and
- audit reports on compliance.

Senior executives stated during our meetings that since the risk assessment methodology in place (or to be established) impacts both on internal control and auditing, it should reflect a deep understanding of business activities and the exposure associated with them. Analytical assessments should focus on the types of exposure inherent in a given business line. These must be able to highlight current *and* potential risks due to control deficiencies. This is a process in need of regular update to reflect changes in products, services, markets and business policies, and also in market liquidity and volatility (D.N. Chorafas, *Understanding Volatility and Liquidity in Financial Markets*, Euromoney, London, 1998).

7 THE SUPERVISORY AUTHORITIES EMPHASISE THE IMPORTANCE OF A COMPANY'S AUDITING PROGRAMME

Whether we talk of an Internet company or of a credit institution, any sound auditing plan is based on an objective assessment of risks and organisational weaknesses. For this reason, the regulators of the financial industry now require that it includes an evaluation of internal controls, means and measures within each significant business activity, the timing and frequency of planned internal auditing work, and a resource budget for internal supervisory duties. Performance criteria should incorporate:

- the timeliness of each audit;
- comparison of overall and departmental performance to plan; and
- other measures which indicate if top management is in charge.

Based on these new directives, a company's auditing programme must describe the objectives of the audit work and list the procedures that will be performed during each internal audit review, as well as the sophistication of the tools to be used. The auditing report should present the purpose, scope and results of the audit, including findings, conclusions and recommendations. Work papers should be maintained which adequately document the nature and detail of deliverables.

Internet companies can gain a great lot from these directives. They must see to it that their audit reports are explicit enough to permit members of the Board and senior managers to identify the risks inherent in operations, and assess whether internal controls are effective. All four regulatory agencies in the USA recommend that institutions must conduct their audit of internal control in accordance with professional standards, such as those promoted by the Institute of Internal Auditors (IIA, 'Standards for the Professional Practice of Internal Auditing'). The standards in reference address the:

- independence;
- professional proficiency;
- scope of work;
- performance of audit work; and
- management of internal audit.

Also covered are the frequency and extent of internal audit reviews and testing, which should be consistent with the nature, complexity and risk of the institution's on-balance-sheet and off-balance-sheet assets and liabilities. This directive by regulators is valid both for American banks and for foreign banks operating in the USA. The internal audit function of a foreign institution should cover its US operations in regard to:

- risk assessment;
- auditing plans; and
- auditing programmes.

This directive by the four major US regulatory agencies is an excellent paradigm on the convergence of supervisory criteria, and at the same time on the precision and accuracy needed in management controls. The framework to which I make reference should retain the attention of the Board, the CEO and CFO of every Internet company for a reason other than that of a strictly financial implementation. With some rewording, it can be used to describe the requirements to be fulfilled by accounting and logistics:

- in any company;
- at any time;
- anywhere in the world.

The InterAgency Policy Statement to which reference was made in section 6 also specifies that central bank examiners should have full and timely access to an institution's internal audit resources, including personnel, works papers, risk assessment methods, work plans, programmes, reports and budgets. Armed with such information they should evaluate the quality and scope of the internal audit work, regardless of whether it is performed by the institution's employees or through outsourcing. They should also consider whether the Board of Directors and audit committee promote the internal audit director's impartiality and independence (see D.N. Chorafas, *New Regulation of the Financial Industry*, Macmillan – now Palgrave, London, 2000), and whether the internal audit function is adequately managed to ensure that audit plans are met and programmes are carried out.

The InterAgency Policy Statement further specifies that results of audits must be promptly communicated to the Board, the CEO and senior management. This includes risk assessment by internal audit. The Board must ensure that auditing plans and programmes are appropriate for the institution's activities and that the company has promptly responded to identified internal control weaknesses. This clause, too, can find a useful implementation in Internet commerce, particularly in regard to the evaluation of *our* company's logistics system.

Other issues on which the regulators have focused attention is whether management and the Board of Directors use reasonable standards when assessing the performance of internal audit; whether internal audit programmes have been adjusted for significant changes in the institution's environment, structure, activities and risk exposures; whether the activities of internal auditing are consistent with the bank's long-range plans; and if they are responsive to its ongoing internal control needs.

These fairly recent rules should be seen as the Bible in *any* industry characterised by rapid development of new products and services, where six months' delay threatens obsolescence. In banking, for example, federal examiners currently pay attention to whether the audit function provides high-quality advice and counsel to management and the Board of Directors on current developments crucial in fields such as risk management, and regulatory compliance.

Internal auditors are not expected to spend time on non-issues, or to sweeten their findings to avoid offending somebody. Examiners of supervisory authorities now assess the competence of the institution's internal audit staff by considering the education and professional background of the principal and other members of internal auditing, and by looking into what they have produced as deliverables. This is a relatively new practice, and one which applies nicely in a critical evaluation of:

- technology leadership;
- accounting systems; and
- logistics solutions.

It is not that regulators expect an institution's internal auditors to make no mistakes, for they know the person who makes no mistakes does not usually make anything. What they are looking at is the track record. Examiners also aim to determine whether the institution maintains or improves the quality of its internal control and internal audit functions, and whether the scope of work is revised appropriately as the company's business evolves. This is basic to the effective management of change by the Board and the CEO.

This can be stated in conclusion: internal control intelligence can be of invaluable assistance in providing a preview of what might happen to so far unassailable reputations. Internal control intelligence might also prepare the ground for very useful reflections on common issues and possible directions for improvements aimed at safeguarding the reputation of *our* company, of its Board and of its CEO. 'The life of the law is not logic but experience,' Justice Oliver Wendell Holmes once said.

2 All Professionals Must Adapt to the Forces of Internet Commerce

1 INTRODUCTION

The members of the Board, CEO, CFO, CTO, and their immediate assistants are not the only persons who should understand and appreciate the challenges of Internet commerce. All professionals must adapt to the new market forces. Because of world-wide competition, the driving gear of the twenty-first century is markets, costs, know-how, technology and globality. Their synergy has altered, and continues changing design, manufacturing and marketing practices, as well as relative priorities. The new priorities are:

- investing for competitiveness on an unprecedented scale;
- swamping costs to compensate lack of pricing power;
- developing and sustaining an online delivery system; and
- exploiting to full extent the Internet-enabled new communications capabilities.

The New Economy is no 'Old Boys' Club' of people sitting around and never doing anything. The so-called 'professional survivors' have no place in it. Only those productive and able to deliver can survive.

Many experts now regard the Internet as a global megatrend similar to the advent of the printing press, rail transport, cars, aeroplanes, the telephone and the computer. Products and services supported by the Net are changing the way people and companies communicate, search, buy, sell and distribute goods. They also alter the way people look for information and spend their leisure time.

Whether in America or in Europe, 1999 statistics and 2005 projections suggest the population of Internet users is greater than that of Internet shoppers by a wide margin. As Swiss Re's *Sigma* was to remark: 'The first generation of Internet users mainly consisted of young people with high incomes who were inspired by the new technology. Now a second wave of users has emerged: people less interested in the technology who use the Internet mainly because it is convenient and saves time' (*Sigma*, No. 5/2000, 'The Impact of e-Business on the Insurance Industry', Swiss Re, Zurich, 2000).

Based on Swiss Re statistics, Figure 2.1 shows this progression and contrasts US leadership in both Internet usage and Internet commerce to the second position taken by Europeans. The top two reasons given by the same publication are just as valid for Japan: English is not the common language of European countries and the employment of credit cards is not as widespread. I would guess the fact the Internet is an American invention and the US public is more open to novelty are two more reasons which should be added to the above two.

Whether for information gathering or for commerce, the Internet has invaded our business and our daily life at a pace much faster than any new technology in history. It has also brought home the fact that, amidst the wave of change, an overall theme of an industry in full restructuring is *convergence*. With the net, converging business includes publishing, television, telecommunications, radio, cable, computers and software.

Widespread acceptance of the need for R&D, just-in-time (JIT) manufacturing schedules, fast flow replenishment (FFR) of inventories, emphasis on quality assurance and the coming new era of smart materials are convergence themes related to engineering and management breakthroughs. At the same time, new management priorities in logistics impact on accounting procedures and standards and, in consequence, on business practices. Accounting is after all the most basic information system after the service of management.

The object of this chapter is to bring to the reader's attention why all the professions affected by the Internet must adapt to the new driving forces of rapid innovation and global competition. Foremost among them is the impact of the Internet technology (discussed in section 2), and of the increasingly more sophisticated world of Net-based purchasing (to which Chapter 3 is dedicated).

2   THE FAR-REACHING EFFECTS OF TECHNOLOGY ON THE NEW ECONOMY

The best way to start the discussion on this section's theme is through an example. The American information economy is growing at *twice* the rate of all other sectors which make up the Gross Domestic Product (GDP). Since 1995, information technology (IT) has contributed more

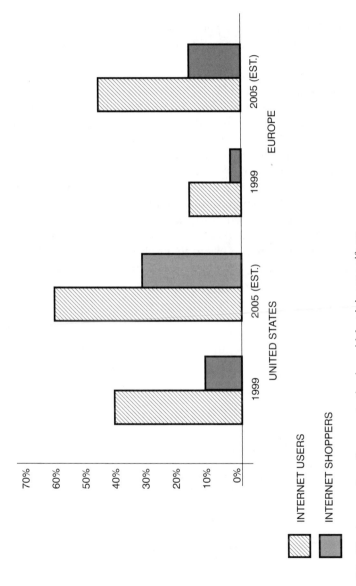

Figure 2.1 The increase in online penetration is rapid, but it is not uniform
Source: Swiss Re, *Sigma* No. 5/2000, by permission.

than 45 per cent of economic growth in the USA: roughly 45 per cent of all new business equipment spending now goes to information technology-related wares:

- since 1993, Americans have purchased more PCs than televisions;
- as of 1997, they purchase more PCs than motor vehicles.

In 1997, for the first time ever, there were more messages sent by e-mail than by traditional letter post. These and similar statistics are important not only because they identify the moving gear behind growth characterising the US economy in the mid- to late 1990s and the early years of the twenty-first century, but also because they contribute to the definition of *how* the new economy ticks.

New economy is the name given to companies benefiting directly from the latest revolution in information technology, intelligent software, Internet-based communications, rapid innovation cycles and the globalisation of markets. By contrast, *old economy* refers to that section of the economy still embedded in decades-old business models, and/or product lines which do not re-invent themselves to answer developing market needs. Figure 2.2 gives a bird's-eye view of the transition from the old economy to the new.

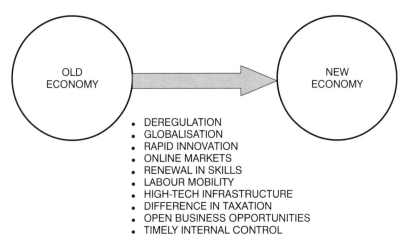

OLD
ECONOMY

NEW
ECONOMY

- DEREGULATION
- GLOBALISATION
- RAPID INNOVATION
- ONLINE MARKETS
- RENEWAL IN SKILLS
- LABOUR MOBILITY
- HIGH-TECH INFRASTRUCTURE
- DIFFERENCE IN TAXATION
- OPEN BUSINESS OPPORTUNITIES
- TIMELY INTERNAL CONTROL

Figure 2.2   Ten factors characterising the migration from the old economy to the new economy

1 The new economy paradigm motivates imaginative minds, and leads them into taking bold business steps.
2 The value of education and know-how rises exponentially in a world based on ideas and analytical thinking.
3 The Internet creates new opportunities but also destroys corporate pricing power, by allowing people to compare prices from a thousand sources.

Few old economy products and processes can serve Internet commerce without adaptation and special care. Products and services particularly suitable for selling online are those that can be *identified*, *described* and *rated* through a small number of factors (D.N. Chorafas, *Managing Credit Risk*, Volume 1, *Analysing, Rating and Pricing the Probability of Default*, Euromoney, London, 2000). Few and easily understood parameters are vital to marketing on the Net. Complex schemes:

- cannot be explained in an effective manner to a wide population;
- are not easy to personalise to customer wishes as the need arises; and
- they always risk being misunderstood, or at least unappreciated.

This is true even if some of the processes underpinning the majority of products are similar from one situation to another, and from product development to after-sales service there is a continuum. Based on a concept by Swiss Re which addresses itself to insurance, this continuum is shown in Figure 2.3. The careful reader will appreciate that several of its basic elements are shared by different industries: for instance, global marketing by trading companies, financial service providers, virtual brokers; claims management by insurance professionals, repair companies, call centres; and of course information technology by all sectors of the economy.

Within this continuum of products and services, and their interaction with the market, new economy companies make extensive use of electronic systems, implement real-time, and capitalise on digitisation. By contrast, old-style business models range from batch-based supply chain mismanagement, to average quality manufacturing, near-sighted financing, excessive inventories and lack of marketing punch. Sure enough, when we talk of advanced technology we do not just mean IT, but *high technology*.

34

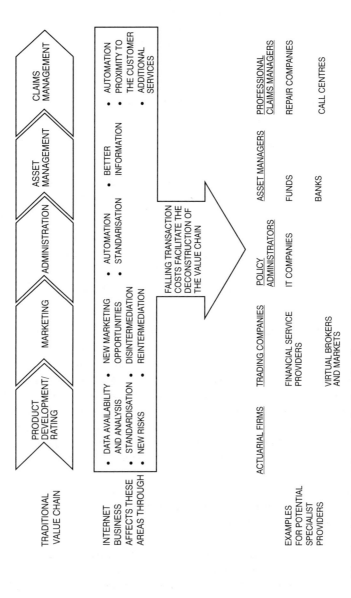

Figure 2.3 Specialised providers exist in virtually all steps of the value chain: an example from the insurance industry
Source: Swiss Re, *Sigma* No. 5/2000, by permission.

- Advanced IT solutions are on integral part of running our business and caring for its future. We should be satisfied with nothing but the best.
- The definition of high-tech changes with time. The only constant is that it acts as the force driving our company's growth and survival.

Technology choices must respond to *our* strategic objectives and this must be safeguarded through internal controls. This is something tier-1 companies already do, as Chapter 1 has explained. But the careful reader will appreciate that few managements are willing and able to adapt the technology they use to changing market conditions and to the actions or reactions of their competitors.

Still another important element in the definition of new technologies is that globalisation forces firms to drive for personalisation of the goods and services they offer. This has resulted in the demise of concepts targeting mass production, and the abandonment of the cloning of engineering design and marketing operations. This has been a fundamental cultural change of which every company and every product designer must take account. Increasingly in the new economy products are designed for *a* specific user, not for an amorphous mass, and when company size leads to insensitivity to the user's wishes, then the economies of scale turn into disadvantages.

This issue of sensitivity to market drives and individual customer wishes is among the basic reasons why in many fields economic activity has moved from large firms to small, more innovative and more flexible ones: from IBM to Compaq, and from Compaq to Dell; from Sears Roebuck to Wal-Mart; and from AT&T/Western Electric (now Lucent Technologies) to Nokia and Cisco.

The new economy does not come free of costs. Challenges have to be faced individually in an efficient manner, just to keep a level playing field for ourselves and our firm. The search for individual solutions in a dynamic economy is never ending. Because with the Internet products and processes get *personalised*, solutions cannot be uniform. The way to bet, however, is that:

- they will obey the law of *volatility in returns*, significantly increasing and diminishing profitability;
- they will create a world of instability, not of equilibrium; and
- they will penalise those staying behind to the point of going bust.

Chapter 1 has demonstrated that a crucial factor deciding about success or failure in the new economy is how well each person and each company can absorb and manage change. Inability to do so puts one immediately at disadvantage. At the same time, change engenders many challenges, some of which are visible and others are not, as we will see in subsequent sections.

3   IMPACT OF INTERNET TECHNOLOGY ON THE EVOLVING COMPETITIVE LANDSCAPE

One of the basic strengths of the new economy is the impact B2B commerce is having on all sectors of industry, reducing the amount of required working capital through implementation of more efficient modes of supply-chain management. The size of realisable economies can best be appreciated if we keep in mind that companies such as BP Amoco, Sears and Carrefour have launched an electronic market which brings around 50 000 suppliers together (see Chapter 3).

Sears alone makes around 100 million purchase orders per year, concerning goods which eventually slip down to consumers. This is a critical mass which helps in documenting that whether we talk of B2B or business-to-consumer (B2C), contractual power has shifted from the *sell side* to the *buy side*, leading some experts to suggest that the most pronounced impact of the Internet has been to empower the consumer.

A more refined way of making the same statement is that until now companies typically have considered the aggregate of consumers as a big amorphous cluster. Now emphasis is on personalisation because technology gives each buyer what he or she needs to be in control of purchasing chores. The Internet enables consumers to get together and tell companies what they want them to do. This is not exactly in the interest of those companies who would rather tell the consumer what he or she needs to buy.

Some organisations are, however, capitalising on the opportunities offered by this twist. A number of examples will help in documenting this statement, and one of the best is Ford's use of the Net to empower its clients and employees. Ford bought a Web-based computer for each of its 350 000 employees, world-wide. Then, it announced a joint venture with Sprint PCs to put the Internet inside passenger cars. This imaginative move addresses two levels:

- productivity; and
- product development.

The first offer of car-based Internet services is with the 200 000 top-of-the-line Lincoln models Ford is selling every year. The Sprint PCs link will make it feasible to communicate via the Web with home and office; and, alternatively, with the car from home and office.

Many experts expressed the opinion this would end car crime as we know it. I do not agree, because thieves also get smart, and hackers who do things for their own pleasure will not fail to take advantage of the new facility, enabled by the Internet (see also Chapter 11). They have the experience of doing so. An example is the 'I Love You' global bug of March 2000. Crime will remain crime, but at a higher level of sophistication.

This being so, what benefits does the Internet provide to its users (at least those conceived today as being important)? Such benefits fall within the realm of all four quarter spaces of Internet commerce: business-to-business, business-to-consumer, consumer-to-business (C2B) and consumer-to-consumer (C2C) exchanges. The following six bullet points answer this query concerning benefits:

- a platform for globalisation;
- marketing through B2B, B2C, C2B, C2C;
- means for reaching the clients of other companies;
- purchasing through B2B, B2C, C2B, C2C;
- a framework for online reporting services; and
- a means for developing and advertising new products.

These top six issues both drive and are driven by, the expanding horizon of Internet commerce (I-commerce). They promote the trend to dynamic pricing, the growing emphasis on cost reduction, mobile computing and communications, and the fact that the Web is becoming increasingly more intelligent, and also the ongoing bandwidth explosion (see section 5).

The cutting edge of the market sees to it that product and process obsolescence comes rapidly and without warning, as we saw in Chapter 1. This leads experts to suggest that our epoch can best be characterised as one of *creative destruction*. The introduction also spoke of convergence in business as another characteristic of our time. The Internet's supporting sectors can be better understood when divided into focused but integrative business lines which cut across old divisions:

- *Internet commerce*, for buying and selling merchandise, and also facilitating the matching of buyers and sellers;

- *software*, both Web routines and add-ons, primarily designed for inter- or intra-enterprise communications and I-commerce;
- *content* – firms providing 'what you see is what you get' (WYSIWYG); a sector including both *portals* and *destinations*;
- *wider access*, through dial-up lines and/or dedicated networks, as well as network management services; and
- *infrastructure*: radio, cable or fibre, which supports any-to-any communications, and uses basic software for diagnostics.

There is a large array of infrastructural services necessary in an online environment and its exploitation. Designing, offering and sustaining these services should take account of the fact that 300 million people use personal computers at work, and 900 million homes world-wide have television. There are also organisational prerequisites which go beyond what we have known so far in terms of requirements (see Chapter 6).

The use of the Internet as a platform for globalisation and the rise of business-to-business I-commerce work in synergy. Still, one of the hard-to-estimate forces is the extent of B2B online commerce ten years down the line. According to Goldman Sachs, less than 0.5 per cent of inter-company transactions currently take place electronically. But from retailing to manufacturing, traditional old economy firms began to realise that it is tough to bypass Web-based merchandise exchanges and survive. Insensitivity to the Web means abandoning the slashing of procurement costs in a radical way. Precisely for this reason, as Chapter 3 will explain, America's top three car makers announced a web-based exchange for parts. Aware of the challenge, automotive suppliers are doing the same. Morgan Stanley suggests that such initiatives could reduce costs by $2000–3000 per vehicle over the next 3 to 5 years, which is no mean feat.

Users of B2B procurement software such as Cisco Systems (see Chapter 6) and IBM suggest they are saving 20 per cent or more of their purchasing costs. Leaders in B2B procurement software include Commerce One, whose programming products connect buyers and sellers into online market places for clients such as COVISINT (see Chapter 3); other leading companies are Ariba, Oracle and i2 Technologies.

Some companies espouse Internet commerce for defensive reasons as well as for renewal of past policies which are no more effective. Allstate Insurance is an example. Created by Sears Roebuck, Allstate first sold car insurance by mail order, expecting to cut expenses by 40 per cent. It stuck to this sales policy for three years, before sensing insurance sales required human contact.

- In 1982, Sears began a 10-year process of moving Allstate agents out of shops and into offices.
- By 2000, Allstate had difficulty in competing through bricks and mortar due to its huge costs; hence it espoused I-commerce.

To make the transition to Internet sales Allstate management invested more than $1 billion. This money helped create nation-wide Internet and telephone operations. Part of the cost has been that Allstate had to hire 6000 people, also adding 35 000 PCs and more than 10 000 phone lines. These employees do not follow normal hours. They work in the evenings and at weekends, and they are part of the transition the work-force must undergo to continue finding employment.

4   COST SAVINGS WITH INTERNET COMMERCE: REALITY OR FANTASY?

Section 3 brought to the reader's attention a couple of examples from the growing body of evidence from Internet commerce in the USA. These pressed the point that the Net helps in cutting costs in some spending areas. Savings are thought to be at the 10 per cent level or higher. Preliminary findings show similar effects for some Scandinavian and British firms. In principle, and this is written in a general manner, the Internet should reduce prices through:

- reduced costs of executing sales;
- cheaper after-sales service;
- fewer staff (albeit better qualified);
- lower procurement costs;
- the swamping of inventory holdings; and
- lower distribution costs.

Some recent American studies conclude not only that prices on the Internet tend to be lower than for conventional retailers, but also that as Internet commerce expands to cover a broader part of the popula-tion, competitive pressures on prices should become more intense.

Another school of thought believes that online commerce will have to attain a critical mass before having a significant impact on conven-tional shop prices. What is meant by critical mass has to do both with shoppers and the range of products. Roughly 50 per cent of goods could conceivably be sold on the Internet. *If* prices for all these goods and services fell by 10 per cent, *then* the general price level would fall by about 5 per cent. Assuming it takes 10 years for half of the cost effect to come through, inflation could be around 0.5 per cent lower a year. This does not look like being a big deal, and there is also a divergence of opinion about the size of cost-cutting. While some experts say that there are areas of both business procurement and consumer spending where the direct impact of Internet commerce should be extensive, others suggest this is counterbalanced by the fact that in some domains the effects are fairly limited.

Examples of products and markets where cost reduction through I-commerce is less pronounced are fuel, power, personal services, restaurants, household services and recreation. The trouble is that these areas make up around 50 per cent of consumer spending. In these areas of business activity, the Internet can be used to check prices from different suppliers, and to provide information regarding purchasing habits and spending levels. Under these conditions the effect will be indirect, through increased competition, rather than direct. Furthermore, such assumptions are made on the basis of present-day knowledge. It is still no less true that in a world of rapidly changing technology, different agents are likely to have different levels of capitalising on what Internet commerce offers. Unavoidably there will be information asymmetries, and these will result in different types of market imperfection.

Could the Internet lead to a new type of monopoly? In the USA, the Justice Department is concerned that this could happen by keeping public information privy: for instance, a ticket-vending site to be run by, say, two major airlines from and to rival carriers. It could also get exclusive fare information from the parent carriers and refuse to share it with online rivals.

Another fact of which the careful reader should take account is that the transition from lower costs to lower prices, because of the Internet's impact, is not necessarily rapid or automatic. Amongst other things, it depends on the presence of sufficient competition and motivation, as well as:

- the size of the reduction in business costs;
- the speed with which cost savings are made; and
- the extent to which the cost savings are passed on.

This in turn is a function of the pace of online wholesale and retail business, which depends on the growth of both Web-based business supply chains and Internet usage for household purchases. Still another factor is the success of online wholesalers and retailers in establishing brand image and brand durability in spite of rapid innovation in products. Figure 2.4 provides a composite picture of these conditions by bringing into perspective the Internet's impact on commercial channels and the results which can be expected.

Based on concepts and statistics available today and those reasonably foreseeable, the way to bet is that as Internet commerce expands to cover a broader part of business enterprises and of the population, the competitive pressures on prices should become a lot more intense. In both business and consumer terms, wider access is likely to result from a shift away from technical factors; the new keyword is ease of use.

Extranets linking business partners should shy away from complex formulas and relatively expensive computers. For consumers, the answer is cheap and easy to use televisions and portable phones. At the same time, evaluating products online could lead to interesting changes in buying practices. Consumers might rely more heavily on perceived signals of quality, such as brand, thereby softening price competition; and these companies would look after the creditworthiness of counterparties, established by independent rating agencies (D.N. Chorafas, *Managing Credit Risk*, Volume 1, *Analysing, Rating and Pricing the Probability of Default*, Euromoney, London, 2000), rather than rely only on posted prices.

Not long ago, an American study compared the price elasticity of groceries sold through conventional and Internet outlets, and it concluded that price sensitivity is lower among online grocery shoppers than it is for conventional shoppers. This might reflect the relative affluence of Internet users and the largely automated nature of grocery shopping with a core weekly shopping list. Alternatively, it may be a prognosticator of shifts in the markets; only time will tell.

5 BROADBAND NETWORKS, INTERNET COMMERCE AND NOMADIC COMPUTING

Section 3 made a brief reference to the likely effects of broadband and section 4 spoke of purchasing through portable phones. One of the key factors affecting the future of the Internet is that increase in channel capacity, at steady cost, overtakes processor speed. This is in the process of happening; 1999 was the year when the US market spent more on bandwidth than on processing power. Decisions in favour of

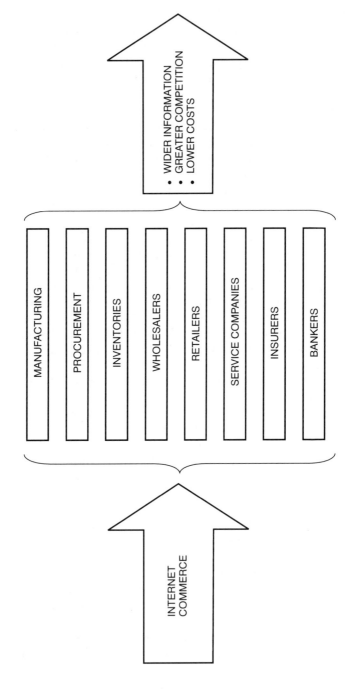

Figure 2.4   The Internet's impact on commercial channels and expected results

bandwidth are expected to intensify in the coming years. This is seen as an Internet-centric development, and top-tier companies are taking advantage of this new trend.

Both B2B and B2C markets stand to profit from current trends and their likely evolution. In 1999, 40 per cent of Dell's sales were done over the Web, while in 1997 this figure was only 8 per cent. Even if the major beneficiaries of bandwidth market are carriers and companies providing communications, hardware and software, the aftermath can be far-reaching. An example of what I mean by this statement is given by the 'Internet in everyone's pocket', a solution projected by Nokia.

Companies manufacturing and marketing portable phones are quick to capitalise on the fact that, because we are living in a mobile world, *nomadic computing* is one of the fundamental characteristics of this decade. A requirement posed by nomadic computing is that every device on the network should be able to communicate its identity with everything else, whether this 'else' is a human user, or another device.

Speaking in terms of a business architecture and of system design supporting it, a major distinction between current and future solutions is between *adaptive* devices and those which are *explicitly guided*. Adaptive devices exist today; the thermostat is one. But they are standalone. The new generation of adaptive devices will be able to network seamlessly with human users and other devices. These adaptive entities will be contact sensitive, automatically identify themselves, and able to tune their actions to the context of a given situation which they are confronting.

The characteristics described in the preceding paragraph are, to a large extent, those behind the forthcoming merger of the Internet and cell phones into an even more potent global communications network. Experts believe this merger will be followed by a rapid rise of nomadic computing services. Its growth will be akin to the characteristic curve radio and television have shown, which has been steep, rather than that characterising classical telephony and motor vehicles, where product acceptance and market growth was rather slow.

Without any doubt, if effectively done this merger of technologies will unleash a swarm of new products, but it will also pose rigorous managerial requirements. Both *our* company's internal control system (see Chapter 1) and its restructured accounting must be ready to track the changes taking place. The system solutions we develop should be flexible and adaptable because projections on product acceptance and market growth of new inventions are notoriously inexact.

The tracking of any product in the fast evolving global market landscape must be in real-time and capillary. This is an obligation for every company which operates in the new economy. Interactive systems need a great deal more attention in online tracking of costs, risks and returns. Also, the aggregates handling them should be designed from the start as big systems. Big systems are not small systems which grew up over time; they have totally different requirements. Well-managed companies know that and therefore they follow up their new designs closely.

1   In principle, no product (no matter how promising) should use as a decision-making paradigm market response to other, earlier products.
2   There is no assurance whatsoever that the Internet's and the cell phones' curve will not bend, because of reasons we presently do not understand.

Power production is a good example of the ups and downs of launching new products. The time lag from discovery to practical applications has been more than 20 years, which is understandable. More puzzling is the fact its growth curve dipped some 50 years down the line. As already mentioned, slow growth also characterised the car industry; then came acceleration of market acceptance largely due to deep cost cutting with the Model T, followed by a flat curve during the period of the great depression. Only a longer term of market acceptance can tell whether a product is a jewel or a lemon.

Finally, practically unlimited broadband capacity put at the disposal of business and of consumers is a dynamic, quickly changing market phenomenon with many unknowns. In an all-you-can-use broadband environment, users need to quickly assess where their business is headed and learn how to compete using virtual companies and strategic alliances, and how to operate, then dissolve, virtual organisations to make new ones.

Senior management must also account for the technological risks facing the ongoing business. In 1980, there was the accidental complete collapse of the Arpanet (today's Internet). In 1990, there was the accidental collapse of AT&T's long-distance system. In 1999, a bug called Melissa spread itself widely through e-mail, infecting Microsoft Outlook users. The year 2000 saw extensive distributed denial-or-service attacks, the 'I Love You' bug, and others.

Professionals willing and able to adapt to Internet forces must appreciate that even simple security attacks can have far-reaching consequences. Trojan horses do not require an unsuspecting user of Internet resources to open an attachment, or even to read e-mail. Any reading of Web pages on a machine without significant security precautions represents a threat.

In all likelihood, with any-to-any broadband networks, penetrations, misuses, damages, system crashes and outages will be relatively easy to perpetrate on any system at any time, no matter how secure it might look. The same is true about stealing sensitive information and systematically compromising backups. Professionals should never be complacent about a fundamental lack of adequate information security measures. We will talk more about this issue in Chapter 11.

6 A BUSINESSMAN'S VIEW OF THE INTERNET AND OF THE MANAGEMENT OF CHANGE

Chapter 1 brought the reader's attention to the management of change. According to Michael Bloomberg, to manage change one has to appreciate that the *Internet is an equaliser* (this idea was expressed in his lecture at the Monte Carlo Investment Forum, 30–31 March 2000). Online marketing makes it difficult to distinguish one firm's product from the next. In an ever-evolving environment, where whatever is already available becomes highly visible, the challenges are:

- how to make money with cost-free services; and
- how to find something to do that the competitors cannot.

For instance, *common buying* (see Chapters 3 and 4) can be a source of liquidity by capitalising on current market inefficiencies. Supply chain examples document the fact that when we allow the components of our business to co-operate with each other, we create *a new, more profitable* environment. The challenge is that if we are not careful, its effects might benefit competitors rather than ourselves.

In principle, online ordering, and (even more so) common ordering, reduces costs, permits more business per sales representative, and produces an improved information flow. But it also brings to the foreground substitution possibilities, pricing transparency, and competition based on quality, as well as possibly creating some friction between business partners leading to agency costs (see Chapter 8).

On the upside, supply chain management through B2B solutions helps in reducing inventory shortages, sees to it that less time is required to fill orders, and provides shorter delivery schedules. It also makes feasible early recognition of customer preferences. But seasoned management would appreciate that for every upside there is a downside.

When a new product or process is launched, we do not always appreciate that it does not have only strengths. Electronic document interchange (EDI) provides an example. Electronic links between companies have been around for more than a decade in the form of EDI. Large manufacturing firms are the main users of the different parochial and incompatible versions of EDI, but only a small portion of their suppliers (no more than 20 per cent) are connected to their EDI system.

Complexity, cost, 'not invented here' thinking and incompatibilities have killed EDI's chances from the start. Happily some lessons were learned from these failures, and the same basic mistakes have not been repeated with electronic mail. This led the way for successful e-mail implementation. Quite similarly, system solutions should see to it that the wider adoption of the Internet:

- is flexible in a system-wide sense;
- draws in a wider range of firms (many of whom do not know each other); and
- means that the links being provided are much cheaper than those of EDI.

All three points are important because in all likelihood the largest impact of business-to-business is likely to be on small to medium-sized enterprises, since many large companies already have electronic links between parts of their empire (intranets) and with their business partners. Also, in B2C terms, by placing the necessary information in an accessible format, merchants could transfer some transaction costs to the customer. This could not happen with EDI because practically no consumers have ever used it, given its complexity, heterogeneity and cost.

Many businessmen now believe that costs can be radically reduced if they are careful about how they plan and implement B2B and B2C solutions. Judging by the processes which inevitably began in the USA and are now rapidly spreading to Europe and Asia, companies in the old economy can significantly improve their results by ordering from new economy companies B2B, especially in an environment of rising material and commodity prices in the manufacturing industry, and higher salaries for IT and other specialists in banks.

Companies also aim to capitalise on enhanced customer proximity over the Internet and customised orders, as well as accurate and quantifiable marketing campaigns which are very important in the new economy. The result is superior supply chain management and a greatly improved customer relationship. To better appreciate these statements and their aftermath the reader should think of the Internet as the new frontier:

- in speed of business transactions;
- in acceleration of information transfer; and
- as a means for swamping costs.

According to some estimates today, we have about 1 per cent of the information that we will have available in 2050. But how many people and companies will be able to distil knowledge from this information overload? This is by no means an idle question because people who fail to interpret in real-time the market's signals may be visionary one day, and blind the next.

Few companies have positioned themselves in a way which permits them to appreciate that when we change the rules of the game, we introduce new variables, new actors and new facts, and these may greatly upset their current business. Easier access and knowledge engineering-enriched datamining greatly facilitates the distribution of services, and brings to the foreground new winners.

No doubt, there will be surprises. Whether in banking or in any other industry, the *killer application* comes from people and companies with a clear vision and a tip-top team able to make things happen. When we wish to get the most out of available technology, we need skills which may not be available today in the organisation, or at least not in the large majority of cases. We also need an environment where these skills can flourish.

Best results are often obtained by an entity which may be a new economy spin-off, works from a high-tech ground, uses unconventional approaches and ends by having a much better price:earnings ratio than its old economy parent company. It is not uncommon that the new economy daughter company emerges as a leader, faster and better than its parent could have done.

7 INVESTMENTS IN TECHNOLOGY WHICH ESPOUSE THE VIEWPOINT OF ALERT BUSINESSMEN

In the life of organisations, and their evolution over time, the factors that determine growth or decay tend to be autocatalytic. Reputation, exploitation of business opportunities, the ability to challenge the obvious, financial staying power, and the drive to maximise one's chances reinforce or undermine each other with the same efficiency.

As so many factors come into play, the advent of new economy entities must be followed up most carefully because that will ultimately lead to the gradual transformation or decay of old economy companies. This will probably take place after we see a few painful disappointments connected to new economy firms, which will be more likely to hit the *laggards* than the *movers*. The first companies to launch a good product and capture a good share of the market stand a better chance than those who stay behind; but, as this transformation happens, mistakes in judgement are magnified by the same forces propelling the new entrants, and they fall behind.

At the same time, the price:earnings (PE) ratios of old-economy companies that are further along the road to the new economy become higher than those rooted in the old economy practice. For instance, Charles Schwab's PE is 3–4 times higher than that of a traditional brokerage firm, because analysts and investors consider Schwab's leadership in information technology and the Internet as an engine for economic and earnings growth. Such stocks are trading at a premium.

Price:earnings ratios, however, do not tell the whole story. More worrisome to the laggards is that they suffer from *cream skimming*. Old economy companies are losing their most profitable customers, leading many financial analysts to believe that the next ten years will be a world of instability in the financial markets, with those companies who stay put going bust.

This being the perceived trend of events, it is not surprising that investments in technology are on an up-trend. But the pace of these technological investments is uneven, and the same is true about what companies obtain in terms of return on investment (ROI). Based on US interviews, the following best estimates exemplify the likely growth in technology investments doing the next years:

Internet	57%
Software	43%
Telecommunications equipment	41%
Semiconductors	40%
Computers	31%

These investments will, by and large, follow the predominant trends in the implementation of technology: Internet commerce, much greater bandwidth, mobile computing, and the Web becoming increasingly intelligent. Among projected top applications are dynamic pricing (through auctions) and B2B exchanges, expected to hit $3.2 billion in business terms in 2001.

Whether a company is a provider of equipment, software and other wares, or a user of Internet services, its senior management is well advised to ask: 'What will be our weight in each of the top business fields of the first decade of the new century?' This question evidently makes sense only among companies which have already established an Internet presence. Taking Europe as an example, the latest statistics among industrial companies is that 50 per cent of British and German, 33 per cent of Italian, and 25 per cent of French firms are on the Internet, though not all practise I-commerce. Three reasons explain why some firms are not yet Internet-enabled:

- lack of skills;
- imperfect security; and
- financial costs.

By contrast, the motivation for those who are involved in I-commerce is that the Internet provides a crossborder level playing field; their projection of turnover in electronic commerce suggests that it will double every year, at least until 2004; and the result of 'not being there' can be an important loss of market share, reducing by so much their ability to meet expectations.

Is it enough to be on the Internet in order to taste the new economy's goodies? The answer, of course, is: 'No, it is not.' One has also to be ahead of the curve and in 2001 being ahead of the curve means espousing *smart technology*, the next big frontier in technology's rapid course. Smarter-and-smarter is a pivotal point of the new economy. In their fundamentals, smart materials capitalise on the development of low cost and low power microprocessors, which permit use (in the best possible manner) of technology's breakthroughs in a range of applications, from automatic identifiers to the work these wares do.

How fast smart technology will enter everyday life, and therefore all aspects of business and industry, depends to a large extent on how fast the cost of electronic tag (e-tag) microprocessors drops towards 1 cent. The new pyramid of computing technology ranges from the peak of supercomputers with prices of $10 million or more, to the new generation of chips with an integrated antennae for any-to-any communication.

In a couple of years, these chips will be costing 10 cents, and by 2005 or thereafter their price might drop to 1 cent. This will be instrumental in making smart technology the catalyst of the new wave of computation which will be available everywhere in the coming years, providing personal access to resources which may be located anywhere in the world.

It is most likely that the return on new high-tech investments will be expressed through much greater efficiency. A characteristic example is what has happened with the use of energy in Western countries. Today oil accounts for a much smaller part of the Group of Ten (G10) economy than ever before:

- in the year 2000 this stood at about 1 per cent;
- it was 2.5 per cent in 1990; and
- it was 6.5 per cent at the end of the 1970s.

That's the way to look at the advances of technology. In the bottom-line Internet commerce is a proxy for consumer spending. John Chambers, CEO of Cisco Systems, said that 'the Internet Revolution will be over in a decade or two when all corporations become e-companies, completely incorporating the Net, in their operations' (*Business Week*, 12 February, 2001). The consensus is that companies have been able to offset rising energy prices by becoming more efficient, particularly through the efficient use of technology.

3 Strengths and Weaknesses of the GM, Ford, DaimlerChrysler and Renault-Nissan Supply Chain Partnerships

1 INTRODUCTION

It has been unavoidable that the supply chain gets restructured as the old economy is replaced by the new, and traditional companies form vast partnerships to take advantage of business-to-business deals on the Internet, as well as compete with new economy companies. Alert management is aware of the fact that whoever falls behind in product innovation, greater productivity and cost-cutting will not be able to hold his own in global competition, and will be left in the dust.

The Internet is not only an equaliser, as Michael Bloomberg says, but also a means to compensate for the fact no company accounts for more than a small fraction of the online market as a whole. To gain the benefit of size in negotiating rock-bottom prices, old economy companies such as GM, Ford, DaimlerChrysler and Renault-Nissan get together in supply chain agreements (see section 3), while other companies such as Cisco and General Electric opt for a lone wolf Internet strategy (see Chapter 4 for General Electric, and Chapter 6 for Cisco).

Internet auctions and reverse auctions radically change the rules of competition. They also require rethinking many accounting rules which were not made for multiple counterparties simultaneously involved in online transactions, some of which are tentative. Alternative supplier accounting is an example of changes needed to face the new terms of trade, and their mapping into *our* financial system.

It is projected that as early as 2002 every industrial and financial organisation worth talking about will be connected to the Internet. All

51

these businesses target not only significant cost benefits but also a compression of the supply chain to take advantage of:

- auctions used as a mechanism for dynamic pricing;
- reverse auctions ('name your price'); and
- universal visibility of product and price information.

The goal is to reduce costs by 10–15 per cent or better, and capitalise on the dynamics of online execution. From all the evidence, this trend expands through business and industry on global scale. To face the challenge, survivor companies have to thoroughly revamp their policies, rethink their system of internal control (see Chapter 1), adapt to the forces of Internet commerce (see Chapter 2), restructure their accounting system, and make their logistics more efficient than ever before.

At least theoretically, the crossborder nature of the Internet also helps to bypass the fact that Europe has not been a very stable landscape of nations and jurisdictions, as its borders changed with some frequency. But the Internet cannot do away with another fact, which is that over the years European society has built a social system that makes it difficult to respond to ongoing challenges from globalisation; the rapid personalisation of products and services; and restructuring for cost cutting. A similar reference is valid for Asia, including Japan.

Those countries and those companies will be able to gain the most from the forces unleashed by the Internet that can best capitalise on the five topmost change agents of the decade 1995–2005, as presented in Table 3.1. All sectors of business and industry can feel their impact. The common factor underpinning all five is *much greater flexibility*, which can be dramatised through the following example I heard in one of the research meetings: 'Be able to change the colour of a car while it is in the assembly line.'

Table 3.1   Change agents and their impact on products and services

Change agent	Impact
Internet	• Greater reach; market and price visibility
Technology	• Drive to capitalise on greater efficiency and productivity
Deregulation	• Freedom to enter a competitive market; fewer hard-core rules
Globalisation	• World-wide market; need for real-time consolidation
Greater customer sophistication	• Increase in demand for innovation and personalisation of products and services

2 BASIC NOTIONS UNDERPINNING THE IMPORTANCE OF THE SUPPLY CHAIN IN THE NEW ECONOMY

The theme of this chapter and Chapter 4 is the supply chain. It has been a deliberate choice to start not with many rather general references but with a case study on the larger and most important example so far, the joint effort in Web-based purchasing. The fundamental notions underpinning this, and any other, Internet purchasing activity are presented in a nutshell in Figure 3.1. Notice the dichotomy between the vendor's viewpoint and that of the purchasing organisation.

The background Figure 3.1 presents will be better appreciated if we keep in mind the contributions of the Internet and of technology at large; namely their ability to create a greater efficiency and to keep the purchasing system flexible. As Chapter 1 has underlined, this requires a cultural change, abandoning preconceived notions, stereotypes and ossified structures of the past. To capitalise on evolving business opportunities we must reset our core values such as

- *fully online commercial services.*

In banking, for example (see Chapter 5), this means all the way to payments, settlements and online exchanges. Alert customers will also require the provision of factual and documented investment services which can be consulted interactively online. The rub is that investment services have become commoditised, while at the same time they require significant amounts of analysis and research.

At root, investment services may range from consulting about choices connected with individual accounts, to complex capital raising activities, initial public offers (IPOs) and transborder money flows. The more important the customers, the more they would want their supply chain to provide business intelligence. This leads to another prerequisite:

- *sophisticated risk management services.*

Sophisticated risk management services should both teach *how to* carry out damage limitation and *how to* implement algorithms and methods. They should not be limited to modelling, but also call for a first-class methodology able to improve upon current risk control, ensure secure transactions (probably through digital certification: see Chapter 11), and provide financial advisory capabilities.

54

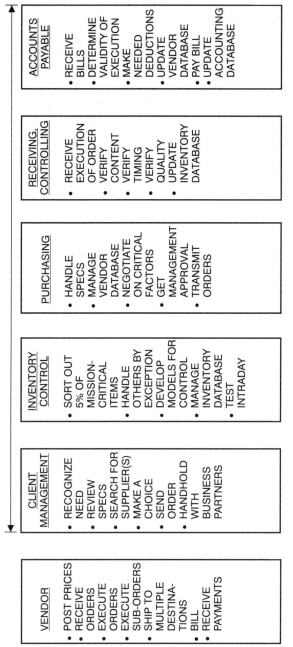

PURCHASING ORGANIZATIONS

VENDOR
- POST PRICES
- RECEIVE ORDERS
- EXECUTE ORDERS
- EXECUTE SUB-ORDERS
- SHIP TO MULTIPLE DESTINA-TIONS
- BILL
- RECEIVE PAYMENTS

CLIENT MANAGEMENT
- RECOGNIZE NEED
- REVIEW SPECS
- SEARCH FOR SUPPLIER(S)
- MAKE A CHOICE
- SEND ORDER
- HANDHOLD WITH BUSINESS PARTNERS

INVENTORY CONTROL
- SORT OUT 5% OF MISSION-CRITICAL ITEMS
- HANDLE OTHERS BY EXCEPTION
- DEVELOP MODELS FOR CONTROL
- MANAGE INVENTORY DATABASE
- TEST INTRADAY

PURCHASING
- HANDLE SPECS
- MANAGE VENDOR DATABASE
- NEGOTIATE ON CRITICAL FACTORS
- GET MANAGEMENT APPROVAL
- TRANSMIT ORDERS

RECEIVING, CONTROLLING
- RECEIVE EXECUTION OF ORDER
- VERIFY CONTENT
- VERIFY TIMING
- VERIFY QUALITY
- UPDATE INVENTORY DATABASE

ACCOUNTS PAYABLE
- RECEIVE BILLS
- DETERMINE VALIDITY OF EXECUTION
- MAKE NEEDED DEDUCTIONS
- UPDATE VENDOR DATABASE
- PAY BILL
- UPDATE ACCOUNTING DATABASE

Figure 3.1   Software-supported functions entering into play in Internet purchasing activities

The effective management of assets and liabilities (ALM) is for any practical purpose a matter of inventory control and logistics. ALM concepts and models were originally developed in the 1970s to address interest rate risk which looms in any portfolio. This became a major concern in the inflationary decade of the two oil shocks as interest rates increased sharply, and they became much more volatile than in the past.

In the uncertain financial environment of 1972 to 1984, credit institutions had to become more qualitatively minded in order to survive. In turn, the models they developed helped to forge a new management culture which found its way into accounting and logistics. Helped by an advancing technology, it also promoted full online real-time solutions connecting any-to-any not only in all places where *our* company operates, but also our company with its business partners both:

- its customers and
- its supply chain.

Based on personal experience, I would add that the methodology prevailing in the way most companies are keeping accounts and are exploiting them should change. Partnerships forged by fierce competitors to capitalise on Web-based procurement is only one example of what needs to be done in order both to take advantage of business opportunities and to keep costs under lock and key, for the benefit of both our firm and its customers.

Improvements to the accounting system are a tall order because the services to which reference is being made must be supported anywhere, at any time, for any product and for any counterparty. They must be personalised and steadily updated, in order to help understand the meaning of transactions and their associated exposure, as well as the interactions underlying the new business perspective.

What the previous paragraphs have stated will be the key to customer handholding in the future, as well as a characteristic of sound management. Sophisticated methods of interactive visualisation, based on solid management accounting principles, must be able to tell whether a company (and an economy) is producing economic value, or is unproductive and decaying. Ratios can be instrumental in this regard. For instance, the dollar / euro exchange rate tells us a great deal about the European economy.

From January 1999 to September 2000 too much European capital continued to be invested in the USA. The inescapable conclusion from this accounting evidence with exchange rates is that if Europe is indeed the new playground of international business, then why do portfolio investments and acquisitions keep going from Europe to America, and not vice versa? What the shrinking Euro tells us is that the market looks to America as the business playground of the first decade of the twenty-first century.

'We also see a society based on technologies that are old,' said one of the participants in this research. The great skill of Europe has still to do with metal. The strong base for biotechnology, semiconductors, broadband and the exploitation of technological breakthroughs is in the USA. All this has a great deal to do with procurement, and no co-operatve effort, such as the one between GM, Ford, Daimler-Chrysler and Renault-Nissan (which we examine below), can forget about the impact of exchange rates on purchasing costs.

A similar reference is valid in connection with the way the banking system functions, and the way in which it reaches globality. The banking system around the world is still trying to digest a couple of bubbles, such as superleveraging with derivatives and overlending, which are still inventoried in its balance sheet. The business of banking is injecting liquidity into the economy by buying and selling time. Credit institutions do this by taking deposits, giving loans and by trading.

If the analysis of accounting information suggests a bank is not over-exposed, the news is good: its condition is not unhealthy, but it may not be innovative either. If so, it is not leading. European institutions who try to imitate others, particularly the Anglo-Saxons, in blending commercial and investment banking are doing themselves a disservice as long as their hand is guided by their old culture.

There is also the question of a cost structure in the banking industry which is too expensive, because of low technology, too much employment and scant attention to overheads. Whether we talk of a credit institution or of a manufacturing and merchandising company, the internal accounting management information system (IAMIS) should be positioned in a way such that it will show if the current organisation is:

- competitive or extremely expensive in a cost-conscious environment;
- strong and able to face the challenges of deregulation or ossified and retrograde.

As Chapter 5 will demonstrate, Internet banking makes cost issues more transparent than ever before. In many countries, banking has been a protected industry, and protected industries do not get so much mileage in a globalised economy. One of the reasons why cartel-type managing is counterproductive is that it allows one's costs to move up to reach and exceed one's revenues. By contrast, surviving companies are those which are strong and productive and therefore able to continue playing a role when confronted by tough competition.

In conclusion, the message this section aims to bring to the reader is that while Internet purchasing agreements, and the revamped supply chain at large, should be welcome, their contribution will be limited if they try to change the economy single-handed. The reader must appreciate that when we talk of growth and survival, a complex web of factors comes into play. The Internet supply chain is just one mode, albeit an important one, in this web of strategic moves for greater efficiency.

3 THE AUTOMOBILE INDUSTRY IS RE-INVENTING ITSELF AND THIS HAS GLOBAL CONSEQUENCES

With more than two dozen industry exchanges now publicly traded, high technology analysts increasingly learn about the aftermath of supply chains on costs and efficiency on both new and old industries. Automobiles are 110-year-old products. The motor vehicle industry had its heyday as the growth sector of the economy in the 1920s. By the 1950s, the auto industry and its suppliers, as well as its sales and service network (including that sector of the oil industry serving autos), was an established industry representing one in seven jobs in the American economy.

Since then there has been a decline. Like steel, motor vehicle companies have been classified as part of the decaying smokestacks of the economy. But the year 2000 held a surprise. Experts now think the car is the next big frontier on the Internet, all the way to the mobile Internet market, and its vertical take-off in Chapter 2 brought this to the reader's attention.

Is it really the bodyshop work and the engines, or is the car's electronic amenities which attract the market's attention? Is it not true that these amenities start to upstage the auto's traditional selling points, such as styling, colour, mileage and antiblock brakes? Is it possible that automobile manufacturers might lose direct control of their customers and become another component – albeit a key part – of global supply chains?

These are by no means idle queries as car companies now have to compete on brand clout and profit potential with their own parts suppliers. Some experts think carmakers could end up paying hefty fees for the privilege of carrying the latest software supports and consumer electronics gadgets on their vehicles. The top brand may shift out of the metal body and the car's motor, as some studies tend to indicate. The statistics presented in Figure 3.2 speak volumes about the trend.

The best scenario for the traditional manufacturers of motor vehicles is that the auto industry is finally reinventing itself. But this scenario has shortcomings because it is still too early to tell which way the laurels will go. Since the DaimlerChrysler merger in 1998, the motor vehicle companies have been consolidating rapidly. Today just six groups produce roughly 75 per cent of the 44 million cars sold year after year. At the same time consumers have developed surprisingly different tastes in cars, more than in other products.

For most auto manufacturers this variety of tastes poses a particular problem because it both collides with and helps a policy of alliances, in search of a faster and more capital-efficient way to grow. This policy of alliances accounts for the reality that some companies do not want to be bought out outright. As a result, the surviving organisation keeps the management of the 'partner company' in place and committed, and tries to bypass political problems that arise when national brands are swallowed up by foreigners.

The trouble is that with loose alliances of that sort come many other problems. For instance, auto companies find that they are competing in

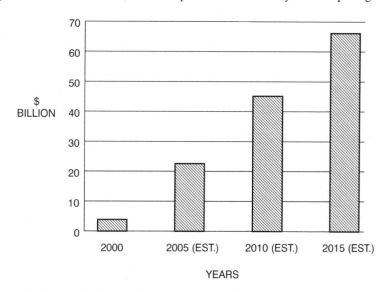

Figure 3.2   Trends in spending on motor vehicles, computers and software by the Japanese auto industry during the coming years

one area while co-operating in another. When the worlds of competition and co-operation collide, things can become rather awkward for all parties, as well as confusing to the market.

Can this collision happen with joint purchasing agreements made to capitalise on the Internet supply chain? The answer is that it *might*, as we will see in section 6. What sort of effect may incompatible information systems and overcapacity have on these alliances, on supply chain agreements, or on cost cutting? The answer is not positive to any one of these queries.

Let us start with what might well be the most important flow. The world over, the plants of auto manufacturers are producing, or have the capacity to produce, too many motor vehicles – much more than the market needs. Overcapacity is expensive, therefore some companies, such as Ford, arc cutting back by selling off and closing plants. Others, such as Audi, Nissan and Honda, appear to be doing the opposite.

Overcapacity and supply chain relationships correlate, as clear-eyed management can see that it is harder to hold on to existing markets just by modernising ageing plants. To cope with a growing global competition we need new departures rather than holding on to old connections. In many cases, it is easier to:

- open up greenfield plants, and
- forge supply chain alliances.

Behind both these options is the drive to cut costs and search for a piece of an existing market which can be sliced from the cake. Lower and lower costs for better quality is one of a modern strategy's pillars. Another is customisation: for instance, in the auto industry tailoring vehicles to answer a specific need at attractive prices. Still another strategy is co-operative engineering design.

GM seems to have designated its European Opel operations to serve as the liaison with Isuzu, Suzuki and its other affiliates which can plug into the global GM digital design system. For instance, a new small car, dubbed the YGM, was drafted simultaneously on Suzuki and GM computer screens that were 6000 miles (10 000 kilometres) apart while designers co-operated with one another through networks.

This example underlines a consequence of employing analytical computational technology to generate computer images of new cars and their components, rather than mocking up every part or sculpting clay models during the design process. The system to which I make reference also permits effective collaboration among designers who are thousands of miles apart. That transition to modelling and simulation has many facets.

New vehicles now go from drawing board to showrooms in about one year instead of the traditional three or four; even one year is unacceptable. This lead time is rapidly shrinking and some car makers, such as Toyota, talk of delivering a custom-made car to client specifications in 3½ days.

Neither would this be the 'ultimate' advance in supply chain management. During the Smart World Conference at MIT (12–13 April 2000) the ability to change car colour while the body was on the assembly line was discussed. Emphasis was also placed on the need to value-analyse any vehicle, and any one of its subsystems and components on a steady basis rather than as a one-off.

At GM, for example, analytical computational technology made it possible to slash $1 billion in product development costs. 'It has potential to get better yet,' says G. Richard Wagoner, Jr, GM's president and CEO, 'because math-based tools aren't fully integrated' (*Business Week*, 10 April 2000). If the experience from banking is any good, they will be integrated in a relatively short time (D.N. Chorafas, *Credit Derivatives and the Management of Risk*, New York Institute of Finance, New York, 2000).

The message the reader should retain from these paragraphs is that computers have become both a process and a product in the car industry. According to an estimate made by Matsushita Communication, by 2003 – which practically means tomorrow – some 40 per cent of all cars sold in Japan will have onboard computers with Internet access (see also the reference to Ford Lincoln in Chapter 2). By 2015, Japan's digital auto drive will constitute a market worth about $67 billion a year in hardware and software. By contract, in 2000 onboard computers were featured in less than 1 per cent of auto sales of $8 billion.

It is not too far fetched to suggest that this projected 850 per cent increase over 15 years, from $8 billion to $67 billion, in market potential is fuelled by software, computing gadgets and the Internet. At the same time, the Internet acts as the auto industry's new sales channel and highway for purchasing (see section 4). The number of cars sold on the Internet when this text was being written was still small, representing less than 1 per cent of auto sales. Statistics, however, say that by June 2000 over 60 per cent of car buyers used the Internet for research and price comparison.

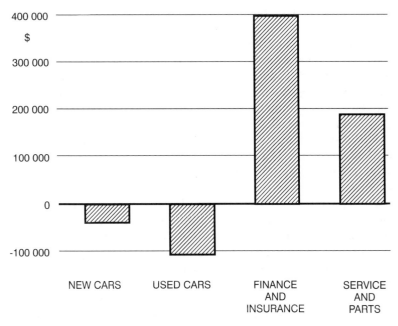

Figure 3.3   The biggest profits for American auto dealers now lie in logistics, from finance to servicing (statistics on an average auto dealer's business)

The larger share of that traffic is going to independent Internet players such as autoweb.com, autobytel.com and cars.com, but the auto companies themselves are quick to exploit this new market through their presence. Not only does this make good sense given the Internet effect, but there are also reasons to believe that for auto dealers profits from finance and insurance have replaced the income source from new and used car sales, as statistics in Figure 3.3 document.

4   COVISINT: THE BIGGEST SUPPLY CHAIN ON THE INTERNET (GM, FORD, DAIMLERCHRYSLER, RENAULT-NISSAN)

On 25 February 2000, GM, Ford, DaimlerChrysler and (with a minor delay) Renault-Nissan abandoned their standalone purchasing policies and joined forces to create the world's largest virtual market. Current estimates suggest that joint purchasing will buy $250 billion worth of parts per year, from thousands or even tens of thousands of suppliers. (Section 5 will review the background of this agreement and its snags.)

Not to be left behind, three days later, on 28 February, Sears Roebuck and Carrefour announced a retail consortium, called GlobalNetXchange. As we briefly saw in Chapter 2, this will bring together $80 billion of annual purchases. Some 50 000 companies sell to these two retailers, and those of their suppliers not ready to face the cost-cutting challenge are running out of luck.

A day after the Sears/Carrefour announcement, on 1 March, Cargill, DuPont and Cenex Harvest, a US farm co-operative, let it be known they were setting up Rooster.com, which will both supply farmers and sell their crops.

The agricultural industry has been slow to embrace the Internet, but this is changing, at least in the USA. Among 2.1 million American farmers, the 380 000 largest ones produce most of the crops and buy most of the farm supplies. About 60 per cent of these bigger farms are now connected to the Net. They are shopping around regionally and nationally, even internationally.

According to the US Agriculture Department, 29 per cent of all American farms, big and small, had Internet access in 1999. That is more than double the per centage in 1997. Of the farms with sales of $250 000 or more, 52 per cent had Internet access in 1999, and this share is growing. Cargill, DuPont and Cenex Harvest capitalised on this Web-awareness when they set up their Net exchange. An interesting characteristic of these consortia is that they aim to be independent, while betting on online sales services as *the* market of the future. To cover their overheads, they will take a small cut on large numbers of transactions, rather than depend on allocations from their parent companies.

The entities resulting from these joint purchasing and sales agreements will probably be big enough by virtue of combining the buying power of their founders. The latter will benefit not only from price cuts but also from the fact they can hold fewer inventories, because the exchange will smooth out demand.

Along this frame of reference from different sectors of the economy, in all likelihood the net effect of COVISINT will be to make the more efficient of its members even more so. As far as effectiveness in operations is concerned, today the COVISINT members are dissimilar, if one judges from net profit per vehicle in second quarter of 2000 shown in Figure 3.4. The partners who would reap the greatest benefit are those who are already the more efficient.

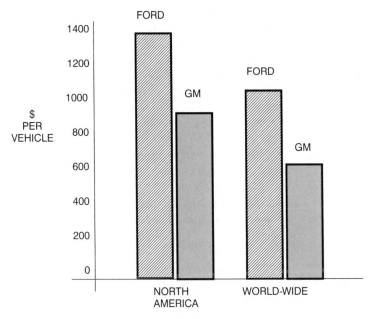

Figure 3.4   Ford versus GM: net profit per vehicle in the second quarter of 2000

Cognisant people who participated in this research also underlined the fact that the massive entry computers and electronic gadgets in the car industry's end product will inevitably have a far-reaching effect. According to their statistics and projections, today in the USA about 90 per cent of the installed power is under the hood of cars; tomorrow it may well be that 90 per cent of installed electronics are embedded in automobiles. If this prognostication is worth its salt, eventually the integration of GM, Ford, DaimlerChrysler and Renault-Nissan purchasing activities on the Internet will become the most potent supply chain in the world in purchasing electronic gear, including computers and communications wares as well as software.

Industry analysts suggest that the more immediate (but still projected) benefit from COVISINT is at least *a 10 per cent cut in costs*, or $25 billion per year. Ten per cent savings represents a margin which can make many automotive manufacturers salivate. Some of them currently have a bare 1.2 per cent profit margin. This 1.2 per cent, for instance, is the profit level Ford has on its operations in the UK, as revealed in the May 2000 decision to close down its assembly operations in England.

To be able to stay in this increasingly more demanding motor vehicle market, and compete in cost terms, auto company suppliers are now obliged to rethink their products and processes. To do so they need a first-class cost accounting system fed by real-time data. Automobile company suppliers, too, who are not up to this challenge will throw themselves out of the market place. In my book, the basic principle is that nobody can resist the forces of the new economy; however, nobody can adapt to the fast developing environment without first-class technology and logistics.

It is somewhat early to say whether companies go for B2B on the Internet because this is a strategic decision, or whether they merely follow a trend. A short while after the GM, Ford, DaimlerChrysler and Renault-Nissan accord, six of the largest automotive parts suppliers joined forces to examine potential Internet commerce initiatives in an effort to:

- Face the challenge set forth by their corporate clients, and
- Accelerate cost-savings on the supply side through I-commerce.

The six are: Delphi Automotive, Dana, Eaton, TRW, Motorola and Valeo (of France). All six are global tier-1 suppliers to the automotive industry. Together, they have annual revenues in excess of $100 billion. If current projections by the car manufacturers that they will be able to shave 10–15 per cent from their suppliers' bills hold true, then the aforementioned six automotive suppliers must do just as well; otherwise, they will not be able to survive.

Since B2B Internet commerce sets the challenge for the coming years, the more clear-eyed suppliers have identified several areas of mutual interest involving I-commerce. They also understood that after having been for a long time support services, accounting and logistics have now come to the frontline. The target of a dynamic logistics system benefiting from models and real-time computation is:

- better supply-chain management;
- immediate customer support; and
- interactive after-sales activities.

The six automotive industry suppliers I made reference to have not been explicit on whether their co-operation would ultimately involve the formation of an Internet-based trade exchange, or would centre more simply on common standards and systems. One way or another, however, the message is that by working together on joint technology they can:

- avoid repetitive costs; and
- establish common solutions.

This is seen as a way to improve effectiveness throughout the supply chain. At Wall Street, one of the analysts I met commented that the response of the six suppliers was to be expected after the big US car manufacturers announced plans for a jointly owned trade exchange. He then added that, in his judgement, only one or two of these supplier companies would really gain a great deal from the common exchange.

Let me conclude with this thought. Not everything depends on the Internet in terms of cost control. Management's attention should start at organisational level (see Chapter 6); and it should look after every detail which has an impact on expenses. Sun Microsystems, for example, put intelligent switches in its offices and factories to switch off lights when nobody is there. This reduced the power bill by an impressive 15 per cent.

5 TAKING THE PROVERBIAL LONG HARD LOOK AT THE INTERNET SUPPLY CHAIN

On one hand, procurement arrangements between industrial organisations (whether in the same industry or cross-industry) mean that additional cost-savings will have to come from further down the food chain. On the other, the pressure coming from the drive for greater cost-effectiveness through Internet purchasing is tremendous, and those companies with blurred management accounting systems who want cost control and who lack high quality standards will not be around for long.

The case studies we have seen in this chapter help to demonstrate that a growing number of companies from both the old and the new economy want to capitalise on the efficiencies the Internet can provide. But while business-to-business exchanges have many characteristics of a sprawling market, significant cost reductions are by no means a foregone conclusion at the level of each individual company. It takes much more than 'B2B magic' to get results.

There is no doubt in my mind that the winners will be those companies which have renewed their culture and are capable of an ingenious implementation of new technology. Only a deep-rooted policy of innovation, not just catchwords and presence in I-commerce, can transform old technology companies into more efficient and more profitable ones. An example is what GM intends to do by using its Hughes Electronics satellite capability: it plans to offer new technology services, through products such as direct satellite television, and to enter into a variety of satellite / Internet locator services and similar domains.

GM and some of its competitors also hope to incorporate modular approaches to building their cars, further exploiting B2B Internet commerce to put pressure on their suppliers. One of the expected results is the ability to provide the consumer with *on demand* access to new products, such as cars and trucks, made to order in a timeframe as short as a week.

This initiative goes beyond the present confines of COVISINT, whose goals have already been pursued individually by some of the automotive industry suppliers. For instance, in August 1999 Visteon conducted its first online bidding activity among its suppliers to competitively award nearly $150 millions in circuit board business. Pre-qualified suppliers were invited to bid online for providing the company with the latest printed wiring circuit board technology. This hour-and-a-half long event was the first of many that Visteon has been conducting to source online a variety of commodities. The company's goal is to leverage the most advanced global automotive resources for its customers, while cutting its own costs.

In a way, Visteon's entire electronic commerce strategy should be seen from the COVISINT perspective. The aim is to forge strong, reliable partnerships with the best suppliers anywhere in the world. Therefore, management has explored the possibility of employing the concept of Internet retailing to supplier sourcing at the beginning of 1999. Within months a team had designed and implemented an electronic procurement system that would accommodate real-time, online bidding from anywhere around the globe. Suppliers have been accessing the bidding site via a standard Web browser and a password.

Unlike target pricing, where a customer typically sets a target price for a commodity, the suppliers' bidding sets an effective market price for the technologies and commodities being sourced. This is in a way similar to bid / ask in the foreign exchange market, and it can be analysed through similar tools (D.N. Chorafas, *How to Understand and Use Mathematics for Derivatives*, Volume 1, *Understanding the Behaviour of Markets*, Euromoney, London, 1995). Once they are online, suppliers have been able to view the prices being bid for a particular commodity. But they do not see the names of the other organisations involved, therefore preserving a certain degree of confidentiality. Throughout the event, submission of bids is in strict confidence in the same way the bidding system worked prior to the advent of electronic commerce.

If one ignores day-to-day business and takes a long hard look, it is possible to appreciate that Internet commerce and steady innovation in business ventures share a common background. The strategic question underpinning them is, 'What is the most likely model of a successful company in the twenty-first century?' There are different variations on this theme but all well-managed entities are looking at what exactly is an affordable business structure. From this perspective we should examine:

- business-to-business Internet commerce; and
- supply line co-ventures on product improvement.

Those are two related approaches to the same strategic question. At Visteon, for example, the Board seems to appreciate that the automotive industry is on the edge of a consumer-driven revolution; one that it has never experienced before in its 110-year history. Therefore, the way to bet is that the complacent will perish, which induces alert executives to move on.

It is only reasonable to expect that other old technology industries, even those without direct consumer products (such as steel, aluminium, chemicals and machinery), will also try to become new technology users. They have to do so if they wish to improve their efficiency and productivity, which is practically synonymous with saying 'if they wish to stay in business and prosper'.

One of the signs pointing in this direction is the fact that old technology industries are consolidating and restructuring in an effort to redefine themselves and establish their place in the new global economy. This economy is merciless to people, companies and nations which stay behind, as I have stated so often. Not all these new departures are going to be successful, however, and to escape bad surprises we should learn from the problems other people have found in their way.

6   LEARNING FROM THE DIFFICULTIES THE COVISINT PARTNERSHIP IS GOING THROUGH

The collaborative Internet purchasing agreement of four major players in the motor vehicle industry, of which we spoke in section 4, illustrates how big competitors can put aside their rivalries and work together. The predecessor to the concept underpinning COVISINT dates back to November 1999 when GM and Ford independently started their own Internet market places for autoparts. Subsequently, they realised they could get more mileage by combining forces.

The trigger to collaboration in purchasing has probably been the fact that, early in January 2000, some major suppliers complained about having to deal with multiple market places which pose largely hetero-geneous demands and use incompatible specifications. The rumour has it that thereafter GM made a suggestion to the president of Oracle, Ford's software partner, which planted the seed of a combined exchange.

Before going on, let me define the difference between Internet com-merce exchanges and collaboration hubs. In I-commerce, exchanges work in a way similar to stock markets. Buyers and sellers meet, more or less anonymously, to agree on prices of commodities such as energy or telecommunications bandwidth. The buyers and the sellers may be independent dot-coms or entities acting on behalf of major industry players. A crucial element in this interplay is the neutrality of the exchanges.

By contrast, I-commerce *collaboration hubs* go well beyond the trans-action phase. Their goal is to help companies complete projects, from design and manufacturing to distribution. The underlying concept is to provide an online workplace, for instance, for contractors to collabor-ate with architects, handle blueprints, administer permit processes, purchase building materials, and do whichever other chores are neces-sary to see the project through.

In the case of the automakers in the COVISINT consortium, the joint effort was that of an exchange. Its potential did not fail to attract the eye of investment bankers who acted as catalysts. In January 2000, at separate meetings with GM and Ford in Detroit, Morgan Stanley Dean Witter executives raised the prospect of combining forces.

- Such a combination, they said, would bring forward the world's larg-est B2B agreement.
- It also had the potential to create worth up to $10 billion on the stock market within 5 years.

The way it has been reported in the financial press, J.P. Morgan was not far behind in joining forces. It launched its pitch at the 1 February dinner with GM's top executives, including the company's president, G. Richard Wagoner, Jr. The investment bankers argued that manufacturers of motor vehicles and their suppliers could use Internet power to save billions of dollars in costs.

Neither were the profits of the exchange itself forgotten. It was calculated that by charging transaction fees for both companies' $600 billion in annual purchasing, the exchange could generate billions of dollars in new revenue. The seeds planted by investment bankers blossomed when Ford's president, Jacques A. Nasser, called GM's president to talk about a joint venture. Three weeks later, DaimlerChrysler joined. The deal was done and it was made public on 25 February 2000 (see section 3). Insiders, however, say that while it is pace-setting, the I-commerce deal was not without its problems. These began with the allocation of responsibility and accountability at the consortium's CEO level.

The automakers' Internet market place found itself with four CEOs (Tom Colberg, who has been an interim CEO from Pricewaterhouse-Coopers, and co-CEOs A. Alan Turfe from GM, Alice Miles from Ford and Peter Weiss from Daimler) with the result that, according to insiders, even the most basic decisions led to lengthy debates.

The fact that choosing a name for the new venture took nearly three months is not so disturbing. More fundamental is the fact that, as should have been expected, there were technological conflicts and these arose almost immediately. Ford settled on Oracle for software to run its exchange; but GM chose upstart Commerce One's market place software, and DaimlerChrysler asked why SAP's software should not be employed.

The three software companies themselves were not strangers to these arguments. Oracle, Commerce One and SAP understood very well that whichever company's technology dominated would stand a much better chance of getting lucrative business from auto-parts suppliers (a very worthwhile market). This debate about suppliers is very relevant to a great array of off-the-shelf software vendors, and most importantly to developers of Enterprise Resource Planning (ERP) systems.

The conflict underpinning the choice of software technology drives home another issue which will show up time and again with Internet commerce. When fierce competitors combine forces to gain mass market advantages, it is unavoidable that their incompatible information technology will stand in the way. By providing an integration of formerly discrete islands of applications, the vendors of ERP systems have plenty to gain provided they are retained as the common solution of the partners.

7 COST CONTROL MEANS A BETTER BOTTOM LINE, BUT ALSO REQUIRES CHALLENGING THE OBVIOUS

On 21 March 2000, Morgan Stanley, Goldman Sachs, BP, Royal Dutch Shell and others announced they would combine their purchasing. Contrary to the automotive industry deals we saw in sections 3–6, this agreement on Internet trade is cross-industry. As such it opens a different vista on the way online purchasing exchange may evolve in the years to come. The concept of a restructured supply chain is expanding.

In quick succession, on 29 March 2000, Boeing, Lockheed Martin and Raytheon of the USA, and British Aerospace & Electronics Systems of the UK, made a similar announcement about joining forces for purchasing on the Internet. These four big aerospace companies sell a combined $400 billion per year, and expect cost cuts of 10–15 per cent. This means $40 to $60 billion cuts on price lists of their suppliers in the aerospace industry. It also represents a squeeze down to *pure cost* in a sector of the economy which tries hard to survive. The end result is the disappearance of aerospace industry suppliers unable to *re-invent themselves* on an ever lower cost basis in:

- product design;
- manufacturing; and
- distribution.

The Internet-enabled exchange of four out of the world's five largest aerospace companies is bringing together thousands of suppliers and customers, including airlines and governments. Therefore, this joint venture promises to be one of the most important electronic trading platforms, allowing its partners to buy parts from some 30 000 supply chain businesses online.

Analysts think the presence of these four companies should ensure that the Internet-based exchange becomes the leading site in the defence and aerospace industry. In a way, this Internet-level partnership has been a response to the merger of Germany's DaimlerChrysler Aerospace and France's Aerospatiale Matra projected for late 2000, which created the world's number three aerospace and defence group. In an industry renowned for its global sales, registered buyers from the group of four can source from a pool of spares and equipment, but the joint Internet site will stop short of offering aircraft or military hardware. Still, the way Phil Condit, Boeing chairman, put it: 'This will transform the way we do business. A global e-marketplace is absolutely essential to drive new levels of efficiency for the industry' (*Financial Times*, 31 March 2000).

During the same interview, Vance Coffman, Lockheed chairman, said 'easily half' of his company's annual $13 billion purchases could be transferred to the new Internet exchange. Even at 10 per cent cost reduction, which is the lower level of the projected range, this represents $1.3 billion in savings for Lockheed and a corresponding loss of earnings for its suppliers, leading to some critical questions:

1   Are these suppliers ready to face the challenge with similar cost cuts, and still maintain a healthy profit margin?
2   Do they have in place a cost accounting and logistics system permitting them to turn the screw on *their* internal costs and on *their* suppliers?

As I never tire of repeating in my seminars, the twenty-first century will not be kind to those companies who do not know how (or do not want) to manage their costs, or whose culture does not permit them to challenge the obvious. The more merciless becomes the global competition, the more the old standard bearers of business and industry who do not re-invent themselves are in peril.

Neither is the wave of co-operative Internet-enabled exchanges ready to subside. Another major drive targets electronic parts. Several competitors are eyeing the leadership in online business exchanges for computers and other electronics. IBM, for example, has made agreements with Nortel Networks, Toshiba, and some other companies for a consortium, *e2open.com*. Its goal is buying and selling semiconductors and passive elements over the Internet, with the aim of streamlining the purchasing process, and bringing down the costs of semiconductors. Typically such exchanges are not limited to their original partners. For instance, IBM is also negotiating with Nokia, L.M. Ericsson, Motorola, Seagate Technology, Philips Electronics, Matsushita Electric and Hitachi Electronics in order to enlarge the original group of partners.

This IBM-led venture has been preceded by a similar agreement between Compaq Computer, Gateway, and Hewlett-Packard who joined forces in creating an online market place. Similar exchanges have been established or are in the process of doing so in the chemical industry.

As is to be expected, the leading partner stands to profit from an I-commerce exchange. IBM will build the online market place using its own hardware and software, as well as products and services from its electronic commerce partners, Ariba and i2 Technologies. An initial public offering of the exchange has also been considered, though it might be several years away.

These and the other initiatives on procurement of semiconductors and other gear on the Internet come at a time when practically all electronics companies are already pretty much procuring online and have the ability to share connections with their suppliers. It is not always necessary to aggregate purchasing on a co-operative basis; a lot of Web-based procurement is already happening on the initiative of different independent agencies.

Extending corporate intranets to include indirect procurement has, for example, helped British Telecom to save as much as £5 billion ($7.5 billion) in purchasing costs. Other carriers are in discussions with a number of equipment and service providers across the supply chain in order to determine:

- how best the portal should be run; and
- what sort of services it should offer.

Though admittedly the telecommunications industry has not been highly active when it comes to building extranets that unite competitors along the lines followed by the automobile industry, no sector of the economy wants to be left behind as regards the prospect of big savings. Few companies, however, are ready to challenge the obvious; yet, in the years to come, this will be a big factor in separating winners from losers. This is the important message to keep in mind. The rest is projections and estimates. Just prior to the Nasdaq meltdown of 2000, several analysts projected that, before this decade is over, 40 percent of business and 15 percent of retail trade will come from Internet-related services. By March 2001, even longtime I-commerce boosters have been questioning growth assumptions. They wonder if Internet commerce will capture more than 5 per cent to 10 per cent of all retailing revenue, not the 15 percent that was expected earlier. All these are guestimates influenced more by the stock market fortunes than by a factual market research.

*   *   *

The Nasdaq blues have spread to executive positions. As the first quarter of 2001 came to a close, some of the better-known names in dot-coms find themselves without a chief executive officer. These include COVISINT, BarnesandNoble.com, and Alitalia. Yahoo! and Terra Lycos have lost seven senior executives between them, while Ebay cannot find a sales manager. All this bodes ill for Internet companies which are in sore need of experienced management talent.

4 Why Supply Chain Relationships Require Very Efficient Accounting and Logistics

1 INTRODUCTION

The practical examples presented in Chapter 3 come, to a very large extent, from the USA. Today, the American market makes up around 80 per cent of world-wide Internet commerce. Western Europe represents about 10 per cent and East Asia 5 per cent. The rest is dispersed. Over the near-term, the US share is expected to decline to about two-thirds to three-quarters of the world's total online commerce, as Europe catches up, followed by Asia. It is appropriate, however, to distinguish between:

- retail trade, or B2C; and
- wholesale trade, or B2B.

It is also necessary to appreciate that, as documented by a survey by Webmergers (*Business Week*, 4 September 2000), in the first 7 months of 2000, out of 238 dot-com start-ups, 41 collapsed, 29 were sold in fire sales and 83 withdrew their plans for initial public offerings. The Internet world is a tough place.

The Internet will continue to grow in spite of this mortality rate, however. In total numbers, many projections suggest that Web-based commerce is likely to progress rapidly, as shown in Figure 4.1. Some sectors will move faster than others. As regards B2C, even after 5 years of online retail sales in the USA it is only expected to be worth around 6 per cent of total retail sales. The careful reader will recall from Chapter 2 that only 50 per cent or so of consumer spending will probably be affected, even in the longer term.

Current projections indicate that total world-wide Internet commerce would be worth between 3 and 5 per cent of global GDP in 2005. More impressive are the figures regarding Internet users. Lehman Brothers forecasts that by 2005 the world will add 70–80 million new Internet

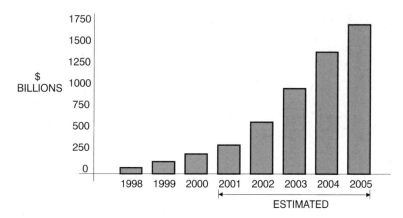

Figure 4.1   Higher end estimates of current and projected transaction revenue through Internet commerce

users every year, and some 70–75 per cent of these new users will reside outside North America.

The first forecast looks to me too optimistic, especially as there are other statistics to be considered. According to Essex Investment Management, over half of the world's population has never made a telephone call. Even in markets which are trying to accelerate their development, the demand for traditional voice telecommunications is sluggish, at 3–5 per cent per year. Demand for voice telecom may, however, be getting a boost as Internet-based telephony comes of age.

Different projections characterise the B2B growth in Internet commerce as companies become cost-conscious and take advantage of the Net. In Chapter 3 we spoke of the automotive and aerospace industries. Health care companies, too, are joining forces to squeeze costs out of purchasing: Johnson & Johnson, Abbott Laboratories and other firms entered into agreement and were joined by General Electric (see also section 2). As we will see in the present chapter:

1   transparent supply chains mean *exposed pricing*, as everyone sees everyone else's bid and auctions serve as discovery processes (see sections 3 and 4).

This evidently worries all business players and motivates them to take both measures and countermeasures. In late March 2000, in a move to block Internet health care companies from usurping their relationships with patients and doctors, and eventually taking away large portions of their business, some of the biggest health insurers developed their own Internet project: Aetna, US Healthcare, Cigna, WellPoint Health Systems, Oxford Health Plans, Foundation Health Systems and Pacific Care Health Systems. This initiative pits these insurers against Healtheon / WebMD, a leading Internet health care company.

The six insurers hope their project will make it easier for patients to enrol in health plans, and choose doctors and hospitals by replacing paperwork and telephone calls with online channels. They also expect to smooth relations with disaffected physicians by speeding communications, as well as cutting business costs. The online solution would handle administrative services too, such as approving or denying medical procedures and processing payment claims. This sees to it that:

2   real-time accounting and financial reporting procedures have become the pivotal point in any well-documented management action on Internet procurement and sales.

As these examples demonstrate, the forces of the Internet are changing the business landscape. From auto manufacturers, to aerospace, electronics, health care and insurers, entities are coming together with an eye on costs. It is not enough, however, for the different providers to appreciate that common buying is a new source of liquidity, and it is wise to capitalise on current inefficiencies in the supply chain. Whether as a lone wolf or in unison with others, a company must be prepared to capture the Internet opportunities. This needs lots of preparation, as the case study on General Electric (GE) documents.

2   GENERAL ELECTRIC'S EXAMPLE: A LONE WOLF STRATEGY IN INTERNET COMMERCE

The emphasis Chapter 3 has placed on joint ventures for Internet-based purchasing exchanges should not be seen as the only way to go. While by grouping together the resources of several companies we can capitalise on the effects of scale in purchasing agreements through I-commerce, lone wolf approaches, too, can pay dividends as this case study documents. The coming years will prove what constitutes the better solution:

* lone wolf solutions; or
* cross-industry agreements.

Neither discharges our company from the obligation of re-inventing itself and its business. To better appreciate the reference to General Electric's and its Internet strategy, we should keep in mind that the process of restructuring and re-inventing started long ago when Jack Welsh became the CEO. There is no better reference to this than the colossus that became GE Capital Services and its subsidiaries. One of them is GE Equity.

With holdings in more than 250 companies, GE Equity has become the top performer among the 28 distinct operations that make up GE Capital Services. In the fourth quarter of 1999 GE Equity made about $300 million in after-tax gains by selling shares in the Internet Capital Group and other companies. An April 2000 tally showed GE Equity to be sitting on $4 billion in unrealised gains in the publicly traded stocks it held. This is a far cry from the former GE, which depended on hardware manufacturing for its income.

Holding Internet stocks and trading in them is not the only way GE capitalises on the new economy. Its management has set out an ambitious programme of I-commerce under which virtually all its sales are scheduled to be carried out electronically. The concepts behind this programme underscore the company's determination to use the Internet as the proving ground of the new economy. GE's top management thinks that ultimately 100 per cent of the company's transactions could go through the Internet. This is a general strategy, whether sales concern medical equipment, aircraft motors, speciality plastics, domestic appliances, lamps, turbines for power production, or financial services marketed through GE Capital. As a company, General Electric wants to graft the I-commerce discipline on to its basic strategy of boundaryless selling.

Under the notion of *boundaryless selling*, marketing through a policy of product specialisation gave way to teams of managers and representatives who sell items across the company's product range. This cross-product marketing works in synergy with GE's Internet strategy, but it also poses several organisational prerequisites (see also Chapter 6). It requires, among other things:

- sophisticated design of Web sites to make them work in a range of products, services and languages, which is a marketing challenge;
- a thoroughly revamped accounting and logistics system which can handle, often in real-time, a golden horde of products and currencies; and
- advanced risk management solutions able to cover (both individually and in an integrative way) credit risk for counterparties anywhere in the world.

For global trading, for example, payment systems have to be configured to suit a number of currencies and settlement conditions. GE did that. It also made sure that its sites were able to target a spectrum of customers, from distributors, retailers and consumers, to individual businesses: small, medium and big.

General Electric did not re-invent the wheel in terms of capturing business opportunity on the Internet. In its way, it took the best practices from companies such as Microsoft, Dell, Cisco and Wal-Mart, even if GE itself and its people are highly inventive. A major advantage in doing so is that at GE the 'not invented here' mentality disappeared long ago. The new corporate culture imprinted by Jack Welsh prompts employees to learn from other practices, then act fast to get results. At the same time, workouts broke down a lot of the bureaucracy inside GE, and a new corporate culture encouraged everyone to speak out.

This new culture and structure saw to it that ideas move quickly through General Electric's echelons and divisions. This is what senior management calls a *massive knowledge transfer*. Such constant flow of ideas and experiences seems to make the majority of GE employees welcome change, while the company positions itself to face the forces of the twenty-first century.

From concepts connected to globalisation to the implementation of Six Sigma (a system design for high product quality and cost control) and strategies relating to Internet commerce, new notions about business practices have moved horizontally through the different business units. There are plenty of deliverables: take Internet auctions and online procurement as an example.

General Electric suggests that Internet auctions brought significant savings through both price reductions and process improvements. Here is just one example. Prior to B2B auctions, GE had purchased 103 varieties of safety glasses but, realising that it could not effectively run an auction on the Web on specifications for 103 varieties of glasses, it set in motion an organisational study that consolidated them down to eight. GE is the first to suggest that it could have done the consolidation earlier, but somehow it did not.

- purchasing in volume online requires a smaller number of varieties to be effective.
- internet trade was the *catalyst* to a significant process improvement.

Leading on from this, on the profit and loss side of the equation, online procurement saved GE some $200 million per year, while the company also received an additional $87 million in savings on the cost of the glasses. There were also other savings which upped the total figure of cost reduction.

It was the focus on the Internet auction, and preparation for it, that spurred the change. The end result has been major economies in procurement of safety glasses from an original $468 million to only $113 million. Other practical cases of Internet commerce also led to commendable results as they contributed by:

- expanding GE's market;
- improving productivity;
- lowering all sorts of costs; and
- helping to reinvent the corporation.

It is precisely this multiple effect, rather than I-commerce alone, that has allowed GE to grow faster than its markets and its competitors on both its top and bottom lines. The big change took place in the mid- to late 1990s, when GE transformed itself thanks to the aforementioned initiatives. Its whole corporate culture changed, from a renowned engineering company that produced original equipment and had big shares of relatively stagnant markets, to a global financial and high technology entity with smaller shares of huge dynamic markets.

As Internet auctions are a potent factor in price discovery and in restructuring century-old concepts about trade, sections 3 and 4 will examine how and why they contribute to real reform. This will help to put into perspective several issues connected with online business activities which both help to expand the market and assist the reader in deciding whether certain growth projections are oversold, undersold, or just right.

3   INTERNET AUCTIONS AND THE NOTION OF TRESPASSING ON THE WEB

Auctions connected with Internet commerce address a range of items, old and new: for instance, new materials, all kinds of machines, surplus inventory, used equipment, perishable foodstuffs, arts items and other goods. In I-commerce auctions are becoming a popular sales channel, driven either by sellers or by buyers. For example, AdAuctions.com runs auctions of advertising space while FreeMarkets does reverse auctions of industrial equipment and materials.

In itself, the concept of auctions is not new. It has been practised by all sorts of companies, including central banks: for instance, there is a variety of methods for selling securities, depending on the type of securities or the aim of government debt management. No two reserve institutions follow exactly the same procedure, yet practically all are conducting auctions. In Germany, for example, Federal bonds, Federal Treasury notes, Federal Treasury discount paper and parts of five-year special Federal bond issues are sold by auction through the Bund Issues Auction Group. Tap issues of the federal Government (five-year special Federal bonds of the current series, Federal savings bonds, Treasury financing paper) are sold in the *open market*, with no fixed issue period or issue volume set in advance.

The policy of auctions can change over time: for instance, until the end of 1997 German Federal bonds were issued through the Federal Bond Consortium using a combined syndicate and auction procedure; but five-year special Federal bonds, Federal Treasury notes and Treasury discount paper were issued exclusively by auctions. All domestic credit institutions holding a giro account with a Land Central Bank were entitled to bid in this auction procedure, which is schematically presented in Figure 4.2.

By contrast, since January 1998 Federal bonds, parts of five-year special Federal bond issue amounts, Federal Treasury notes and Treasury discount paper have been issued uniformly by auction through a restructured Bund Issues Auction Group. Domestic credit institutions, securities trading houses and securities trading banks may become members of this auction group, provided they have a certain minimum placing facility.

Compared to the procedure followed with Federal debt paper, auctions on the Net follow a much simpler approach, but they also are subject to a much greater security risk. Internet companies try to have it both ways: greater flexibility with the least possible exposure. Real life, however, does not work like that. In a 31 March 2000 e-mail, Jeff Bezos, the CEO, informs us that Amazon.com Auctions is now open, then he makes the following points.

1 In the past, when one bought something at his online store, one was always dealing in specific items supported by Amazon.com, such as books.
2 Starting from the above-mentioned date, the Amazon.com community itself, of almost 8 million customers, can sell anything they want to on the Amazon.com Web site.

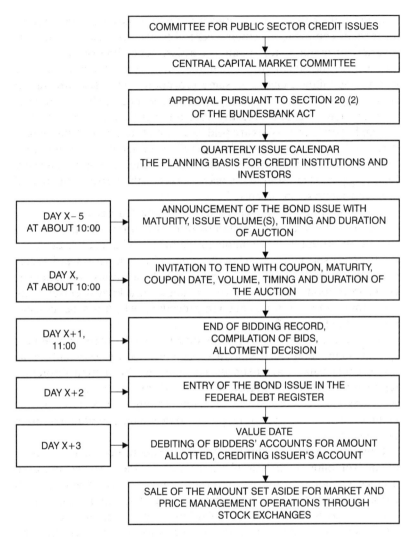

Figure 4.2   Block diagram of the procedure characterising a German Federal bond auction

The issue raised by Bezos is that letting millions of sellers participate in Amazon.com is another way to give his clients the broadest selection possible. They can find rare books and signed first editions, rare music, vintage toys, antiques, sports memorabilia, collectables of all kinds, and so on. Evidently, they can do so at their own risk.

The CEO of Amazon.com did not fail to note that with its new business move his company aimed to do something bold. That is what its auctions policy is all about. It presents buyers with an interesting auction experience, through the honour system. Essentially, the company will take the client's word for it, if one is ever the victim of fraud. In my opinion, only after this system is tested in court can an idea about its soundness be formed.

The risks associated with the new auctions scheme have not escaped the attention of Jeff Bezos and therefore there are some restrictions: for instance, the Amazon.com guarantee does not apply to purchases above $250. This might not matter so much because the majority of items in this sort of auction sell for less than that, but it is a useful limit to liability.

Buying and selling involves risks to the host company, and not only to the players in the auction. Exposure can come from many sides. In May 2000, a French judge's decision forced Yahoo's auction service to make Nazi memorabilia inaccessible in France. The judge cited a French law that renders the sale or display of anything inciting racism illegal.

Yahoo objected to this ruling, saying its international sites could not be held responsible for respecting all laws in all countries. Experts, however, think that whether or not such arguments by Internet portals and service providers have any legal value in any and every sovereign country is an issue which will keep many lawyers busy in the years to come.

Neither can Internet auctions be free of fraud. One type of fraud is beating up prices in a price discovery auction (see section 4). In May 2000 eBay suspended the seller and voided the sale of an abstract painting whose price shot from 25 cents to $135 805. The reason for this action had nothing to do with the authenticity of the painting. Rather, on the second day of a 10-day auction, the seller had entered a bid of $4500 on his own offering, a practice known as *shill bidding*.

Analysts were quick to point out that the Internet auctions world faces a deeper problem than lone self-bidders acting as partners who have engaged in cross-bidding activities. There are many schemes, some of them illegal (this one included), that may influence the outcome of online auctions.

The *New York Times* datamined eBay's auction records and assembled a list of 33 Internet names that repeatedly bid on one another's offerings. These participants have also prompted other bidders by posting glowing testimonials to one another on eBay's feedback system, the *comment forum*.

eBay does not deny this is happening. 'We look for rings,' said Robert Chesnut, the company's associate general counsel. 'We have detected rings. But there is a limit to *shill bidding*. And there are things that look like *shill bidding* that are not' (*International Herald Tribune*, 3–4 June 2000, emphasis added).

The company does not divulge how many people it has expelled for shill bidding so far, but the practice of beating-up prices can have a disastrous effect on Internet-enabled auctions. The case of the cancelled abstract painting auction, for example, drew 95 bids although the bid history contains just 17 names. Such a concentration of bidders provokes questions about:

- the reliability of bidding on the Web; and
- the practice of masquerading under a variety of Internet names.

These people regularly bid on one another's items but have rarely placed the winning bid. Their tactics consist of attracting public attention, thereby pushing the prices higher. With this, they are biasing the pricing process, and are reducing the confidence consumers and other entities have in the online auction system as a whole.

Another counterproductive online practice is that of trespassing on the Internet. In May 2000, a US Federal judge in California ruled that the practice of collecting information from third-party Web sites through automated search programs, also known as *crawlers*, constitutes trespassing. Judge Ronald Whyte issued a preliminary injunction barring Bidder's Edge, which indexes online auctions, from presenting users with the best deal by automatically harvesting information from eBay.

The judge found that Bidder's Edge was trespassing by using the resources of eBay's computers without the owner's permission. 'The law recognises no such right to use another's property,' the ruling said. In effect, the judge's design outlawed deep linking and reaching beyond the online auctions.

The characteristic of deep links is that they take their users directly to a relevant item on a given website which typically belongs to another firm. This is modern-day trespassing, yet their work is part and parcel of the Internet's fundamentals. A similar job is done by search engines, content aggregators, comparison-shopping sites, and other software constructs performing basic search functions on the Web.

4   DYNAMIC PRICING THROUGH B2B AND B2C AND INTRINSIC TIME

Many companies have accepted the wisdom of using a sharp knife in cutting costs, but few have figured out how much money they are giving up by using static pricing strategies for their products and services. Part of the reason for this failure is cultural. Another part reflects the fact management often lacks detailed information about the price the market can afford. As a result, companies:

- routinely overprice some products,
- while most often underprice others.

Different incentive schemes amplify this failure. In many entities the sales force works on poorly studied quotas and/or is compensated on how many units it sold regardless of profit margins. As a result, salesmen tend to push the low-margin items because it is easier to sell more units when these are underpriced; even underpriced products have marketing dollars to spend.

This is precisely the opposite of what should be done, and it could be corrected through *dynamic pricing* using the Internet as a vector. Also known as *smart pricing*, the process described in this section draws on a web of supporting mechanisms including costing, market research, buyer psychology and computing power. The latter is needed to sift through lots of data on spending patterns.

A prerequisite of smart pricing is sophisticated software. Atlanta's Talus Solutions developed yield-management programming products for airlines and hotels, which provide a test-bed for smart pricing through a novel experimental approach. A basic tenet of this revenue management solution is that an item's price should not be static: it should vary constantly with changes in supply and demand.

This concept is relatively new, but it is catching up fast. Ford is a good example of a new pricing approach. Starting in 1995, the motor vehicle company stepped up market research to find features that the customer was willing to pay for, but the industry was slow to deliver. It also:

- set up its sales units as profit centres accountable for Profit and Loss (P&L); and
- told them which vehicles and option packages made Ford the most money.

By being informed about costs and margins, the sales units can focus their marketing effort on products with higher profit potential. Ford also re-engineered pricing to encourage customers to move up to better, higher-profit vehicles. That required segmenting the market so that full-price customers could not see the bargains that others were getting.

Hotels in Las Vegas have a different smart pricing strategy. For the same room at the same hotel prices can vary by up to a factor of five depending on whether there is a major event in town, such as Comdex, or any other reason increasing demand for available rooms. Unlike big cities such as New York and London, in Las Vegas hotels room rates over the weekend are higher than in the middle of the week when demand is low.

Dynamic pricing, however, requires lots of homework. To start with, it should not be used without careful market study. In some industries too much price variance can backfire. Coca-Cola found that out in 1999 when it floated the idea of changing the prices of drinks in vending machines depending on the weather. Marketers warned that Coke could damage its brand by price volatility, and customers howled at the thought of paying more on hot days.

Evidence so far available indicates that varying the price constantly works best in situations where there is no firm bond between the buyer and the seller. It should not be done in transactions where relationships matter. A thorough marketing study should make sure the company is not antagonising its customer base but, on the contrary, offers its clients the chance to benefit from a pricing variance, as is the case with the hotels in Las Vegas.

Another issue to be carefully examined is how far services provided in one industry can affect the prices charged for services in another. An example is the pricing model announced in April 2000 by UGC, the French cinema operator. Its offer to the public has been that instead of paying for a ticket every time you go to a movie, you can opt for a yearly fee of Ffr1176 ($178) paid in twelve monthly instalments. This not only emulates the pricing by Canal Plus, the French private television operator, but it allows subscribers to visit at no other cost as many cinemas as they like throughout the national UGC network. UGC capitalised on the fact that its network features 700 theatres throughout Europe. This network has been suffering from pay-TV competition, since pay-TV too offers the latest feature films. UGC management bet on a smart pricing solution which, it hopes, could reverse the downward trend.

Dynamic principles similar to those examined in this section apply also to Internet commerce, and their implementation can be enriched through an array of online capabilities. Where companies sell directly to customers on the Web, the multiplier effect of a customer base lies in the fact that marketing's reach is becoming truly global, and portable telephones are scheduled to be Internet terminals. Because of this, some experts believe that in the near future B2C might increase sales exponentially with only a limited initial investment in the Internet. Another positive fallout is that the costs of B2B and B2C tend be lower because of a substantial reduction in the amount of required inventories to meet customer demand. The downside is in the need to face specific costs on the Net.

The message the reader should retain from this section is that there are new types of pricing which can influence business-to-business and business-to-consumer relationships. Current experiences are leading to different pricing models which can potentially be used in Internet commerce. Indeed, one of the less well-known consequences of business-to-business relationships is the flexibility associated with dynamic pricing.

Fixed pricing, as we know it today, is about 150 years old. It was invented for ease of mass marketing, and better management control of income from sales, but now the Internet provides auction platforms for price discovery and makes negotiated pricing a reality. For example, a company called FreeMarkets lets buyers bid for the amount they are willing to pay for an item. As pricing by negotiation returns to favour, auctions and exchanges can become the key price-setting mechanisms.

To a substantial extent, dynamic pricing is based on *faster clockspeed* and this is bringing both new opportunities and new risks for companies on the Web. An integral part of this reference to faster or slower clockspeed is the concept of *intrinsic time* and its impact on financial and other types of transactions.

While the laws of physics are universal, the use of time is not uniform from one market to another. Some markets work faster than others, and the same is true of some traders in the same market. Not only is the Internet global, but it is also a market characterised by rapid execution. Figures 4.3 and 4.4 bring to the reader's attention the idea that there is a difference between physical time and intrinsic or time in business. When business activity is slow, ten minutes of clock time may represent the normal trading activities usually completed in five minutes of physical time. However, in a very dynamic market, ten minutes of physical time may include the amount of trades normally completed in 20 minutes.

PHYSICAL TIME

INTRINSIC TIME

VOLATILITY

JUST NOTE
DIFFERENCE
(JND)

JND

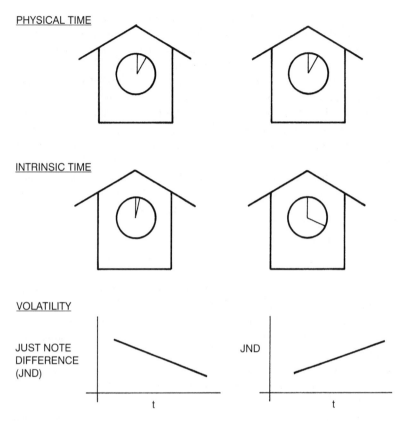

t

t

Figure 4.3   The impact of intrinsic time on market activity and volatility

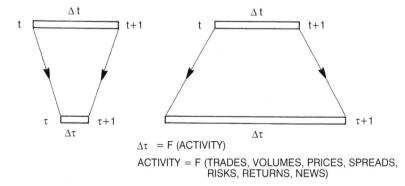

Δt   Δt

t   t+1   t   t+1

τ   τ+1   τ+1

Δτ   Δτ

Δτ = F (ACTIVITY)

ACTIVITY = F (TRADES, VOLUMES, PRICES, SPREADS,
             RISKS, RETURNS, NEWS)

Figure 4.4   Intrinsic time is essentially a process of physical time deformation
to account for market activity
Note: F(.) stands for 'Function of'.

Intrinsic time would impact on dynamic pricing because, as the pace of trading increases, the level of volatility also shoots up. At the same time much faster business activity done online tends to alter the so far prevailing trading rules. Because the rules and structures are changing, the processes that make supply chains tick need regular redesign and this can be effectively done only when companies master the mechanics of supply chain design, and are ready to adapt as their industry structure and its procurement habits change.

5 HIDDEN COSTS ASSOCIATED WITH INTERNET COMMERCE

Setting up, running and servicing a Web site to ensure it is 99.99 per cent reliable is by no means easy or cheap. Both human capital and strong financial backing are necessary. The same is true of rigorous solutions for logistics and distribution which are critical to the success of I-commerce.

The costs associated with being present on the Web are by no means limited to opening a site. There are also major expenses connected with customer acquisition. As the case of Amazon.com shows, this may require a significant amount of capital investments made up front over several years, which leads to a paradox: many online retailers have managed to undercut their bricks-and-mortar rivals on price, but they have done so by investing in marketing thrust all their earnings and some red ink, over a period of time.

There are also other hidden costs to account for. Because price comparisons become far easier online the Internet has been a strong price-deflator. The irony is that sharp price cutting has hurt the bottom line of Internet companies much more than that of bricks-and-mortar outlets, though it did affect the latter's business.

As competition in electronic commerce prices is so cut-throat, many experts now suggest that the most important impact of the Internet will be felt when it gives rise to entirely new products, as happened with earlier technological revolutions. Typically, with entirely new products, price comparisons are nonlinear. By contrast, with established products which transit from the old economy, it is much easier to obtain sharp price reductions online than offline for both B2B and B2C trades, whereas vendors find it harder to raise their prices when customers can instantly compare their price list with everyone else's.

Other things being equal, the economies a client realises on the Internet offer a powerful incentive to have a Web site, the more so as they can be scaled up to take advantage of globalisation. Classical bricks-and-mortar outlets cannot do that; the nearest thing to it has been the hypermarket, Wal-Mart model. But usually other things are not equal, and therefore every company must make a soul-searching analysis of risk and return.

One of the returns many companies sought to obtain on the Internet was the *first mover* advantage. If an early starter gets everything right (Web site, order fulfilment, distribution, payments, and so on), newcomers find it much harder to catch up. With the first company's success, each challenger's entry price rises. By contrast, *if* the Web site is poorly designed, choice is minimal and delivery uncertain, *then* the downturn would be faster than in the bricks-and-mortar world.

Another interesting issue is the *scalability* of the Internet market. Among I-commerce performers, Amazon.com has been testing the inherent scalability of the online business by expanding well beyond its starting point of bookselling. Jeff Bezos, Amazon's founder and CEO, has said that he is willing to sell anything except cement. But this raises the question of whether Web retailing favours focused enterprises or general type stores?

Another one of the hidden costs associated with Internet commerce is the failure to reach one's objectives in spite of important entry costs, because the chosen solution is half-baked and cannot possibly compete with well-organised sites. A parable I heard on Wall Street compares established, successful Internet companies to the creosote bush, a tall desert plant that drips poisonous oil, killing off all vegetation that tries to grow anywhere near it.

An example of a company which cannot organise itself to gain leadership on the Internet, or in its business-to-business plans, is Unilever. The company's CEO expects online activity to transform the way in which the firm obtains its products and materials. Within two years, he says, half of all purchasing will be done on the Internet. He also hints at several big B2B alliances 'to come' (*The Economist*, 26 February 2000). This is a flawed argument: Unilever's Internet strategy was unveiled in February 2000, with a huge delay over the original 1998 plans. Two years later is like a century in Internet time, and several big alliances 'to come' is a thinly veiled admission that there is nothing yet.

The only exception to this statement, when this text was written, was a $200 million joint venture with iVillage, one of the lesser strength American portals aimed at women aged between 25 and 54, who are prime consumers of lucrative personal-care products. It was also vaguely stated by Unilever, in conjunction with this announcement, that another alliance would test how European teenagers interact with brands on the Web. That is hardly a blockbuster.

As we have already seen in Chapter 3, other old economy companies have been bolder in transforming themselves. GM and Ford have embraced the Internet for many of their activities. Section 2 explained how General Electric has reinvented itself using the Internet as a catalyst. Such moves by big enterprises mean that their suppliers, as well as intermediaries through whom they sell, must take to the Internet too, and they should try to do so from a position of leadership, not in a 'me too' way.

6   CONGESTION PROBLEMS OF INTERNET COMMERCE AND TRUCKING SERVICE EXCHANGES

Transport is the lifeblood of any Internet commerce business. The benefits described in Chapter 3 and in the present chapter as deriving from I-commerce and trading exchanges are not to be interpreted to mean that they are the twenty-first century's equivalent of penicillin for business ills. They have been intended to inform the reader that there is no better policy for survival than living with one's time, somewhat ahead of the curve. This, however, requires:

- reaching hard core decisions about a change in course, which do not come easily (see Chapter 1);
- revamping our culture, our tools, our accounting, our logistics, and our way of doing business; and
- appreciating that not only are there constraints to overcome, but also unwanted effects about which we have to be careful.

One of the things that is not wanted, yet it is around and it is inescapable, is the severe transportation problem which in all likelihood would accompany the growth of Internet commerce, particularly because of direct deliveries. Current studies predict that a congestion beyond what we have so far experienced would follow, with only a minor timelag, the trucking services exchanges in the making. With this, many packages may arrive late or damaged.

There is a correlation between traffic congestion and each company's effort to optimise its inventories. With just-in-time, indeed real-time inventory management, large manufacturing conglomerates, as well as merchandising concerns, have practically transferred their warehouses on to trucks. This means inventories on wheels, clogging highways and streets. To a considerable extent, formerly warehoused goods are now on the move.

Through JIT and FFR companies have compressed their inventories to a minimum, but to keep production lines running and merchandising racks full, manufacturing and merchandising entities have been obliged to put in motion their formerly warehoused stocks. Internet commerce gives a further impetus in this conversion. The ugly side of fast delivery is that:

- trucks are practically running half empty to execute rapid ordering requirements;
- turnpikes, highways, city streets get clogged; and
- the level of pollution is increasing, contrary to what the different 'climate' summits seem to suggest.

Based on the proliferating studies on traffic congestion, experts believe that item by item delivery of merchandise bought through electronic commerce will exacerbate the current transportation bottlenecks. Therefore, it will magnify the need to control the resources allocated to the delivery of goods and their timing. This is true both for B2B and B2C, and most particularly for the latter.

- *If* delivery at home leads to congestion of transport channels;
- *then* it is necessary to proceed with simultaneous multiple deliveries, accepting a certain timelag.

To satisfy this requirement there has been suggested a solution, nicknamed *the Internet of logistics*. This aims at a thoroughly restructured accounting and logistics approach, designed bottom-up for the realities of Internet commerce, rather than through updating of old procedures. The new design must involve simultaneously:

- electronic bookkeeping;
- computerised dispatching; and
- auction-based fleet management.

New developments are necessary to make it happen, including smart technology and electronic tags (e-tags), road sensors, variable traffic signs and rapid upgrade in electronically allocated road capacity. This is planned to be a dynamic allocation procedure, in contrast to the classical use of road capacity for traffic reasons.

A different way of putting this is that new and highly imaginative solutions are necessary, because the likelihood of congestion of transport channels due to I-commerce deliveries and other reasons is not to be taken lightly. Even without need overcharge of rapid delivery in response to piecemeal client orders received online, cities and highways are faced with an explosion which requires several competencies at once, including:

- creating a market which is independent of distance, rather than divided by geography; and
- managing the needs of this market online, without aggravating traffic problems because of deliveries.

One way to solve this problem is to see to it that transport becomes more efficient. The challenge lies in the fact that at the present time there are not many ideas around about how to increase transportation efficiency, whether on the ground, by air or by sea. It is one thing to use the virtual world of the Internet to tie together supply chains and their users, and another to solve the physical chores, with pick-up and delivery problems which existed well before the Web.

Transportation by land, air and sea is a problem with many variables, some of which are non-linearly connected to one another. Oscillating demand and supply, with its shortages and excesses, also involves many hidden costs. The Internet helps to solve a big chunk of the ordering problem through a click. The Net can also be of assistance in transportation management, because it provides greater visibility and permits a fair amount of experimentation. What the Internet cannot do is to solve the physical transport problem single-handed.

In other words, Internet or no Internet, the transportation problems afflicting the real world remain to be solved. FFR and JIT inventories solved some issues but added to others, because it is not possible to track the shipment until it arrives, yet companies only have a few hours' inventory with JIT.

Can automatic identification and smart materials help to tackle the fundamentals of this problem? A tentative answer is that auto-ID could play a major role in some areas. For instance, it could improve the concept of trucking service exchanges which is now developing in the USA, because smart materials transmit their identity, location and status. Trucking services exchange aim to address, among other issues, that of B2B delivery congestion and associated pollution. The verdict, however, is not yet out as to whether they can alleviate the congestion associated with B2C deliveries, or will make matters worse.

Enthusiasts of trucking service exchanges count as profits the time saved through the increased frequency of deliveries, but they fail to factor in the time lost to extensive delays as well as the cost of traffic congestion. This problem is not so different from that of air transport. Can market incentives be used to reduce airport congestion?

Some economists propose variable pricing, so that travellers who fly during rush hours pay for the privilege (see, in section 7, a similar scheme regarding California roads). Other economists have suggested a different system of landing fees to discourage small private jets from clogging highly congested airports.

However, such traffic-based market incentives and disincentives are a form of government regulation. They override how markets would otherwise price a given type of service, in order to serve public purposes. At the same time, none of these disincentive schemes compensates for lost time or environmental effects.

Besides congestion and pollution, few companies truly account for delivery costs of Internet commerce, let alone costs relating to insecurity of payments (see Chapter 11). In absolute terms delivery costs can be rather insignificant in monetary terms, but they are significant in social effects, as in the case of clogging the streets. That is why experts advise that vendors should consider the costs of delivery, and shippers should bid for their chosen routes. To do so, they must make their routine schedules, account, compute expenses, and project asset utilisation in considerable detail. A great deal of preparatory work is necessary in order to optimise delivery plans.

MIT's Dr Yossi Sheffi advises that instead of bidding only on individual routes, carriers should specify both the price for a requested route and a lower price which is possible if this route is combined with another route and/or with a return schedule. This kind of combinatorial bidding would permit carriers to set prices based on expected greater efficiency which takes account of schedules as well as of traffic density in the chosen delivery route at a given time.

In conclusion, next to the insecurity of payments, traffic congestion could be the sword of Damocles over the head of I-commerce. To attack it successfully we must project traffic densities, account for cost optimisation issues, and tackle pollution problems. There is a horde of issues waiting to be solved in connection with Internet commerce. If anything, these problems risk becoming worse over time. In fact, the situation is already critical.

7 IF TRUCK-BASED HOME DELIVERIES ARE PART OF THE PROBLEM, WHAT IS THE SOLUTION?

Optimists think that home delivery of goods bought through Internet commerce will do away with the need to go to the market by car, but there is no evidence to sustain such an argument. People drive by car to the news stand or to a store just to buy a pack of cigarettes. They do not need to have their refrigerator empty to jump behind the wheel.

While several studies have looked into the projected aggravation of current congestion issues, none has given convincing results that the growth in truck-based home deliveries could be offset by a reduction of suburban shopping trips. This lack of an effective approach to a critical problem is further aggravated by the fact that most B2C companies do not know how to optimise their deliveries service.

The sense of a meeting in which I participated not long ago is that many enthusiasts of I-commerce forget the fact that not everything is going together smoothly at the payments and the deliveries end. Returned goods are an example. Statistics suggest that returns from I-commerce are at the 30 per cent level, which is way too high. It is also wise to remember *consumer power*. Many consumers know what they want, and when they order on the Web they want it now. Rapid delivery makes its own contribution to road congestion, because it adds new inputs to the traffic equation.

Should truck deliverers run half empty because of reasons related to the immediate satisfaction of customer demands? Nobody has a rational answer to this query. The prediction of consequences is difficult because one of the carefully kept secrets is that most of what has been tried so far as a better approach does not work. Both in city streets and on highways the current infrastructure is not designed for sophisticated solutions involving dense traffic.

Some ideas are being tested but the results do not give ground for much hope as regards solving congestion problems. For instance, Singapore is now trying *congestion pricing* in the central area, fixed by time of the day. As another example, in June 2000, the California Environmental Dialogue (CED), a 32-member group whose membership includes oil companies, motor vehicle manufacturers and environmental protection outfits, published a paper on the state's transport policy, which approximates Singapore's model.

By endorsing the principle that the 'user should pay' for road use and that 'tolls and congestion pricing should be utilised whenever possible', CED's paper put on the table an issue which will lead to significant debate during the coming years. In the past, road pricing has been championed by people intent on imposing more of the external costs of driving on road users by charging them a fee that reflects both the:

- distance travelled (which is what fuel taxes do); and
- the time and route of the driver's journey, which so far has not been taxed.

The concept underpinning road pricing is that driving imposes a heavier burden during rush hours and in congested streets. Hence, when an itinerary which clogs the road is deliberately chosen, such routing should cost the company and/or the driver more money.

In the years to come, some form of congestion pricing will probably be necessary when using the roads (or airspace) at times most in demand. Therefore, this concept has merit, but how it is to be implemented is still unknown. Some people suggest that rather than just imposing new charges on currently tax-free but crowded roads, state authorities should examine all possible alternatives. For instance, California could make use of its network of underused high-occupancy vehicle (HOV) lanes on existing roads: these could be opened to single drivers who choose to pay a toll.

To understand what this suggestion is all about, the reader should first of all appreciate that in California's case we talk of highway traffic, not of city traffic. In the state of California are two of America's four working examples of high-occupancy toll lanes (HOTs). Another one is in Florida, and one is in Texas. Of the two California settings, SR-91 is in Orange County, and it allows drivers to pay an amount (depending on the time of day) for the privilege of using an HOV lane.

Interstate 15 is north of San Diego, and this example is closer to CED's model of adjusting price to demand. Its fee varies from 50 cents to $4, depending on the volume of traffic in the HOT lane, with the current price flashed up on screen half a mile before the pay lane starts. At the same time, an electronic transponder system sees to it that there is no need to stop at a toll booth.

Can this selective payment system be converted for city traffic? I doubt it, but other people think it may be possible. When in a recent symposium I objected to the lecturer that what he was suggesting was too theoretical, he suddenly switched from getting congestion pricing information, to paying for consumption of street traffic resources through static pricing, by charging $1 and debiting the credit card (or, even better, the chip in the card).

Of course I did not fail to inform the lecturer that, before talking of using the often failed smart card to pay tolls in city streets, he should visit Italy to get first-hand information on the chaos created on the *autostrade* with smart card payments. I do not know if he took the advice, but a reality test can be unparalleled in its effectiveness.

If chip-in-card payments on the *autostrade* are a mess, which *is* the case, it would be ludicrous to think that cities have the technology required for solutions which can provide dynamic congestion pricing information to the users of paved roads, for their optimisation, or that they have the skills and can find the money necessary to put such solutions into effect appropriately, sustaining them over time by accounting for dynamic conditions imposed by:

- time;
- traffic density;
- weather; and
- other events.

In practice, it would take a huge amount of driver discipline to have even a modest hope of success, and driver discipline can be a scarce commodity, particularly in Latin European countries where every driver does as he or she pleases and in more than 99 per cent of cases gets away with it. Besides cultural change, which is not around the corner, dynamic solutions require truly advanced technology. Computers have to do the optimisation and communicate it in real-time; it cannot be done by hand.

Not everything is, however, hopeless. While a small sample of cities might wish to try the idea of inner road tolls – at the expense of their residents – as far as business-to-consumer Internet commerce is concerned my advice is to try (at least in the interim) more down to earth solutions. A good example comes from Japan and it combines I-commerce deliveries, money dispensing and classical bricks-and-mortar commerce.

Let us call this experience '*order at the Internet, take the goods and pay at the store.*' Japan's Seven-Eleven, a supermarket chain known for being ahead of the curve, has installed automatic teller machines

(ATMs) at its 8200 outlets. Since most of these stores operate 24 hours a day, the ATMs allow round the clock banking, and safe payment for online purchases.

The idea of using ATMs installed by the cashiers in supermarkets and other stores is not new. It was successfully tried in the late 1970s in Boston in a Bank of Boston project called 'Money One'. But it was not associated with the delivery of remotely made purchases, and somehow it did not catch the merchants' and the public's eye in other countries.

Using modern technology, Seven-Eleven has improved upon this concept. Its ATMs are eventually expected to work as multimedia terminals as well as accepting orders. This is an imaginative extension of another forward practice. Since 1987 Seven-Eleven has been accepting payments on behalf of utilities. In 1999 it collected some $6 billion in associated fees. Earning commission is a new product line for supermarkets.

The concept of 'order at the Internet, take the goods and pay at the store' is an extension of this commissions policy. It is simple but ingenious. After placing orders on the Web, customers pick up and pay for them at any Seven-Eleven shop of their choice. This solution capitalises on the fact that Seven-Eleven attracts 2.6 billion customers yearly, a daily average of 950 per shop.

Why not pay for I-commerce by credit card over the Net? Let me answer this query in two ways. First of all, polls indicate that as many as 70 per cent of Japanese dislike using credit cards for online purchases. The response of Europeans is not so different. With the exception of the UK, and (to a lesser extent) of France, the credit card culture has never really taken off in Europe. People are cash oriented and also like to use cheques or giro payments.

Second, the big negative is *security*, the Internet's Achilles heel. We will return to this issue in Chapter 11. As we will see before this book ends, one can write off security only at one's own (high) risk. The magic formula or device which will do away with the security risks associated with online payments has not yet been invented, and I doubt it will ever be.

5 The Selling of Banking Services on the Internet puts Current Accounting Systems under Stress

1 INTRODUCTION

The theme of Chapter 3 and Chapter 4 has been cutting costs with a sharp knife by means of *purchasing* on the Internet, whether through joint ventures or a lone wolf approach. The subject of this chapter is *selling* services. I have chosen selling banking products and services as the main topic because there is no better example than online banking with the opportunities and risks it presents, including its effects on the institution's accounting system.

As I have had already the chance to underline, for all practical purposes the business of banking is *buying and selling time*. That is what banks do when they take deposits and give loans; also when they make investments and when they engage in derivatives trading, whether for interest rates, currency exchanges, equity indices or other deals.

Services and products offered by a bank which positions itself against the challenges of the new economy are characterised by a number of distinguishing factors. Starting with liquidity, a credit institution must be able to handle deposits in a wide range of currencies and extend credit facilities for personal and corporate loans, including overdrafts, margin trading, guarantees of many sorts, import and export facilities, factoring and leasing.

The accounting system must be polyvalent, able to effect payments and settlements in a number of currencies, including foreign exchange and currency swaps, options, futures, forwards, caps and collars. Because *virtual* balance sheets are now produced intraday, the bank must manage its portfolio and its logistics in real-time, not through night runs.

A modern bank must also work as a network whose corporate finance and advisory services include: equity raising, IPOs, private equity, structured debt, mergers and acquisitions, and leveraged financing. For investment management purposes the new economy bank finds itself obliged to offer discretionary, advisory, execution only, and research services. These address equities, bonds, mutual funds, hedge funds and structured products, and also trust and custody services.

The new economy bank must also master all the details of taxation in practically all countries in which it operates (see Chapter 7), as well as manage inheritance planning for its clients, taking into account ways and means to optimise taxation. The effects of globalisation on taxation are widespread. There is plenty of opportunity for optimisation regarding individuals, small businesses and large corporations.

Many of the activities I have just described have to do with buying and selling time. This has been classically done in bricks-and-mortar establishments: the credit institution's headquarters and its branches. Today it takes place increasingly online, and the Internet is fast becoming an important carrier, particularly for consumer banking and brokerage services, while private networks are used for trading because of vulnerability considerations which a public network cannot waive (see also section 7, and Chapter 11).

In conclusion, many senior bankers whom I met in my research said that within 20 years the institutional structure of banking and finance would not be the same as that which we have known for over a century. A great deal of buying and selling of time will be done through the new generation of broadband Internet, and the credit institutions who win will be those way ahead in the technology race.

2 THE CHANGING CONCEPT OF FINANCIAL SERVICES BECAUSE OF INTERNET BANKING

The careful reader will remember Michael Bloomberg's dictum: 'You have to appreciate the Internet is an equaliser.' *If* the most common medium currently available is an equaliser, *then* companies have to search for value differentiation. They must also find a solution to a problem which surfaced with Internet technology: the fact that it brings the *zero pricing* challenge to the table. This is what Bloomberg calls 'How to make money with cost-free services.'

Zero pricing of commonly available services reinforces the search for imaginative solutions because it brings to the foreground the need to find something *we can do that our competitors cannot*. This way, we can charge a fee. By contrast, charging a fee for flat earth services discourages customer adherence to *our* online offers.

Value-added solutions are not easy to find. There is a precedent for what is today called *Internet banking* for consumers, and this reference is not positive. In the late 1970s/early 1980s, when interactive videotext became available, many banks jumped into home banking and got burned. Losses of $50 million or $100 million were not unusual. They came from the First National Bank of Minneapolis test in the Dakotas, to Chemical Bank's Pronto, the joint venture of Knight-Ridder with the Florida banks, and so on. Internet consumer banking repeated this experience. In the year 2000 Bank One revealed huge losses (see section 3).

Let's face it: barebones online consumer banking is a non-starter. It needs other goodies and plenty of sugar-coating. Barebones offers are a nasty way of discharging responsibilities rather than serving the public, and the public understands that. Therefore, I am not at all impressed by statistics and projections which show that there is a rush towards Internet banking among retail and commercial institutions.

Figure 5.1 presents an estimate which was given in the course of my research. As far as I am concerned it poses more questions than it answers about entering into Internet banking with flat earth products. The majority of Internet banking offers are no different from the 'Press 1, press 2, etc.' supposedly in the name of automation, but in reality to avoid having to serve the public. 'We got rid of push 1, 2, 3', said Michael Bloomberg. 'That's nuts. We want people who ring one number to have somebody to help them:

- Give advice
- Do hand-holding, and
- Explain what, why, when' (Monte Carlo, 30–31 March 2000).

That is a sound principle. Another thing Bloomberg underlined is that in the financial world (and by extension in any other industry) everything we do these days has to provide a *seamless* interface to the client. This is the best way to keep the client calling back. Our Internet offers should also support seamless access to *our* public databases. This has to be done in real-time while providing for high efficiency, and high security.

This seamless interface must be interdisciplinary and capable of addressing all product and service channels of our institution. When we want the components of our business to co-operate with each other for cross-selling reasons and in order to create a new, more effective business environment, we must also provide efficient means for doing so. This leads to three strategic considerations.

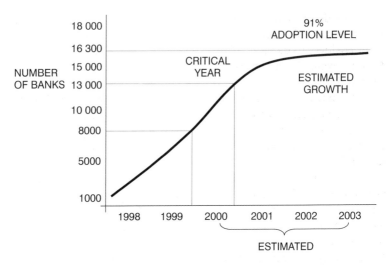

Figure 5.1   Number of banks in the USA adopting Internet banking
Note: However, not all Internet banking is successful. Bank One did not fare well with Wingspan.com

1   Value differentiation online is a 'must', even if it is a menace to the classical bricks-and-mortar line of business.

Value differentiation done online is also bringing to an end the classical segmentation between retail banking, investment banking, insurance, and other financial services. At the same time, cross-selling obliges the modelling of the customer profile for asset management and other reasons.

What I just said is true about any product line. For instance, as Figure 5.2 suggests, every loans officer should be operating online to at least four databases, some of which are shared with other channels. Internet selling *with a punch* avoids a sort of dis-intermediation through B2B, bringing banking-type customer initiatives into a broader landscape where they might not have gone on their own.

2   Brokerage and banking on the Internet, the way it is done today, is the tip of the iceberg of new strategies.

Online clients, and most particularly the higher net worth individuals, want to see a pallet of services offered along with the ability to do more than the classical banking functions. Few institutions are able to offer their Internet clients such a pallet of alternatives. Brokers and fund managers have been better able to do so than retail bankers.

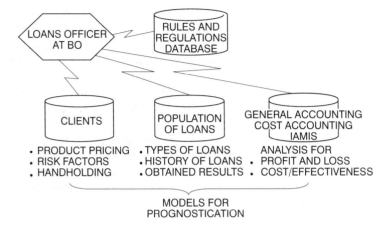

Figure 5.2 Every loans officer should be operating online to four databases

Notice as well that with Internet selling there are alliances not too dissimilar from those we have seen in Chapter 3 with Internet purchasing. Charles Schwab, the broker, offers online 33 products of its own. Alongside them, Schwab also exhibits 1650 other products from its business partners. The own products Fidelity promotes number 170; those it offers in collaboration with its business partners number 3200.

3   A rapid response to Internet challenges through well-studied strategies representing both an offensive and a defensive approach.

The value added we are going to offer must be an issue fully open to steady innovation through R&D because our competitors are many, and they too know they have to move fast so as not to be left in the dust. There is a race in modern banking and those institutions who drop out do not have much hope of recovery, and therefore of survival.

Among the above references, numbers 2 and 3 correlate. The fact that Schwab sells online 50 times more products from business partners than his own carries a very specific message. It means that an institution's own R&D must be very active as well as enhanced through bought licences to feed the distribution function.

Rapid response to market moves can take many forms. Quite recently, leading international banks have formed the Mobey Forum, a mobile commerce association. This is their strategy to fence off the threats from mobile network operators with proprietary transactions systems. Mobey Forum represents a significant departure from solutions initiated by telecommunication companies, such as the Global Mobile Commerce Forum (GMCF), and the European Telecommunications Standards Institute's Mobile Commerce standardisation initiative. The Mobey Forum includes some of the leaders in the development of mobile banking services, such as Merita of Finland, SE Banken of Sweden, Deutsche Bank, HSBC and Visa, and also equipment vendors such as Ericsson, Motorola and Nokia.

Mobey promotes non-proprietary standards such as wireless applications protocol (WAP), and the wireless identification module (WIM). This effort is primarily centred on the financial sector; it is not cross-industry. The banks hope that a vertical approach will enable them to move quickly on:

- defining indispensable security needs; and
- finding ways the handset can be used for payments.

The banks also want to promote non-proprietary systems and ensure that financial transactions and payments applications will run in a similar fashion, regardless of the type of handset or network being used, which is not currently the case.

In conclusion, we should be keen to evaluate closely the results expected from the strategy we choose on the future evolution of *our* business. This is as true of Internet banking as of any other issue. It is also important to react swiftly. Schwab reacted within a few months to the E*trade challenge, with an Internet product line of its own. In the modern globalised economy you can succeed only if you move very fast and do whatever it takes to establish yourself on firm ground.

3   RISKS ASSOCIATED WITH FACTORS DRIVING INTERNET BANKING SERVICES, AND THE WINGSPAN.COM DEBACLE

Section 2 brought to the reader's attention that there are both opportunities and risks connected with Internet banking. To take the good news first, the key factors driving Internet banking services can be found in several areas: the Internet technology itself; effects of globalisation and deregulation; hope for major cost savings; ability to reach a wider market (if we are ready for it); and low cost devices available for personal use.

Some of my colleagues add to this list of business 'pluses' customer preferences and the adoption of standards. I disagree with both statements. Customer preferences for barebones services are themselves bare. It is the value-added financial services that generate customer preferences, if *and only if* we can provide these services in a way that beats the competition. Nothing is automatic or guaranteed a priori.

As for standards, with the exception of those *de facto* developed by vendors (for instance, Windows and the Intel chips), they are sparse and largely obsolete. Neither is it true that, in an industry as young and fast growing as the Internet, standards are a good idea. They may become a strait-jacket stifling development, rather than present an unquestionable advantage.

There are also the negatives to reckon with. In my book, the biggest negative is *hype*. In Figure 5.3, I have mapped the statistics presented in a recent symposium. By basing his inference on these curves, the lecturer wanted to show how wonderful has been the effect of networking, and most particularly of the Internet on bread and butter retail banking costs, such as cashing a cheque and other teller transactions. There is no question that a bricks-and-mortar approach is more expensive than networking, but the cost of handling a cheque would not drop to 10 cents because of the Internet. This is highly misleading and opens the way to deception. It is a guestimate largely based on false hypotheses and an overoptimistic view of what is feasible.

One of the false hypotheses in costing is that telecommunications expenses will more or less take themselves out of the cost equation altogether. True enough, such costs are shrinking, but relative to the bandwidth. Bread and butter online banking does not need gigabit networks. For its present unsophisticated status, the available narrow bandwidth is perfectly adequate. Furthermore, even if telecommunications costs are dropping and, with them, those of computer devices, these are still non-zero. There is also the need to face rapidly growing database requirements which cost big money. Storage capacity goes up to 40 per cent per year in some industries, which is an awful lot.

Precisely because costs will never be zero, I do not believe in this approach, which minimises expenditures against all the evidence. In every company I know costs have been reduced not because of vaguely specified reasons (which, incidentally, like the Internet are available also to our competitors), but because the Board and CEO set the goal of squeezing costs by, say, 10 per cent by completely automating back-office operations or by some other means.

It is up to the information technologists to prove that this is feasible and to do it, paying plenty of attention to ROI. Just the same, it is up to the Board to aim at doubling net profits, through properly studied

104

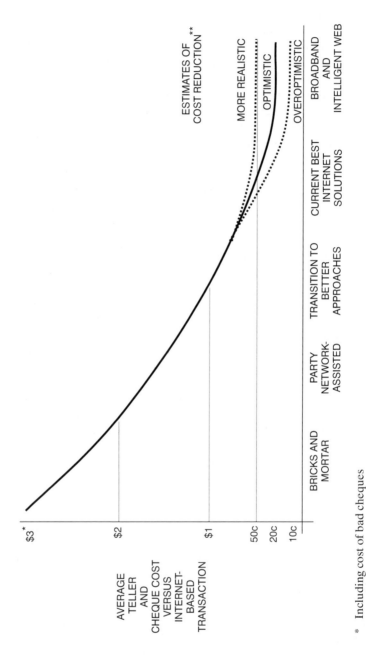

* Including cost of bad cheques
** Including costs of online fraud

Figure 5.3 Transaction costs in banking are dropping substantially because of networking

strategic moves. This will not happen just by being on the Internet, or by hoping costs will disappear on their own.

Let me explain what I mean through an example. Dublin-based Ryanair is a newcomer among airlines. Its speciality is bargain flights between London's suburban Stansted Airport and destinations such as Dublin and Venice. In 1999 Ryanair more than doubled its market cap, to about $1.5 billion. It has established a presence and it survives because its costs are about *one-third* of BA's 21 cents per mile; that is what gave it a big lead over British Airways.

Another hype of which the reader should be well aware is that global-isation provided by the Internet would open up a vast new market of *micropayments* and *microcredits*. The argument goes like this: of over 6 billion people in the world, at least 3 billion earn less than $1 per day. The hype starts after this statistic and it goes as follows. This could be a colossal client population for loans, given the projected 1.5 billion hand-held cell phones. It might even open on a global scale consumer-to-consumer credit, a new business line.

During the Seventh Monte Carlo Investment Forum (Monte Carlo, 30–31 March 2000), Michael Bloomberg answered this argument in the best possible manner when he said that 'C2C credit is like lending money to your brother in law, which is not a very smart thing to do.' But the pros of micropayments do not listen to business logic. I just got an e-mail from friends about participating in a new, ill-defined micropayments venture.

Still another hype is that the missing link in payments on the Internet is provided beautifully by smart cards. Smart cards are a mid-1970s development, pulled and pushed by their fans through vast outlays of money which went down the drain. Any product which, over a quarter of a century, does not take off is a dead duck. But people do not listen to the market's verdict (see also Chapter 11 on security).

This of course does not mean that Internet does not help in cost-cutting and in providing the platform for *novel* services. First, it makes it feasible to create a single market, which is important only *if* we can take advantage of it. Another boost is that it improves the possibility of integrating financial services, such as banking, brokerage and insur-ance. The Internet might also be instrumental in changing customer preferences, *if* the appropriate strategy is put in place by credit institu-tions to exploit the more sophisticated, more demanding, but also more cost-conscious part of the market. That's what Charles Schwab and other top-tier institutions have done. Table 5.1 compares Schwab to Fidelity and E*Trade in terms of online accounts and assets.

Table 5.1   Online accounts and assets of three firms using the Internet

	Millions of accounts	**Managed assets (in $ billion)**
Charles Schwab	3.3	349
Fidelity	3.2	232
E*Trade	1.8	44

E*Trade is a pure Internet company and, as the statistics in Table 5.1 show, its clients tend to be of lower net worth than those of Schwab and Fidelity, who run neck-and-neck in the more affluent market segment. Independently of market segment, however, the online clients of all three firms have come from some other institutions; Internet companies tend to cannibalise the client base of bricks-and-mortar firms capitalising on:

• value migration; and
• the generational shift.

However, management blunders can happen with investments in Internet banking as with everything else. Bank One has $270 billion in assets and is the fourth largest bank in the USA. Rocked by misjudgements at top management level and an earnings shortfall, it has been the subject of rampant take-over speculation after the Board forced John McCoy, Jr, the CEO, to resign. The current Bank One was created by the 1998 merger of McCoy's original Bank One of Columbus, Ohio, and First Chicago NBD. At the time of the merger, it was heralded as yet another example of the advantages of size and consolidation in the banking industry; but Bank One's problems have shown that size coupled to unrealistic business strategies can quickly overwhelm a corporation.

In my personal experience, big size is often accompanied by big problems. Bank One had two of them: credit cards and Internet banking. In late March 2000, following the appointment of Jamie Dimon to the helm, analysts said that his biggest challenge would be reviving the credit card operation, which in good times contributed as much as a third of Bank One's total profits, and finding a solution for the credit institution's Internet venture.

Dimon's salient problem is to decide what to do with Bank One's Internet-only bank, *Wingspan.com*, which consumed cash in massive quantities. The former management of Bank One had put this online banking operation up for sale, and this was another blow to the bank's credibility. Bankers with direct knowledge of Wingspan's financial statements said that Bank One lost about $150 million before taxes on this venture in 1999 alone, yet most Internet banking fans had taken Wingspan as their ideal what the future will look like.

The failure of Wingspan.com makes interesting reading not only because of the huge amount of money spent on it, but also because, at least superficially, there did not seem to be a major design flaw. From the start, Wingspan was (correctly) focused first and foremost on the customer, even adding an *iBoard of Directors* made up of customers who could offer advice on products, services and the strategy connected with them. The customer call centre runs 24 hours a day, 7 days a week, which is the dream of many service organisations. The emphasis on rapid service is exemplified by the fact that applicants for home equity loans get answers in 60 seconds.

Every Wingspan employee has been required to listen to customer calls for at least 1½ hours a month, and its top executive team has a policy of reading e-mails from at least 20 customers a day. The service orientation of Wingspan is further documented by the fact it also features *customer experience* departments and *customer advocacy* teams to address complaints and suggestions quickly. Wingspan invites customers to refine the bank's offerings, and customer feedback led to software changes that permits users to access all their accounts at once, with a single sign-on. Yet, financially speaking, Wingspan failed.

4 AN EXAMPLE FROM CITIGROUP: POSITIONING OUR BANK AGAINST THE FORCES OF THE TWENTY-FIRST CENTURY

Section 3 made two fundamental statements: that market opportunity comes from value differentiation, and that to succeed on the Internet a credit institution must have a polyvalent strategy rather than just technology leadership. Market leaders are focusing on the customer, and in the majority of cases their offerings are *not* channel-specific. What they see in the Internet is that it provides new opportunities to serve the customer but leaves to their bank the initiative to put them to good use. A corollary of this statement is that sustainability of *pure* Internet plays is questionable; therefore it is most advisable to study the different type of Internet opportunities, and pick the best.

To do so, we must be able to develop an *own strategy*. This strategy must account for the fact that there is not one but several possible Internet sales solutions, all of which are exploiting the existence of new

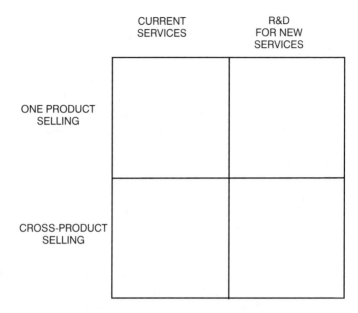

CURRENT   R&D
SERVICES   FOR NEW
                 SERVICES

ONE PRODUCT
SELLING

CROSS-PRODUCT
SELLING

Figure 5.4   Four alternative strategies in Internet banking

distribution channels. Once our strategy is developed and tested, it must be executed quickly with appropriate human, financial and technological resources.

Figure 5.4 describes this business opportunity through quarterspaces. The least rewarding is the top left box of current services and single product selling. The best opportunities are offered by the bottom right box of R&D for steady development of new services and cross-product sales. This seems to be the strategy chosen by Citigroup.

According to John Reed's account at the Monte Carlo Investment Forum of 2000, at Citigroup 60 per cent of the revenue of $36 billion is moving from a terrestrial (bricks-and-mortar) to the Internet model. To reach this goal both banking and insurance are thoroughly revamped, and special attention is given to:

- the development of new services;
- the restructuring of existing services; and
- a wider cross-selling strategy.

Today at Citigroup some 40 per cent of revenues come from cash management services. These are the first to move to the Internet. John Reed also underlined that this change is industry-wide. Capital market services, too, are moving to the Internet. These are addressed to both investors and issuers of securities.

'*Who does not move ahead of the curve is vulnerable,*' said John Reed. Choices have, however, to be made and these choices will define what *our* financial institution will be doing during the next decade. Strategic choices come squarely into this reference. Retail banking at Citibank represents the greater stockholder value; from it derive more benefits than from corporate loans. This contrasts with the strategy followed by most of the better known European global banks, which centre all their efforts on investment banking.

There are also key tactical differences. Citibank has a huge profitable retail base in Germany. By contrast, Deutsche Bank and Dresdner Bank underperform in this product line and are thinking about getting out of retail trade altogether. The United Bank of Switzerland has done something similar. Such tactics do not make sense because they take the commercial bank out of its roots.

Financial institutions which look down on retail banking say they are doing so because they have chosen investment banking instead. But the investment banking market is globally crowded. To be a player in investment banking, an institution either has to confront the leaders in this field head-on or give away to Goldman Sachs and Morgan Stanley.

National Westminster and Barclays went through this frontal attack and they have been licking their wounds for some time. NatWest even fell prey to the Royal Bank of Scotland. However, like Citibank, Lloyds TSB chose to concentrate on value-added retail banking and it prospers. Internet or no Internet, a top management which has unrealistic expectations from fields where it cannot lead drives its institutions to disaster. While the chances for leadership in investment banking are slim and they are *not* getting better, management's attention is diverted and the next generation of retail banking slips out of its control.

This next generation of retail banking would follow the pattern we saw in the right bottom box of Figure 5.4 and, without losing control of the lower net worth strata, it will move up the scale into personal banking for higher net worth individuals. This is what Citibank did in Germany following its acquisition and restructuring of Kundenkredit-bank (see D.N. Chorafas and Heinrich Steinmann, *Expert Systems in Banking*, Macmillan – now Palgrave, London, 1991).

Take the European landscape as an example. According to recent estimates, some 26 million Europeans have investable assets of between $100 000 and $1 million; hence there is plenty of scope to court this affluent market. Citibank now offers both onshore accounts and an offshore service to those people with upwards of $100 000 in assets. Services include:

- advice on a range of mutual funds;
- transactional brokerage; and
- some margin credit capability.

In contrast to investment banking for the high finance class, this type of asset management is a sound option. To those with more than $400 000 to invest, Merrill Lynch offers portfolio management services through its Mercury Asset Management. Those with less than $400 000 are handed to Merrill's brokerage operations. Emulating Charles Schwab, Merrill Lynch operates both through bricks and mortar and on the Internet.

This strategy towards the affluent and less affluent clientele differentiates Merrill Lynch from Morgan Stanley Dean Witter, which mainly accepts clients with at least $5 million in liquid assets. It also bets on the fact that the targeted clients generally have a longer-term potential, particularly for lucrative derivative financial instruments.

The message the reader should retain from this discussion is that private banking can benefit in a significant way from Internet supported services, because it provides a good platform for value differentiation and cross-selling (see also section 5) at reasonable cost. But underpinning this approach must be a sound strategy on client targeting, as in the examples I have given. A similar statement is valid, up to a point, about the more complex capital market services for both issuers and investors. This has to do with different types of securities which are moving to the Internet. Notice, however, that banks whose major activities are concentrated on this market are vulnerable to such trends if they do not have the skills to exploit the Internet connection in an effective manner. The time to react is now, and this brings our discussion back to the strategy *our* institution should adopt in Internet banking.

'I am revolutionary in my personal views,' said John Reed. 'But the Internet model also has cultural prerequisites, not only those of a technological nature.' Whether old institutions will be able to adapt to the new environment is wide open; even if ex-bricks-and-mortar banks have some advantages, those who start with a blank sheet in Internet banking presumably have a culture still missing among many of the older institutions.

5   EXPLOITING THE LEVEL OF BUSINESS OPPORTUNITY IN ONLINE ASSET MANAGEMENT

The careful reader will remember that it has been a deliberate choice to take banking as an example of Internet sales rather than some other industry: for instance, the sale of airline tickets, which is another good example of the Internet's effects. In 1999, four US airlines combined their ticket sales on the Internet. In May 2000, British Airways, Air France, Lufthansa, Alitalia and others did the same. As contrasted to securities trading and personal banking, an Internet-based sale of air travel tickets has shortcomings: an Internet site pits the airlines against travel agents, their traditional sales outlets. These Internet sales partners will be increasingly pushed to compete in fare prices against one another and, as with retail banking, the opportunity for value differentiation is relatively limited.

While price cutting is part of the game, it should not be the only chance because it becomes self-destructive. When John Reed says that Citigroup's 40 per cent of revenues come from all types of cash management services which will move to the Internet, he means that this channel will capitalise on online access to the market to become richer and more rewarding to the bank. Sales activities will move up the value chain.

Something similar is true about payments of all sorts. They will not be made at no cost. What will happen is that the costs will be lower while ways and means will be explored on the Internet to ensure that the opportunity for value differentiation is greater. That is a key reason why consumer financial services are moving to the Internet. The other main reason is changes in use patterns of consumers is that to a substantial extent, though not wholly, intermediation will be through the Internet.

Experts believe this will require rethinking the bank's hierarchy of granting loans, as shown in the lower middle part of Figure 5.5. The concept of the loans book itself will change to become online and interactive. Most affected will be the databases at the two sides of Figure 5.5. All of them must be updated in real-time, as well as seamlessly accessed. This is better because real-time continuous settlement will be instrumental in driving out inefficiencies. To a considerable extent, inefficiencies will be driven out of industry after industry, through Internet-based transactions; but we are not yet there.

What can be done to beef up the value-added aspect of banking services being offered (and to be offered) to Internet-based online accounts? To answer this query in a factual manner we should appreciate

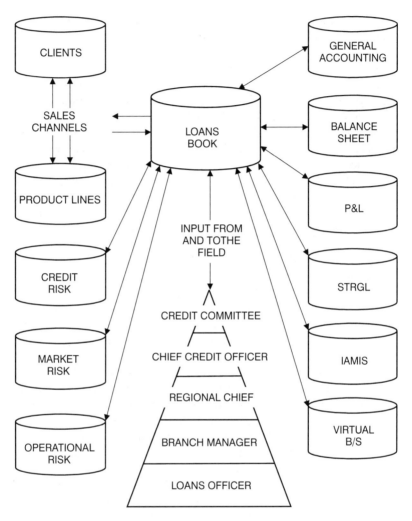

Figure 5.5   Internet banking will force the integration of the loans book within the landscape of other databases

that online services for investors can be distinguished into three main classes:

- financial information;
- aid to choices; and
- aid to asset management.

There is no lack of financial information services on the Internet. There exist today some 70 000 sites (!) which offer news, commentaries and/or quotations. They get most of their value by expanding the geographic coverage of Internet surfers. Can there be value differentiation in financial information? A clear trend developing in the USA is the effort directed at upstaging a site's credibility.

Also in America, credit institutions who act as financial information providers have started offering some of the fruits of their bricks and click strategy without charge. This is not yet the habit in Europe, where companies try to make the consumer pay for the services he gets. What about aid to choices? That is the business of online financial advisors. Some, like Sharp, offer low-cost or zero-cost online advice. Their income comes from sale of models they are developing, including:

- risk management;
- Monte Carlo simulation;
- behavioural finance models; and
- stochastic market moves.

Aid to asset management is what particularly concerns the brokerage firms and their clients. Here a distinction must be made between America and Europe, in terms of policies by the investing public. The pattern is shown in Table 5.2. Other things being equal, asset managers make more money in Europe because the investing public goes for discretionary (full powers) accounts. That is not the habit in America.

One of the particular aspects of the American banking landscape are the *online brokers*. They have more aversion to losses than to risk; and they are ready to play again to recover their losses. They do so without appreciating that this significantly increases their risks. The bottom line is that the priorities set by online brokers reflect an intellectual confusion, leading to an accumulation of different exposures.

Table 5.2 The pattern of investment management habits in America and Europe (%)

	United States	**Europe**
Execution only	45	20
Advisory	35	25
Discretionary	20	55

That being said, the diversity of goals and priorities reflected in the investing population suggests that there is no 'average' client. Therefore an Internet policy based on the average client is going to fail, particularly as we move towards innovative products offered through the Internet. Today, much of what is accessible online concerns tools developed for the average client, *as if*:

- everybody believes in the average entity; and
- everybody bets on the average entity's future.

That is wrong. As the Web becomes intelligent, broadband offers more possibilities, the role of mobile computing is felt (see section 2), and dynamic pricing takes hold, banks betting on satisfying the requirements of the 'average client' will wake up to big surprises. They will find that: the customised financial product is king; knowledge of supply and demand is meaningful in smaller and smaller segments; application hosting must be steadily enriched with new, appealing products; and a wise strategy is to steadily learn about the evolution in customers' drives.

6   THE REGULATORS SEE TO IT THAT MONEY DOES NOT BECOME OBSOLETE

Regulators have a major role to play in this environment. In April 2000, the Office of the Comptroller of the Currency (OCC) published a working paper entitled *The Repeal of Glass-Steagall and the Advent of Broad Banking*, which considers the likely effects on banking organisations of the enactment of the Gramm Leach Bliley Act of 1999, and gives some hints on regulatory measures that might follow.

Basically, the OCC study views the Gramm Leach Bliley Act as extending changes taking place in the banking industry, rather than as being something revolutionary. It also makes the interesting point that it is too early to tell whether the most efficient model for the delivery of financial services will be:

- the *portfolio model* exemplified by Citigroup, which provides in a single company a wide range of banking, securities and insurance products and services; or
- the *portal model*, represented by Yahoo Finance, which uses a single website to access a similarly broad range of products and services through a number of unaffiliated companies.

This brings our discussion once more to the point made in Chapter 4 about auctions and reverse auctions and about alternative supplier accounting. Both the portfolio model and the portal model call for revamping the accounting structure to respond to management information requirements. Other things being equal, the second alternative requires a much more generic approach to permit visibility beyond the portal's screen.

In July 2000, OCC also issued an advisory letter to national bank directors and CEOs emphasising the importance of Board and senior management oversight of audit and control systems to ensure their effectiveness (see also Chapter 1). OCC stated that the risk of audit and control certificates has been heightened by 'new products, services, delivery channels, and other rapid changes in the banking environment'. Accordingly, audit programmes may need to be modified and *strengthened* to address these changes.

This speaks volumes about the responsibility of banks entering into Internet banking, and the new risks they are assuming. OCC noted that it will continue to take into account a national bank's size, complexity and overall risk profile when evaluating the effectiveness of its audit and internal control programme (see D.N. Chorafas, *Implementing and Auditing the Internal Control System*, Macmillan – now Palgrave, London, 2001), which will now be rated:

- strong;
- satisfactory; or
- weak.

Independently of this, one of the OCC comptrollers praised the Securities and Exchange Commission (SEC) for issuing its proposed rule concerning auditor independence. He stated that 'ensuring not only the independence of external auditors, but also the appearance of independence, is vitally important for investors and other users of financial statements, including bank supervisors' (*Financial Services Alert*, Goodwin, Procter & Hoar, Vol. 3, No. 49, 1 August 2000). Let me remind you that external audits are required for all US national banks with $500 million or more in total assets, and the OCC also encourages smaller banks to seek independent audits.

Credit institutions should appreciate the regulators' newly-found activism. Not only does the derivatives boom in the 1990s make it mandatory, but also the projected growth of Internet banking is sure to bring into the picture too many unknowns and associated exposures, in addition to a horde of myths and hypes to which the banks fall victim: for instance, the idea that electronic money (e-money) will make central banks obsolete.

Harvard's Benjamin Friedman has been one of the proponents of this concept that e-money might render central banks obsolete, but many economists who looked into the idea, declared it wrong. In a conference organised in July 2000 in Washington, by the World Bank, IMF and International Finance, Charles Goodhart of the London School of Economics (and formerly of the Bank of England's monetary policy committee) argued that e-money is unlikely to retire ordinary currency in the foreseeable future, stating that the great advantages of currency are simplicity and anonymity; even if the first might be eroded by technology, the second will remain.

Anonymity in transactions is what both buyers and sellers often want, not because they plan to break the law but for their own convenience. Whether in the form of smart cards or electronic funds transfer (EFT), e-money is not technologically capable of providing anonymity. Smart cards bear their owner's identification, while EFT requires that all transactions are written in journals and stored in databases to enhance the trust between the parties. In contrast, cash leaves no tracks and it makes no demands on anybody else's integrity.

What about the demand for banks' deposits at the central bank, a major component of the monetary base? Charles Goodhart argued that banks are no more likely to disappear than currency. Specialised financial intermediaries will always be needed to help people and firms choose their asset portfolios, and distinguish between good and bad credit risks, but these financial intermediaries must reinvent themselves and revamp their products. That is what Internet banking is all about.

7   PRIVACY AND SECURITY CONSIDERATIONS WEIGH HEAVILY ON INTERNET BANKING

Privacy and security used to correlate, and this permitted a fairly co-ordinated approach to both issues which are vital to every financial transaction and to the Internet-based supply chain at large. As far as privacy on the Internet is concerned, current studies indicate that there exist three areas of concern:

- *personal privacy*, therefore protection from entities and people who may be authorised to access private information;

- *confidentiality*, hence the ability to protect the information from non-authorised persons and companies; and
- *obstruction*, or outright damage, by third parties directed to means and media put in place to protect the previous two classes.

A major change with networking at large, and with the Internet in particular, is that today security and personal privacy are in direct confrontation. Every time we click to go to a particular page on the Web, we are logged. Some people say that technology benefits the consumer, even if it takes privacy away. But others do not like to see that happening, and I understand their concerns.

Regulators have every reason to look into the many challenges with Internet banking, and try do something about them. Security is at the top of their list and so is privacy protection. But how? There is a long debate about the benefits encryption may and may not provide. There is also the case of avoidance of vandalism and of the different viruses.

As far as regulators are concerned, protection of investors and of the banking public must be legally guaranteed. This is more difficult than it sounds because of some of the products we discussed in preceding sections, such as advice given by Internet companies. Who is to say if it is factual and documented, or if the public is being taken to the cleaners?

In my judgement, the greatest impediments to Internet banking and Internet commerce are the two subjects under discussion: privacy and security. The violation of one's privacy and safeguarding of one's assets from Internet thieves (see section 8) are major concerns. Companies are faced with both the security of individual transactions, and reputational risk resulting from lack of security. A bank which gets its Internet privacy and security requirements wrong would lose its ability to deal online. Security is not just a technical problem: primarily, it is an organisation problem and, as we will see in Chapter 11, it has to do with people.

Often the media carry the news about hackers' attacks of the variety known as 'Denial of Service', where intruders try to bring down major security walls. To protect themselves, companies use knowledge engineering artefacts designed to understand patterns, including patterns of security attacks. But in the longer term security is a moving target.

Computer companies, and other firms who sell hardware and software for security reasons, usually misrepresent the issues. 'My solution is robust' is a weak argument. No code is unbreakable. Digital certificates supposedly issued 'to secure transactions over the world' are misrepresenting their claims. The ability to audit such certificates in real-time improves upon current security processes, but falls short of giving 99.99 per cent assurance.

Technology-based solutions break down because people try to crash them, and they succeed. Hackers have been particularly ingenious in getting through security walls of financial institutions. Many people are nowadays writing programs to exploit security loopholes in Internet; and there are plenty.

Some of the most frequent security violations happen with what are considered to be established, supposedly dependable programs. This is one reason why I consider statements, such as 'The movement of banking towards Internet will depend highly on secure credit cards', as being light-weight. It is true that if a bank does not have a large credit card population, it is going to cost it dearly in Internet banking because the costs will not be spread over many users. But a large population is increasing Internet risks; it is not reducing them.

People who make light-weight statements do not know what they are talking about, and the same is true of those advocating miracle solutions to be obtained by using smart cards which are 'not well received in the US', while supposedly they 'are well received in Europe'. These are undocumented overstatements, misleading those who listen to them.

On 3 April 2000, Marylise Lebranchu, the French State Secretary for Consumption, made the point that the use of bank cards (credit card, debit cards) with embedded chips is not as secure as it has been supposed to be. According to statistics from the Association Force Ouvrière Consommateurs (AFOC), the level of fraud is 17 per cent higher than the 0.02 per cent posted by the bankers' association for credit cards (GIE CB).

Implicitly GIE CB admitted that much when it agreed to change the current 320 bits chip to a 792 bits chip on smart cards without cost to the consumer. Even the 0.02 per cent level is highly costly to the banks. Officially, given the rate of use of credit cards and debit cards in France, losses have been estimated at least at Ffr178 million ($26 million) in 1999.

This is by no means the only worry. Identity theft is another significant negative. Thieves in Paris have been reportedly sabotaging ATMs to get hold of both cards and personal identification numbers (PINs). Internet commerce is not alien to such events which show a growing level of insecurity. AFOC said about half of credit-card thefts in France involve Internet purchases.

Identity theft starts when thieves misappropriate someone's personal information: address, date of birth, Social Security number and so on, to obtain fake credit cards, driver's licences and other goodies. With that information and identification in hand, criminals are free to operate at the expense of card holders and merchants.

For instance, in the USA, Social Security numbers (when matched with other personal information) enable thieves to apply for credit cards on the Internet, often with minimal scrutiny by issuers. If an identity thief uses a credit card to briefly build up a solid credit history by paying off monthly bills, he or she then has the credibility to apply for items such as loans for cars and rental property. The rise in identity theft crime in the USA is shown in Figure 5.6, and it provides food for

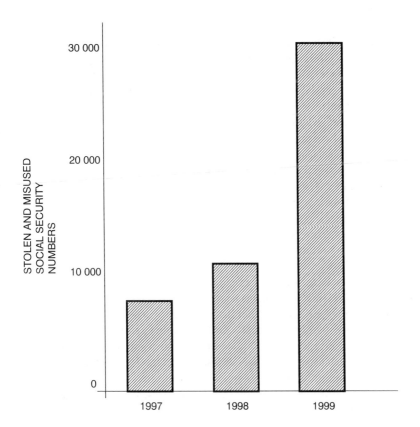

Figure 5.6   As the twentieth century came to a close, reports of stolen or misused social security numbers in the USA increased exponentially

thought for everybody who cares about the security of the financial system.

Matters are getting more worrisome when we account for the fact that fraud stemming from identity theft can channel itself into hundreds of billions of dollars in credit card purchases each year. Indeed, recognising that identity theft could easily get out of hand, with assistance from the Secret Service, several of the largest US credit card issuers are building a database so they can share information on code-breaking and identify geographic locations where credit card fraud occurs more often.

8   CONTROLLING INTERNET CRIME: IS IT POSSIBLE?

The US Federal Trade Commission and other international agencies organised a global sweep to target fraudulent, get-rich-quick schemes on the Internet. In February 2000, this sweep was conducted across 28 countries and it highlighted some 1600 suspect Web sites, which were warned to stop or change their claims. This was part of an intensified effort to combat the proliferation of Internet-based scams aimed at consumers. Practices which were targeted included:

- pyramid schemes and Ponzi games;
- different easy-money claims; and
- unrealistic investment offerings.

For its part, the Securities and Exchange Commission is stepping up its effort to combat online stock fraud by creating an automated system that would listen in on Internet message boards, Web sites and online discussions where stock tips circulate. To many people, this step is controversial because it infringes on personal privacy but, as I underlined in this chapter, on the Internet privacy and security collide.

In its investigation of means and methods currently under way, the SEC has asked more than 100 companies to come up with designs for such a surveillance system, which would scan the Internet for words and phrases commonly used by scam artists. Commission officials said they wanted to automate surveillance activities which their agents are already obliged to engage in on a regular basis, freeing them to do the harder work of interpreting and investigating frauds.

According to the solicitation document issued for project contractors, the projected mechanism would monitor public Web sites, message boards and chat groups. Anything deemed suspicious would be copied into a database, analysed and then indexed for use by SEC investigators in bringing civil proceedings against people suspected of wrongdoing. The SEC also wants e-mail addresses and other identifying information that would help unmask fraudulent message writers.

After reviewing the documents and holding discussions with SEC officials, however, some of the invited bidders declined to collaborate. For instance, PricewaterhouseCoopers advised the agency that it would not participate because the endeavour might impinge on constitutional protections against unlawful search and seizure. Pricewaterhouse-Coopers' chief concern has been that innocent people and their resources would end up in the database.

There are other efforts to stamp out Internet fraud. In April 2000 the SEC issued releases (Nos 33-7856; 34-42728; IC-24426) providing additional interpretative guidance regarding the use of electronic media. This release targets greater security on the Internet and it includes three main topics:

- use of electronic media to satisfy delivery requirements;
- issuer liability for Web site content; and
- use of electronic media in connection with public and private offerings.

SEC's attention is focused primarily on consent to electronic delivery practices and associated treats: for instance, under what conditions an investor may give a global consent to electronic delivery, exposing himself to different types of fraud.

SEC's release also discusses the potential securities law liability associated with hyperlinks on issuer Web sites, and the use of active and inactive embedded hyperlinks. It reviews factors it considers relevant in deciding whether an issuer has adopted information on a third party Web site, and includes treatment of general legal principles that broker-dealers should consider when developing and implementing procedures for online public offering and/or comments on third party Web sites designed to facilitate private offerings.

The SEC warns issuers against reliance on certain types of self-accreditation as a means of qualifying investors for private funds. As with prior guidance on the use of electronic media by the Securities and Exchange Commission, this release includes a number of examples addressing hypothetical situations involving consents to electronic delivery, and the use of online media in connection with different offerings.

It is not too early for such measures because security on the Internet and issues relating to network-based transactions, as well as surveillance, promise to be at the top of the list in the first decade of the twenty-first century. Some people believe that a more open dialogue between hackers, online dealers, companies, governments and the public could help improve Internet security; but others disagree with the inclusion of hackers.

Ironically, the number of experts who now look at hackers as being important for the Internet community as a whole, because they are the ones who dramatise how insecure the Internet is, is on the increase. If a 13-year-old child can bring down the Net and penetrate a highly protected database, maybe the solution is not to go after the 13-year-old child, but to ask on what type of *technology* and *organisational practices* are we dependent?

The initiatives taken by the US Federal Trade Commission and the SEC demonstrate that the online economy is much more vulnerable than most companies would like consumers to know. There are people who can take down the Internet in a matter of minutes, and there are others ready to exploit its weaknesses, while the system as it stands offers little by way of security and protection. We will further exploit the issue of network security, along with some feasible solutions, in Chapter 11.

6 Rigorous Organisational Solutions: A Prerequisite for a Successful Supply Chain

1 INTRODUCTION

The Internet supply chain our company builds, operates and maintains must not only be dynamic but also provide superior services in a cost-effective way. Typically such services are being addressed to customers; received from suppliers; and involve both business partners and internal organisational units.

To accomplish its goals in a commendable way, the supply chain must be designed to expand beyond the provision of transport, and encompass horizontally as well as vertically networked functions of high quality. This must be done in a way which is scalable and adjustable to prevailing business conditions. Simultaneously, it must be capable of espousing different cultures and environments wherever *our* company operates, affording its users flexibility in access, type of application and presentation of results.

Our company's supply chain must also be highly reliable and secure. Even short times of unavailability can result in losing millions of dollars, pounds or any other currency. The policies and organisational principles necessary to deliver value need to be different at each stage of technology or product evolution.

As these comments help demonstrate, the supply chain's reliability is not only a technical matter. It is also, if not primarily, organisational and managerial. *If* our company loses its market credibility, its supply chain will become damaged goods. Said a recent article about the travails of Lucent Technologies: 'On Wall Street, Lucent's credibility has gone up in smoke because of a grim cycle of lowering targets and then failing to meet them ... There are reasons to believe latest growth projections won't be forthcoming next year either' (*Business Week*, 7 August 2000).

The same article was to add that:

> In order to restore its credibility, Lucent must quickly address the operational and technological problems that are behind the slow growth. The company has failed to spot important shifts in crucial markets, such as optical networking. Research and product development have failed in several important respects. Worse, this purveyor of high-tech gear has been slow to embrace the Web for its own internal use. All of which have had a direct effect on performance.

Such comments fit other cases of supply chain mismanagement like a glove. Behind many failures of the type described in this article can be found managerial incompetence and organisational reasons. While embracing the Internet is by no means a sort of present-day penicillin for organisational ills, failure to do so in a successful manner shows near-sighted top management and wanting internal skills.

Since a dynamic supply chain will depend, to a very substantial extent, on publicly available Web software and on the Internet, which are links used also by *our* competitors, superior performance will be a direct result of ingenious organisational solutions. It must also be staffed by skilful people who undergo a lifelong training programme, so that their know-how keeps on being ahead of the curve at any point in time.

Let me add one more reference to the introductory text. Even *if* our company's supply chain is already efficient, and we are proud of its flawless operation, *our* company's organisation and structure must steadily evolve towards an innovative, effective and responsible market-driven solution. The Board, CEO and top management should be the promoters of this policy which is a prerequisite to remaining competitive in the fast changing Internet market.

2   THE MAKING OF A DYNAMIC ORGANISATION AND ITS STRUCTURE

Had the present book been written before the Internet, this section would have opened with the statement: 'One of the main tools for mapping organisational principles into a real-life situation is the organisation chart.' Any human organisation can be charted, but in the fast-moving dynamic world of supply chain solutions both subordinate–superior and peer-to-peer relationships are in a state of flux. They do not exist because of charting. Rather, they are promoted by:

- the business to be done; and
- the project to be completed.

On the other hand, within the same entity organisational charts are both evidence of organisational planning and road maps for decision-making. They are also training devices for those who wish to learn how an organisation ticks. Classical types of charting at senior management level are shown in Figures 6.1 and 6.2. The model of Figure 6.1 is that of a manufacturing company; that of Figure 6.2, of a credit institution.

No organisational chart can be designed until a managerial hierarchy has been established for the enterprise as a whole. Goals will determine structural elements as well as the general character of the company's units: for instance, in a bank, front desk and back office; R&D, distribution network (branches, Internet links); investments; private banking; forex; loans; equities; finance; personnel; supply chain management; and so on.

Few people think about designing their organisational strategies at the same time that they project their technology strategies, yet in the Internet age this is crucial. What sort of strategies will help us move our organisational relationships and our research efforts at the same time? *Where* should we be more creative? *How* can we become more efficient? *When* should we organise by function? *How* do we solve the problem of *organisational lag*?

Since an organisation is something dynamic, charts cannot be allowed to become obsolete through lack of necessary attention and lags in redrafting. Typically organisational charts are two-dimensional (like the examples in Figures 6.1 and 6.2), but virtual companies on the Internet have three dimensions. In either case, the hierarchical structure should be flat, with few intermediate layers; this is even more important for companies working on the Internet. It is the job of an effective management to see to it that:

- hierarchical levels are limited to four or five at the most; and
- the whole concept of structure is horizontal with a *span of control* of more than eight.

By definition, the span of control measures the number of managers and other workers directly depending from a superior. Independently of the number of layers, everybody should appreciate that organisational charts cannot supplant good management, and neither can they substitute the spelling out of relationships defining responsibility and authority.

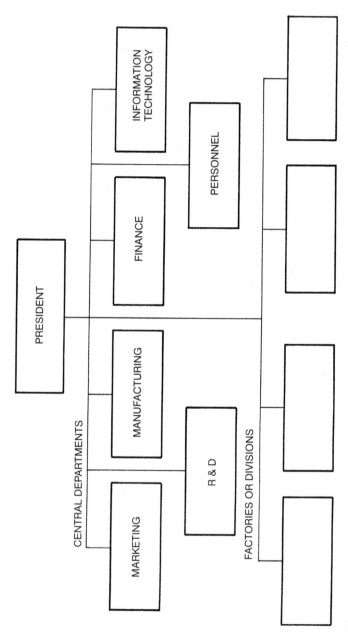

Figure 6.1 Organisational chart of a manufacturing company with many divisions

127

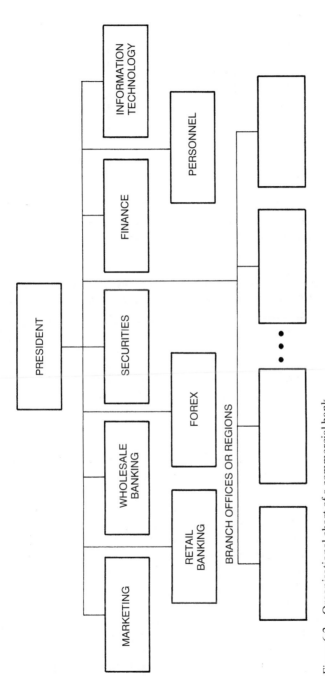

Figure 6.2   Organisational chart of a commercial bank

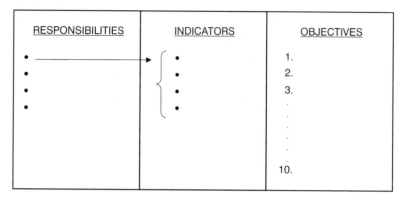

Figure 6.3   The best way to frame a job description is through responsibilities and indicators, with objectives being defined yearly

Any relationships and all of the functions executed by managerial personnel should always be spelled out clearly. Their definition should be concise but crisp, preferably written in a three-fold structure like the one shown in Figure 6.3. This model defines for each job:

- *responsibilities*, of a given managerial position;
- *indicators* of the execution of these responsibilities; and
- *objectives*, for the next twelve months of operations.

The role of responsibilities and indicators is to define and explain what is expected from each managerial post in the organisation. The rationale of objectives is to outline the goals to be reached within a predetermined timeframe by the person entrusted with a given job. The more completely roles and objectives are spelled out, the clearer become the functions performed by the organisation.

It is no self-evident or easy task to define the main responsibilities; outline the interactive reporting lines between the Board and senior management; assess the performance of executives, traders, account managers and loans officers; and ensure that duties are delegated in an appropriate fashion, or even that every executive remains accountable at all time for his decisions and his acts. But *if* the proper culture prevails in the organisation, *then* what I just said is possible.

One of the difficulties with any organisational planning mission is that it starts with people and builds around them. This is indeed unavoidable because, automation or no automation, organisations are made up of people and must operate through people. A company's human capital is the greatest asset in its possession. Organisations which do not take people into account (their strengths and weaknesses) are short-lived. If *our* employees do not fit the aims of the organisation and its mode of operations, then the results will be wanting.

It is in a way unavoidable that in real life organisations build around available personnel and therefore their shortcomings. But if we allow this lack of suitability of some managers and professionals to persist, then *our* company cannot prosper. Whether within the supply chain or outside it, the manager whose subordinates do not understand the nature of their functions and disregard their personal accountability cannot perform any useful function.

This is a particularly serious condition with new industries and with start-ups. When it happens, they disintegrate and disappear. With old economy companies, it leads to rampant bureaucracy. That is how the arteries of the organisation get clogged. A Kodak study in the 1980s demonstrated that it takes about six years of mismanagement to run down a formidable company. In the age of the Internet, decay comes much faster and the company sinks into oblivion.

What about the Internet industry itself? Wall Street analysts believe that many Internet companies have entered a more mature phase of development in which sector opportunities are easier to quantify, and therefore the results of disorganisation and mismanagement have become more visible. The tide is not rising fast enough to lift all the boats. Survival in the Internet world is by no means a foregone conclusion. The novelty effect has gone. An estimated 75 per cent of current public Internet companies will merge or disappear over the next few years.

This sounds quite similar to what has happened to poorly organised old economy companies, especially those which have been in business for many years and have developed a rigidity that hampers their ability to meet the market's changing drives. Therefore, the first test of an effective organisation is flexibility and adaptation to a changing business environment, as the following sections document. This notion will be familiar to the reader from Chapter 1, which focused on the management of change.

3 ORGANISATIONAL PREREQUISITES, RELATIONSHIP STRATEGIES AND TECHNOLOGY

One of the organisational prerequisites within the Internet supply chain is the *relationship strategies* which it imposes. These form the foundation of product and service delivery in all its aspects. From the business partners' perspective, the structure that supports the entire relationship must be sensitive to market moves and capable of change. It must also promote the ability to roll out new and different products, with a short life cycle. Rapid response must reward customers globally in an individualised and tailored manner, ensuring supply chain partners can be serviced in a way satisfying the criteria of:

- accuracy;
- timeliness;
- quality; and
- low cost.

Companies able to compete in such an environment are masters in evolving a variable cost system and an operational infrastructure characterised by global delivery with flexible location management.

Take an institution's private banking activities as an example. When it is well organised and directed, private banking is striving to deliver, on a global basis, a high-quality, consistent service strategy where each one of the clients defines personalised investment goals and risk objectives. These individual goals and objectives must be appropriately matched with products and services offered by *our* bank.

Private banking customers are the high end of consumer banking and their need for special attention, which inevitably has an organisational aftermath. These customers' transactions require a highly secure system and reliable network environment. Quality, timeliness and availability are key elements in this strategy which, when successful, becomes an excellent source of fees to the bank. The successful meeting of such aims call for organisation and staffing which take account of the cross-border market place and its steady growth.

To address the demanding Internet market, both personnel skills and innovative financial products are keys to success. The same is true of skills able to integrate all facets of private banking with information on services. Also, it is important that the products *our* institution offers are characterised by ease of use, 100 per cent availability and a consistent, world-wide customer handling. The organisation we choose must focus on:

- resolving business problems; and
- capitalising on opportunities.

Whether carried out through the Internet, bricks and mortar, or bricks and click, the nature of private banking requires a highly secure, flexible network, allowing firms to aggressively implement a global line of business while making feasible the personalisation of service. One of the primary requirements is sufficient flexibility enhanced by real-time response to avoid long and costly product development and delivery efforts. This flexibility calls for distributed databases, and the incorporation of global security services which:

- continue to reduce the total costs of systems and the unit costs of processing;
- increase emphasis on inter-organisational systems and internal connectivity; and
- consolidate applications while migrating towards an interactive supply chain system.

To execute this strategy, the technology model must move towards an integrated applications architecture allowing high-quality products and services to be developed faster and more cheaply, supporting the use of expert systems and eliminating manual processing and paper in user areas. The network must provide increased real-time peer-to-peer connectivity as well as high bandwidth on demand.

These objectives impose organisational, staffing and technology requirements. These include integrated special functions for internal control (see section 4), and real-time risk management.

Other requirements include the development of quick, low-cost solutions for local business development, and maintenance of a consistent business architecture which accounts for the technology base. Solutions must be characterised by a strong trend towards dynamic services, and the network (Internet or any other) should deliver these services to users in geographically dispersed locations simultaneously.

In answer to these requirements, both rigorous organisational solutions and the chosen application architecture must reflect the business model chosen by the institution and its implementation. For instance, the application architecture will provide an integrated set of intelligent network services supporting basic and complex products, including a service delivery which is globally consistent across multi-country markets (*if* our bank takes advantage of globalisation).

Organisational solutions and the applications architecture should also provide a migration path that permits services developed under new technological perspectives to access old-style server systems, and vice versa. This would minimise the need for system modifications – which are costly and error-prone – if an old-style solution is migrated to comply with the new applications architecture.

In general, the structural approaches which distributed computing environments require in order to support supply chain solutions call for an approach that provides a combination of capabilities, including connectivity, interoperability, ease of use and efficient administration. Organisational solutions must make it feasible for application developers to:

- standardise familiar concepts and techniques;
- feel at ease across a variety of platforms; and
- ensure services in a way that hides the complexity of functions.

The infrastructure must offer administrators single-system view of the services that they manage. It should assure robust distributed operations, and see to it they are managed transparently. A great amount of attention should also be paid to the level and type of security that must be provided for all mission-critical services. This includes privacy, authentication of parties and integrity of information, as we will see in Chapter 11.

4 THE IMPACT OF MANAGEMENT CULTURE ON AN EFFECTIVE INTERNAL CONTROL SYSTEM

Organisation and management culture correlate. What we have seen in Chapter 1 is part and parcel of a new culture able to address longer term issues, but also to tackle day-to-day activities of the nuts and bolts type. Management culture makes all the difference in business ethics which underpin timely and effective decisions, yet it is not a concept economists like to deal with because it is considered to be inherently unquantifiable. But it is qualifiable.

The optimisation and structure an entity chooses is a way of qualification. Like culture, organisation adapts given a number of preconditions, which is practically what the regulators of the Group of Ten countries say when they underline the fact that the bank's Board of Directors bears ultimate responsibility for ensuring the establishment and maintenance of an adequate internal control system (D.N. Chorafas, *New Regulation of the Financial Industry*, Macmillan – now Palgrave, London, 2000) while senior management must be in charge of implementing the strategy and policies set by the board, and therefore for operating the internal controls. Within this frame of reference, the Board of Directors defines the general framework, within which fits the management of the credit institution, and shoulders practically unlimited responsibility for its sound administration. The Board must also ensure leadership, effective supervision of the activities undertaken by management and the quality of obtained results.

One does not need to be a dean of business administration to appreciate the organisational aftermath of this statement. The Board's responsibilities require the appropriate level of competence and sufficient time for its members to be adequately informed about the institution's operating conditions, the terms of business being done, exposure being assumed, and the returns. While specifics vary from company to company, some general organisational principles are valid in all firms, particularly when it comes to the employees' culture.

On 5 June 2000, an article in *Business Week* examined the means industry leaders have used to change the business culture of employees. In Japan, when at Sega Enterprises the management team resisted change, Isao Okawa, the president, defied the lifetime-employment culture by announcing that those who resisted change would be fired, risking shame. Resistance vanished overnight.

In the USA, at Enron, Jeffrey Skilling, the president, moved the energy company from bureaucratic thinking to Internet culture by ripping out nearly all of the elevators at headquarters. His goal was to force people to use the stairs, thus:

- creating more chance encounters;
- boosting collaboration through e-mail; and
- demonstrating that resistance to change has consequences.

At GE Aircraft Engines, James McNerney, the CEO, converted an old warehouse into an *idea laboratory*. Then he appointed 'e-belts', equivalent to Six Sigma black belts, to lead the process of change in his division. This strategy has given commendable results.

A Board's and a CEO's ability to lead is based upon the background and experience of each member. Part of it is education; another part is the values one grew up with; still another, the good and bad practices encountered throughout one's career. The ability to lead in a practical sense hinges on the quality of one's team. Indeed, the quality of the team has much to do with the ability to attract, retain and develop capable associates.

Growth plays an important role in the leadership team. If a company grows by 40 per cent in slightly over 2 years this requires doubling the leadership team to stay where one was before. It also calls for steady improvement in communication skills as the diameter of the groups which inter-communicate explodes, and for cutting down on the number of middle layers. Many companies are today burdened with too many middle managers who resist change.

Managing change in company-wide communications also presents a great challenges. It is no self-evident or easy task to define the main responsibilities; outline the interactive reporting lines between the Board and senior management; assess the performance of executives, traders, account managers and loans officers; and make sure that duties are delegated in an appropriate fashion while every executive remains accountable for his or her decisions and his acts. But *if* the proper culture prevails in the organisation, *then* what I just said is feasible.

Here is another organisational flaw: in an autocratic organisation, senior management does not accept dissemination. It may sound a curious statement, but the proper functioning of an internal control system heeds dissension. Alfred P. Sloan, Jr, the late chairman and CEO of GM, once said at a Board meeting: 'Gentlemen, I take it we are all in complete agreement on the decision here.' When the assembled executives all nodded their assent, Sloan responded: 'I propose further discussion of this matter is delayed until our next meeting, to give yourselves time to develop disagreement and perhaps gain some understanding of what the decision is all about.'

Chapter 1 also brought the reader's attention to the fact that a recent addition to the Board's responsibilities is to ensure that our company's information system is state of the art. One of the tests is if it can effectively support Internet commerce as well as real-time risk management. Analytical studies, simulation, experimentation and interactive graphics can be instrumental in promoting efficient decision-making and feedback control, based on:

- the adequate evaluation of the impact of any decision; and
- the prompt identification of any breaches of limits and tolerances.

For all of these reasons, an integral part of the Board's and CEO's responsibility is to make sure that the company's internal control functions are properly defined, adequately resourced, and take place in the most effective manner. For this to happen, the Board must see to it that *our* institution's internal controls are periodically assessed in terms of their effectiveness and in relation to specific changes taking place within the business environment. For its part, senior management must ensure that adequate mechanisms are in place so that the internal auditors report back to the Board on their findings on a timely and comprehensive basis, and these reports should not then be massaged at senior management level to weed out unwanted findings.

What is the difference between control exercised by the Board and that at other levels of management? The phrase *high-level control* has been coined to help in identifying the role of the Board and CEO in connection with the duties described in the preceding paragraphs. This includes all controls instituted and exercised on the initiative of the Board of Directors in its capacity as a body elected by the general meeting of shareholders, which:

- defines the strategy and general policies; and
- prudentially supervises senior management.

High-level controls are necessary because lack of adequate Board over-sight and accountability, as well as failure to develop a strong control culture within the organisation, can lead to losses. As a general statement major financial losses, even bankruptcy, reflect management inatten-tion to, and laxity in, internal control activities, and also insufficient guidance and oversight, as well as an absence of clear management accountability through the assignment of well-defined, comprehensible duties and responsibilities at all management levels.

5 THE IMPORTANCE OF A MARKETING ORGANISATION AND ITS INFORMATION TECHNOLOGY SUPPORT

A company typically has several organisational units. From an Internet supply chain perspective, two are most vital: R&D to ensure a steady flow of innovative products able to compete in the global landscape, and marketing to promote their sale, whether *our* products and services appeal to a niche or to the wide crossborder market.

In the early 1950s at the University of California in Los Angeles, Dr Harold D. Koontz, my professor of business strategy and a former executive vice president of TWA, taught his students that 'to build an aeroplane and fly an airliner is no problem. The challenge is to fill it up with passengers.' This advice applies equally to Internet commerce. You can fly in the supply chain *if* you:

- offer a superior service or product;
- keep on providing added value;
- know how to market your goods; and
- ensure both high quality and cost-effectiveness.

This requires technical virtuosity. In the year 2000 and beyond, a company whose rocket scientists and systems specialists are an order of magnitude better than those of its competitors has a dramatic advantage over them, and the gap is bound to increase. A well-tuned marketing organisation depends a great deal on advanced information technology. Xerox created specifically focused work teams and hired a top level consultant to train them on:

- rapid software development; and
- the observance of tough deadlines. Management policy has set the objective that information technology produces results in *3 months*, not in *3 years*.

Top management guidelines see to it that:

- all IT projects must be prototyped;
- the prototype must be ready within 3 weeks;
- deployment and operation must take place within 3 months.

The marketing of financial services requires a much more stringent timetable. Taking an example from the experience of investment banks at Wall Street, a major customer may call at 4 p.m. and ask for an offer to invest $500 million in a new financial product, about which he has some vague idea. What the client wants is an offer with risk and return. To answer the client's wish, a trader and rocket scientist (D.N. Chorafas, *Rocket Scientists in Banking*, Lafferty, London and Dublin, 1995) will work overnight and by 8.30 a.m. the next morning they will have ready the institution's offer. This requires a great deal of fast prototyping since no modern financial product can be launched without information technology support. Modelling will not only be done for product development reasons but also for risk management, because without precomputing the exposure the bank (or its client) can turn belly up.

As this example helps to demonstrate, the software development timescales have changed in the most significant manner. What used to be done in years must now be accomplished in weeks. What took a month to see through must be executed in hours or minutes. Figure 6.4 dramatises these reference scales and brings to the reader's attention the most significant difference which exists between coarse grain and fine grain capture, treatment and reporting of information.

Online, real-time *mining* of databases is also of crucial importance to marketing, and organisational guidelines must reflect this fact. The same is true of *directories* and other metadata such as control information, but few organisations create incentives, let alone generate the appropriate know-how, to carefully and thoroughly organise and handle their *metadata* (a higher layer of information elements where meaning and patterns, rather than number, are most important).

There is also the false concept that metadata benefits the organisation, but not the people expected to create it and use it. This is not true because these same people are also computer users – hence direct beneficiaries – and they do take advantage of controls which set limits on the use of information contained in lower layers. To explain the concept of metadata better, Figure 6.5 provides an example with a guaranteed banker's cheque drawn on a demand deposit account.

Real-time data collection at the source, real-time interactive reporting at final destination, datamining and metadata frame a new concept of information technology applications. Senior management must therefore be very clear about the impact of advanced technology on marketing, and vice versa. The worst thing an Internet supply chain company can do to support its marketing effort through technology is to use mainframes. This is because the sophisticated software which needs to be used for an effective technological solution in managing the sales activity requires real-time models, simulators, and expert systems. It also calls for interactive three-dimensional visualisation which eats the mainframe's cycle for breakfast, while extending response times to unacceptable levels.

In conclusion, Internet commerce, particularly B2B, requires interactive computational solutions based on fully distributed systems. Cost-effective approaches are networked any-to-any, based on client-servers, where the servers range from number-crunching to databasing, including disk farms of terabyte capacity for client-oriented information. As many Internet companies have found out, their databasing requirements grow by 30–50 per cent per year.

138

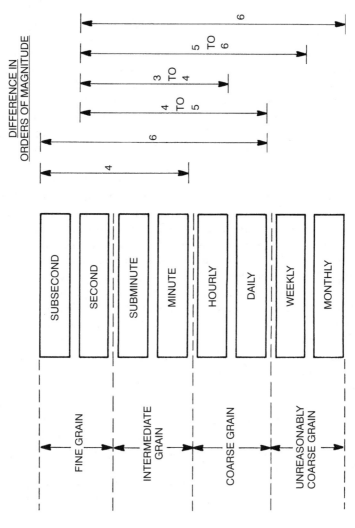

Figure 6.4 There are orders of magnitude in difference between fine grain and coarse grain information

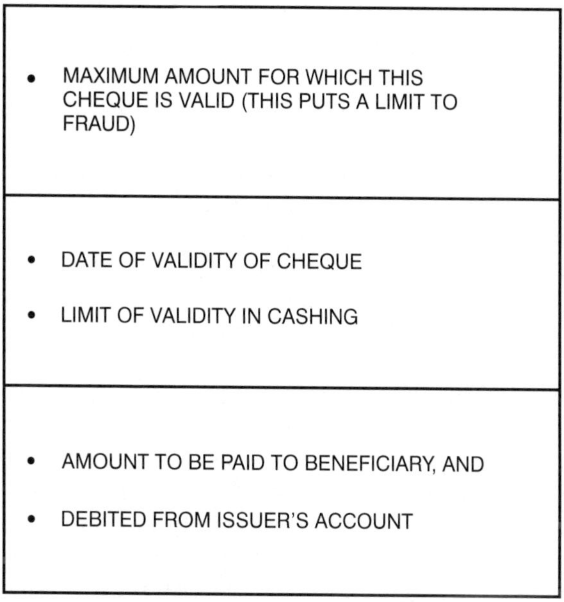

- MAXIMUM AMOUNT FOR WHICH THIS CHEQUE IS VALID (THIS PUTS A LIMIT TO FRAUD)

- DATE OF VALIDITY OF CHEQUE
- LIMIT OF VALIDITY IN CASHING

- AMOUNT TO BE PAID TO BENEFICIARY, AND
- DEBITED FROM ISSUER'S ACCOUNT

Figure 6.5 Probably unknown to its user, a banker's cheque has embedded in it two layers of metadata

6 CISCO: A CASE STUDY ON MARKETING IN THE INTERNET SUPPLY CHAIN

Technologically advanced companies appreciate that to manage themselves and their client accounts in an able manner they need intelligence-enriched network solutions of the type briefly described in section 5. They also need agent-assisted database mining with sub-second response speed allowing them to know about clients, the pattern of their wishes and their individual requirements, ahead of competitors. The need for a new, sophisticated paradigm has been present for some years, but only recently has it been properly appreciated. The problem is that very few companies have the skill and culture which is needed to implement advanced information technology for marketing reasons.

A good example of successful Internet commerce is provided by Cisco. Not only is this firm a key provider of the engines that control Internet traffic, but it is one of the largest I-commerce sites: 85 per cent of its orders are issued over the Web. This says much about restructuring client files and accounting files in a company as big as Cisco's, whose revenue in the April 1999 to March 2000 timeframe was close to $20 billion. Cisco is years ahead of its competitors when it comes to using the Web to link itself to customers and suppliers.

Cisco sells 80–85 per cent of its networking equipment over the Internet, and produces $650 000 of revenue per employee per year. By comparison, its rival, Lucent Technologies, sells just 30 per cent of its equipment over the Web, and brings in just $250 000 per employee per year. Furthermore it has been out of touch with important new areas of the market, with the result that it has missed major growth opportunities.

Other statistics, too, are important. Aiming for profitability, not just sales growth, Cisco has gained some $450 million annually in cost savings by moving many of its supply chain operations to the Web. In a very wise marketing move, supported by the company, its customers can configure products and place orders entirely over the Internet. At the root of this application there have been improvements in customer service, making it easier for clients to interact with Cisco and its management. The next most important gain is that, presently, 55 per cent of orders received by Cisco are shipped without any intervention by one of its employees.

Another major organisational benefit obtained by Cisco is that it is now able to scale its operations without having to proportionately increase the number of people required. This is a brilliant example of the close link between organisation and marketing. The company does the lion's share of its total business over the Net, which amounts to $1.66 billion in monthly revenue.

Also, Cisco's suppliers are able to access the company's ERP system to see product demand and product scheduling on a real-time basis. This makes feasible efficiency processes such as dynamic replenishment, enabling Cisco and its business partners to reduce inventories without compromising production processes or product availability.

Further insight into the organisational and marketing moves which made such breakthroughs possible can be gained through a quick flashback. This will help to better appreciate how to reach such objectives. When, in January 1995, John Chambers was named chief executive of Cisco Systems, the company had 3000 employees and sales of approximately $2 billion a year. Five and a half years later, in mid-2000, Cisco had become a telecommunications powerhouse, with 30 000 employees.

Cisco has grown into the third most valuable company in the world, at one point reaching a market capitalisation of $541 billion. As it diversified into fibre-optic communications and other new computing and networking gear, it continued to grow at a rate exceeding 50 per cent a year. How has Cisco managed this spectacular rise? 'We've always made decisions based on what we think is best for our employees and shareholders and the company in the long run, and not on short-run gyrations', says Chambers (*Wall Street Journal*, 2–3 June 2000).

In a wise move which underlines the impact of organisation and staffing on success in marketing, Cisco ties employee compensation programmes directly to *customer satisfaction* results. Here are, in a nutshell, the principles which guide the hand of its management:

- make your customers the centre of your culture;
- build strong partnerships in an industry more innovative than ever;
- empower every employee to increase productivity and improve retention;
- thrive on change and on the management of change (Chapter 1);
- keep the two-way communication and trust which is required by teamwork.

Cisco's top management appreciates that leading companies focus on internal development, effective acquisitions and a system of partnerships which follows the horizontal business model. It also welcomes competition because competitors are the promoters of innovation forcing *our* company's management to act quicker. 'We will have more market share three to five years from now because we have good competitors,' John Chambers suggests.

Chambers might also have pointed out that his company excels in other organisational domains, such as developing and managing strategic information systems, not only in software and hardware terms but also in training top, middle and lower level managers; setting up priorities; putting ROI goals in its IT investments; and following a dynamic policy in IT implementation.

Both the internal management culture and the support which it gets assist it in preparing for future business, showing sensitivity to market drives, making a timely evaluation of profit and loss, and driving for steady personnel improvement. As cannot be repeated too often, not only innovation but also higher quality of products and services offered ahead of competitors, at cost-effective prices, are the most crucial factors in retaining leadership in the supply chain.

7   INTRODUCING SMART TECHNOLOGY INTO THE SUPPLY CHAIN

Organisational problems are never solved in the longer term. They evolve over time and morph into new challenges. Even if a company thinks that it has achieved 'the ultimate' in structural perfection or marketing solutions, the chances are this 'ultimate' will be short lived. Today, there is no better example of what I am saying than the introduction of smart technology into the supply chain and its expected effects.

The concept of using *smart technology* in the supply chain is new. Yet, practical applications are not that far down the line. Some companies, such as Gillette, which are already active in this way, plan to start implementation by 2002 and foresee a generalisation of smart technology applications by 2005. Other companies, such as Motorola and International Paper, have started an experiment with the former's *BiStatix* chip. Still others are currently engaged in a process of exchanging ideas and sharing visions of the course smart technology should take.

What is meant by smart technology? The simplest way to answer this query is to say that it represents the development of low cost and low power microchip solutions which permit us to use in best possible way the power of the microprocessor. A microprocessor literally printed, say, on a box makes this box *smart material*.

Why do we need smart materials in our daily life and daily business? An easy answer is: why not? A more complex answer is to ask why we need computers, aeroplanes, cars or the telephone? As people do over telephone, the coming generation of smart materials will be able to communicate with each other. The printed microprocessors will also have two antennas. They will both send and receive information.

Smart materials will have an electronic product code and be able to identify themselves. A prerequisite to unambiguous identification is a thorough and rigorous classification. Any sort of material which we use is an object we can classify and identify: it may be raw material, semi-manufactured goods or ready products, to name a few examples; or it may be in process at the factory floor, in an inventory of stored goods or in actual use in the home or office.

Recent advances in low-cost, network-aware embedded processors enable the efficient control of most devices and machines over a shared, open communication infrastructure. The latter may range widely from a small home network to the global Internet and its different supply chains. The cornerstone of this advanced application is the emergence of low-power and low-cost sensing technologies. Its advent makes it likely that a variety of industrial and consumer goods will be tagged with remotely readable identification tags, such as radio-frequency (RF) tags, which are being considered to replace universal product code (UPC) bar codes, and can be read automatically from a distance out of line-of-sight.

The effects will range far and wide. Solutions of the type I am explaining open up vast new opportunities for implementing smart automated systems exhibiting intelligent, collaborative behaviour that can significantly improve both productivity and efficiency of industrial firms. Examples include:

- automatic object tracking;
- inventory and supply chain management;
- control and maintenance of large systems; and
- a whole range of a new generation of Web appliances.

The advent of a smart environment is a world apart from what we have known so far. Classically, inanimate material has been identified as a group: computers, chips, tables, chairs, razors, pencils. Some of this material, typically the more expensive, has a serial number, and therefore individual identification. Cars, all sorts of motors and personal computers are examples. This serial number, however, is issued by its manufacturer; it has no global meaning.

In a globalised economy this is necessary but not enough. Identification should have universal characteristics with synonyms and antonyms avoided as much as possible. This is not easy, but it is possible. Once a piece of material, any material, has been properly classified and uniquely identified, we can proceed to the next step: *automatic identification* (auto-ID). What we need to add to this material is a very low cost chip with antennas; therefore, the ability not only to have an identity number, but also to communicate its identity to other entities, whether people or materials.

Auto-ID solutions will require communication and computational capabilities at low cost. In the years to come, both will be available in abundance practically everywhere. The same is true of efficient, user-friendly personal access to databased resources along the organisational and marketing lines explained in the preceding sections. Several experts now consider the concept of smart materials and their usage as indivisible from the next major productivity strides. Individual item identification, chip technology, antennas and direct access to databases are the pillars of the emerging and growing domain of smart technology.

There are other major organisational challenges which need to be addressed in a rigorous manner. For instance, *when* does a given material become a thing for which auto-ID is necessary, or at least makes sense, because of future developments which we foresee? To a large extent, this is related to cost and to projected effectiveness. Gillette plans to identify every razor blade when the cost of an electronic tag (e-tag) drops to 1 cent from the current 10 cents or so.

Another challenge is the business architecture to be used (see section 1). Without doubt, a global system of automatic identification needs an open architecture. It also requires us to keep an open mind about the nature of e-tags, their communications chores, and the way they integrate into the system in a dynamic manner. Here we are dealing with very big systems which have taxing organisational requirements.

Both from a managerial and a technological perspective, an open architecture and an open mind are made necessary by the fact that the global supply chain is the largest network in the world, and it is steadily growing as well as changing. It is also operating all the time, seamlessly to most people; it is a network which can be easily characterised as:

- sophisticated;
- random; and
- complex.

Because they serve the business partners fully online, larger scope supply chain systems tend to become self-sustaining entities with totally distributed command and control characteristics. One of the marvels of self-regulated supply chains is the way big cities, such as New York, London and Paris, feed themselves without any bureaucrat pulling strings from a Kafka-style castle.

The aftermath of what I am saying has an impact economy-wide. Experts believe that the effect of supply systems on the economy is so profound that when they change the real world as we know it changes as well, and vice versa. Therefore, the challenge for the coming years is to identify how the virtual world of supply chains connects with the real world, how the two influence one another, and how their growth might upset the way we have been working during the last couple of centuries.

8 ORGANISATIONAL PREREQUISITES FOR IDENTIFICATION IN THE PHYSICAL AND LOGICAL WORLD

Classification and identification is one of the most demanding and most complex organisational jobs faced by business and industry. It has always been so, but it is also the next major challenge in information technology, for the simple reason that the real world of entities and the virtual world of data are closely linked to one another. Classically, these links have been *ad hoc* and mostly local; by contrast, the Internet now provides a global capability on which tier-1 companies capitalise.

To take advantage of the capabilities this new state of affairs offers, well-organised online interfaces have to be development through I-commerce. Current solutions are still weak. The next wave of change will make the physical-to-logical (or virtual) world links stronger, and auto-ID will be pivotal to such transition. This is expected to provide a bigger step forward in interfaces than we have seen so far with any other development.

As technology advances and sophisticated approaches come at reasonable cost, it is unavoidable that the interfaces between the real world and the virtual world would change. Today these links are provided through old economy solutions. What we need is to have the two worlds, the physical and the logical, merge their services seamlessly. Key to this is a rational, well-organised classification and identification system.

Classification is indeed a prerequisite to unique and unambiguous identification because it sees to it that every entity has one, and only one, place within the global system. In turn, auto-identification by smart materials and the ability of all entities to communicate their information and/or ask for other datastreams will revolutionise current concepts in the design of large aggregates. Sending and receiving data by inanimate entities will cause changes in the physical world beyond those we have experienced in the past 60 years with computers. It will also give a big boost to supply chain solutions, because it will help to streamline Internet commerce systems.

The first challenge is to appreciate what is behind the concept of classification and identification for inanimate objects. Nobody will dispute the need for identification in human society. We all have a name and many of us have an identity card. Many of us who travel internationally have a passport with name, vital details and a photo, but the identification of inanimate entities, article-by-article, entity-by-entity and information element-by-information element has not yet taken hold.

However, Internet commerce, online supply chain requirements and advances in technology available at low cost have seen to it that this is now changing. We start to appreciate that we live in a physical world with physical objects which need to be uniquely identified to face the challenge of connecting the physical world to the virtual (data) world. This is where the concepts of classification and automatic identification come in. Experts suggest its implementation will be so much of a new paradigm that the next wave of changes in the supply chain will see to it that our notions of handling inanimate objects will evolve as radically as with the assembly line of Henry Ford at the beginning of the twentieth century. The revolution currently under way in merchandising and distribution parallels that of the assembly line in terms of depth.

At the roots of this revolution, largely propelled by the Internet, is a unique identification code for each individual item. As we saw in section 7, it will be embedded in products. It will also be imprinted on microprocessors identifying packages. Auto-identification solutions will be used to store and transmit information to a reader, as well as receive information. This two-way dataflow will update in real-time the intelligent, distributed databases.

Can this be carried too far? Yes, it can. Absurdities in technology should be strictly avoided because they are counterproductive. Let me explain what I mean by this reference through an example. A card manufacturer in Nottingham has produced a smart business card, now being carried by senior executives from BT, Siemens, GEC and GPT (the developer). Each card has £1 of call-time on it. Big deal. This is a good example of the misuse of technology. On the positive side it offers very little worth talking about; but given away as a business card, it may well lead to false identification, with thieves impersonating its legitimate owner.

There is of course talk of adding other information to the smart business card such as hotel and takeaway food suppliers, who in exchange would get orders as well as advertising space; another 'big deal' of trivial value. The developers of these schemes fail to recognise that plenty can be lost in the confusion of getting something for nothing in a scheme which is all-in-one.

The solutions we are after must be *sound*. They must also have clear *objectives* and be *secure*. For over 25 years smart cards tried and failed to take off in the market, because their potential users rejected them. Hundreds of millions of dollars have been lost in fruitless efforts to revive a dead duck. One can lose face by bringing to the market something silly. As an old proverb says: 'If you don't want to be taken for a fool, you should not be doing foolish things.'

By contrast, there is much to be gained by capitalising on the fact that in the post-PC era $100 devices with resident agents and telecommunications gateways will receive and read signals, translate codes, pass information to a computer directly or through the Internet, share the received data stream, and do something with it. Such a system will permit multiple platforms and software modules to talk to each other, while other software modules execute accounting and logistics operations without human intervention. This is the shape of things to come.

Let me add this in conclusion. To gain perspective and appreciate the trends in the coming years we must also have a sense of what went before. Historically the notions underpinning a supply chain did not change until the Industrial Revolution altered the means of transportation, making possible large transfers over long distances. New, efficient means of transportation which did not depend on nuclear power were nineteenth-century developments. In the twentieth century came the assembly line, with the result that a big step forward was taken in production as well as in engineering. However, the change in supply chain among the key nodes did not happen until the advent of the Internet. There are reasons for this delay.

Information about current status, and therefore visibility, has not greatly improved in the first 50 years of computer usage. To make matters worse, there has been reduced visibility, if not downright lack of reliable information about future demand, because of gaps in the feedback from consumers and small businesses towards the main suppliers of goods. A fluid supply chain is now possible but its efficient function calls for thorough organisation. Classification and identification will be the peak technology of 2000–10. (D.N. Chorafas, *Integrating ERP, Supply Chain Management and Smart Materials*, Auerbach, New York, 2001).

Part 2

The Changing Responsibilities of Senior Management in a Modern Firm

7 One of the Big Challenges with Electronic Commerce: Accounting for Taxation

1 INTRODUCTION

Globalisation poses major problems and nowhere is this more evident than in the interface between *legislation* and *taxation*. The taxation challenge is not new, but it has been augmented because of crossborder networking. Crossborder transfer of money, information, knowledge, engineering specifications, logistics models, sales data and other elements is seamless to tax authorities, and there is no way of changing this short of instituting a police state.

As the service economy grows at the expense of manufacturing, the catchment area for taxes shrinks, because tax laws have classically been written for the old, physical economy, not for the new economy. Added to this is the fact that today's legal framework is parochial, and therefore fully incompatible on a global basis. The bits and pieces that seem to converge rest on one or more of three criteria:

- residence of the seller;
- residence of the buyer; and
- type of commerce.

Type of commerce is the most difficult to handle in an Internet sense, but this does not mean that issues connected to the residence of the seller and of the buyer are easy to define. The OECD has been working since 1997 on a taxation system based on these criteria, and has found them elusive. The type of commerce on the Web is steadily changing. As for residence of the seller, a crucial notion in its definition is that of a *stable establishment* (SE). How does one define in Internet commerce the word 'stable'?

Companies in the new economy can play off governments through their decisions about where to locate their operations, including factories and research laboratories. They do so anyway when they use unrealistic transfer prices to shift income from high-tax jurisdictions to low-tax ones (a process known as tax optimisation, which keeps many tax lawyers busy). In 1999, a US General Accounting Office study reported that from 1989 to 1995, an outright majority of corporations, both US and foreign, paid zero US income taxes (*Business Week*, 7 August 2000). This speaks volumes about the obsolescence of the different national tax systems, and their inability to address revenues from a globalised service economy.

Special interest groups capitalise on the absence of crisp definitions for taxes. One of the reasons why today supply chain relationships are thriving is that there are no I-commerce taxes. A company is ordering materials and supplies over the Internet through exchanges that gather together buyers and sellers in a tax-free fashion. It is also holding reverse auctions to purchase more efficiently (the purchaser is soliciting bids rather than the seller) without any great concern about value-added taxes or sales taxes.

There is a growing mass of complex global tax issues. Let us not forget that alternative supplier accounting is a demanding process, even if no taxes were involved at all. Leaving aside the challenge of defining a stable establishment in Internet terms (which is discussed in section 5), such as transborder taxes, transborder alternative supplier accounting for I-commerce will have to deal with a mosaic of laws, rules, rates, ways of withholding tax, and interpretation of laws by the courts, which will make financial reporting a nightmare.

What I am saying is much more than a matter of sharing incompatible information between tax authorities. Even if one accepts the principle that 'Where there are sales there are taxes', as Figure 7.1 suggests, globalisation poses major problems in finding out the proper interfaces between legal issues and taxation, at different levels of reference.

There are also political issues to overcome, and they are not as simple as some tax authorities tend to believe. In the USA, taxing Internet commerce will take an act of Congress, where there are some mighty forces ranged against I-commerce taxation. It is also wise to account for the law's interpretation by the courts. The contours of any legislation are not crisp until it has been challenged in a court of justice. For instance, a 1992 US Supreme Court ruling held that it would be too burdensome for businesses if states enforced sales taxes for out-of-state purchases.

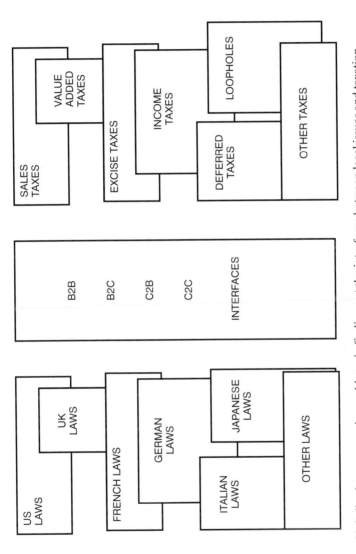

Figure 7.1 Globalisation poses major problems in finding out the interfaces between legal issues and taxation

2   OLD ECONOMY TAXES, INTERNET TAXES, AND CONFLICTS OF INTEREST

In America, where Internet commerce took off before anywhere else, the problem of I-commerce taxation was faced at an earlier time. No clear decision has been reached. The shortcut is a temporary tax exemption for I-commerce. The 1998 Internet Tax Freedom Act put a three-year moratorium on Net access taxes but not on sales taxes. A decision by the US Congress in the year 2000 delayed the final vote on taxes for another couple of years, while an advisory committee is studying electronic commerce with the goal of recommending action on various issues, including online sales tax.

Some people would like to see the government taxing I-commerce. Classical bricks-and-mortar retailers claim that current tax status gives Internet commerce sites an unfair advantage, while depriving state and local governments of billions of dollars in potential tax revenue. In the USA the National Retail Federation is pushing for equitable collection of taxes across all retail channels, including the Net.

Should such legislation pass, it will alter the current status, whereby online retailers are only required to collect sales taxes in locations where they have a physical presence. For instance, MotherNature.com, an online provider of natural health-care products, only collects sales taxes in Massachusetts, because that is where its warehouse (and therefore its stable establishment) is located.

Stakeholders in I-commerce taxation – federal, state and local authorities – seem confident that eventually they will get part of the pie which seems to get bigger by the day. In 1999, US entities (companies and citizens) spent about $20 billion on Internet purchases, double the figure for 1998. And because by all projections online spending will continue to grow, state and local governments are testing alternative tax schemes. Residents of Michigan and North Carolina got a surprise on their 1999 state income tax forms when they were asked to calculate how much they spent online, and a request was made by taxmen to pay the appropriate local sales tax. It is quite interesting that the two states have been applying existing laws that let them recoup sales tax revenue lost to out-of-state purchases. To do so, they use legislation originally created to cover catalogue sales. These have required a business to collect the corresponding sales tax if *the purchaser* has a sufficient physical presence in a state.

Can catalogue sales taxes morph into Internet taxes? Until this case is tested in courts, nobody can have an opinion on whether or not

Michigan, North Carolina and those states which might follow their lead were right or wrong in stretching old laws into new domains such as global I-commerce. In all likelihood, the liberal interpretation of existing laws by tax authorities capitalises on the fact that the majority of people in this world have little or no personal understanding of laws concerning income taxes, sales taxes, or other taxes, and how they work or how they can be legitimately bypassed (read: optimised). The same is true of the majority of small and medium-sized companies who know from experience that conflicting tax laws create confusion, but disobeying the rules of tax authorities can mean prison terms.

Mere size forbids careful study of the different conflicting tax codes. Just one example, the US Internal Revenue Code, is 2500 pages long: this is not a limit but only a present-day statistical reference which will be topped in no time as new laws are enacted by Congress. Tax authorities should, however, appreciate that this is not a one-way street, since consumers have pressure groups, and big companies employ a swarm of lawyers. Both groups will try to clip the wings of the taxmen. Tax laws are neither cast in stone nor are they foolproof. Lawyers and other experts who specialise in taxation appreciate that there is not at present, has not been, and will never be a tax law without *legal* loopholes. In the global market there are loopholes galore. This gives plenty of scope for tax optimisation, as we will see in sections 6 and 7.

Quite often, in the course of business meetings in which I participate, tax specialists comment how surprised they are when in their research they discover the number of loopholes created over the years by the US Congress, the British Parliament and other law makers. By and large, these are made to provide tax relief for certain special interests but they can also have a more general bearing. Bilateral tax agreements are no exception to this fairly universal rule of punching holes in the tax armoury.

Nobody disputes the fact that, in principle, each country has the right to impose its legal taxes. Because transborder taxes overlap and therefore overtax, however, bilateral agreements protect us from double and triple taxation. The rub is that there is no way to apply double taxation principles on Internet commerce which defies the old standard of national borders targeted by national laws. Seamless transborder deals also change the stable establishment concept, to which I made reference in the introduction. An Internet company may have an SE in a country of convenience but in no other in which it trades.

Where is this company taxable? Where should its sales be taxed? The universal principle is that in figuring out its income tax, a company must determine its net taxable income. The amounts of revenue and expense used in this process are usually similar to, but not identical with, amounts measured in accordance with the rules of financial accounting. But there are also significant differences, and therefore it is unwise to rely solely on the income tax regulations of any single country as a basis for solving business accounting problems. Besides that, with the Internet there is an immensely increased possibility of a virtual company to which old economy tax laws do not apply.

Differences in rules and regulations exist in many states within the same country, and between practically all tax jurisdictions. Such differences become very complex indeed in global business settings. The computation of taxes tends to be even more involved because of the practice that a business usually reports the minimum possible amount of taxable income in the current year, postponing tax payments as much as possible to future years. It does this generally by recognising expenses as soon as legally possible, while delaying recognition of revenue for as long as possible.

Another practice, particularly by new economy companies, is to declare no dividends but reinvest all available money in the business of the firm, or in buying back shares. Their shareholders are rewarded by appreciation of their holdings, particularly in rising stock markets, and their officers through the rising value of their options. Some governments which wish to promote new economy companies (for instance, the USA) accept this practice. Others tax the options. An example is recently enacted laws in France and in Spain.

Whenever there are conflicting laws, in the same country or cross-border, there is room for tax optimisation. This is not an illegal practice. As the US Supreme Court has pointed out, the minimisation of current taxes *is legal*, provided it is done consistently and in compliance with prevailing tax regulations. In many countries it is also legal, under most circumstances, to calculate income one way for tax purposes, and another way for financial accounting reasons. This speaks volumes about the polyvalence expected from the accounting system and the tools at its disposal. The objective of optimising current taxes is not by any means the same as that of financial accounting, which is to inform management, the shareholders, and the regulators regarding the income earned; hence the two measurements of income may well be different.

There are other particularities as well. To encourage research, US tax regulations permit most research costs to be counted as expenses in the year in which the research is done; therefore the money has been consumed. But if research is in products that will produce revenue in future years, it is consistent with the accrual concept of spreading these costs over these future years where revenue is earned.

When the laws permit cherry-picking, many businesses choose to pattern their accounting practices in a way which capitalises on the flexibility allowed by tax regulations. But if this policy is carried all the way to optimisation by exploiting tax regulations and their loopholes, then the result may be severe distortions in accounting reports.

Tax accounting, in other words, is by no means an exact science. There is plenty of scope for discovery of tax breaks, whether in one and the same country or in the global landscape. Tax accounting is always in evolution. As an example, in section 3 I will provide the reader with a summary of the evolution of tax laws in the USA, since the institution of income tax in 1913. In Europe income tax started more than a century earlier. Two major events were propelled by the French Revolution and the Napoleonic wars: income tax in Great Britain and universal conscription in France.

3 TAX ACCOUNTING IS NOT AN EXACT SCIENCE, WHETHER IN ONE COUNTRY OR IN THE GLOBAL MARKET

There are not many subjects which generate so much controversy, in popular and professional discussions, as taxes. There are plenty of taxes: corporate taxes, income taxes, sales taxes, property taxes, profits taxes, excess taxes, personal taxes, value-added taxes. Each one of them is strongly advocated by some people and bitterly attacked by others. Taxes tend to rise as if they define gravity, and often they attack completely the wrong target; but most parties are usually acting without clear recognition of the criteria used in tax evaluation and imposition.

Like anything else, taxes should be examined not only in absolute terms but also in reference to expected results. In 1999, a study made by the French Ministry of Finance of the economy proved that some taxes cost more money to collect than they bring to the French Treasury.

Fair taxation standards are necessary, and so is the need for both the legislators and state authorities to analyse and evaluate the rationality of all types of taxes, in full appreciation of their costs and their return. Are current taxes adequate? Too many? Too few? Too light? Too heavy? These questions can be answered only by considering the tax system as a whole, taking government expenditures and their rationale into account. The adequacy of a tax system has meaning only in the light of expenditures society decides it wishes to finance, and thus pays for. Evaluating the adequacy of any particular tax has no sense unless the money derived from it is being used to finance particular, justifiable expenditures.

Designating an expenditure and evaluating its rationale is not that simple, however, even in the same country, let alone crossborder. Neither expense chapters nor the different elements making up the tax system are invariant over time. Sometimes what is derived from a tax instituted for a certain specific purpose, such as the 'vignette' in France (a special tax on cars to aid old people), is diverted to other purposes. In other cases, all the government thinks about is more and more taxes. 'We must tax the poor,' said André Tardieu, a former French socialist prime minister, 'They are the most numerous.'

The nature of taxes, and their rate, changes over time. Take the USA as an example. Prior to 1936, company income tax was always a proportional tax, ranging from 1 per cent in 1913 to 13¾ per cent during the 1932–35 period. This tax was applied to net income remaining after the deduction of business expenses such as the cost of materials; suppliers' bills; workers' compensation; rent; interest; bad debts; other casualties; insurance costs; depreciation, depletion; and losses for prior years.

As is to be expected, however, the rate of taxation grew and it keeps on rising. This is not an American phenomenon. It can be found in all countries, albeit at different rates. In fact in some countries company income taxes take more than 50 per cent of profits. No wonder companies search for legal ways to reduce taxation for 'this' or 'that' reason.

Politics are not alien to the establishment of tax levels which favour some companies (or even whole industries) to the detriment of others. For instance in 1936, in the USA, a new system for providing relief to small business was introduced. It took the form of progressive rates applying to income brackets under $25 000 and a flat maximum rate on income in excess of that amount.

Then, in 1938, Congress amended the corporate income tax system and introduced a taxation algorithm which became known as the *notch* provision. This was effective till 1949. Its purpose was to give a measure of tax relief to smaller firms which benefited in proportion to their income falling below certain thresholds, but to deny any such benefits to larger companies.

There are two reasons why I bring these facts to the reader's attention in a chapter on taxing I-commerce. First, they show a trend of change in the taxation of income, while the positive bias towards smaller firms remains. That is good for small Internet companies in the longer run. Second, they confirm that taxation, and most particularly income taxation, is done in accordance with *ability to pay*: paraphrasing the credo of Karl Marx, 'From each according to his assets.'

Superficially, this looks as if it is fair, but it is not. Progressive rates applied to companies and to people result in the world being most unequal. Income belonging to stockholders in large corporations is taxed at higher rates than income from investments in small firms, and wealthier individuals are made to pay a larger part of their income (and of their wealth, where property tax applies) than other citizens. Therefore, they are officially prompted to optimise their tax returns.

While this happening in a single country is by now a habit and therefore there is no public outcry against it, it becomes a visible problem crossborder with the Internet. *If* taxing I-commerce develops into a global rule and there are no uniform rates, B2B procurement by big firms (see Chapter 3) will be strongly penalised. To other Internet sales like auctions and electronic banking products (see Chapter 5) there will be applied a horde of different incompatible and contradictory tax standards:

- some greedy countries would declare the Internet server as stable establishment, while others would not;
- some countries would have progressive taxation schemes, while others would choose a uniform pattern;
- some countries would apply value-added tax (VAT), others different schemes of sales tax, and still others would not;
- some countries would tax a company (and a person) on its global business and wealth; others only within their borders.

These differences would play havoc with the tax accounting of Internet companies and of other firms using the Net for part of their dealings. But they will also offer the opportunity of optimisation to obtain varying degrees of tax reductions, by channelling more activity towards lower tax rates and careful consideration of where to put the company's Internet server.

The manipulation of tax rates and tax incentives by local and national tax authorities, by targeting corporate size and amount of business being done, would have global ramifications apart from proving to be a complex problem. It would also induce companies to break down their operations into smaller units in order to put their income into lower brackets, adding to the current tendency of relocating them in what are known as 'tax havens'.

Other means of tax optimisation would also be developed. Most serious of all would be the problem of what size of Internet company is desirable and what is not. In spite of what the Justice Department did to Microsoft, and prior to this to Standard Oil, IBM and AT&T, there is no necessary evil in size as such unless other factors, including monopoly and taxes, preclude the entry of new risk capital into competition with established giants. Neither are there rules about corporate size which can be established once and for all:

- some lines of industry require large aggregations of capital for efficient operations;
- in others, large size may be counterproductive because of loss of contact with the market;
- in still other cases, large size may be a matter of natural growth and of astute business policy.

The companies themselves should appreciate the penalties associated with bigger and bigger size. Some of the global corporations today have quite probably exceeded the size of maximum efficiency in terms of unit costs or returns per dollar of investment. This is hardly a matter for public concern so long as the company operates without practising unreasonable restraint of trade, but it does bring to the foreground the issue of equity in taxation, and most particularly of taxation on a global scale.

4 THE SEARCH FOR AN EQUITABLE AND EFFECTIVE BASIS OF TAXATION

Taxes are often presented as the lubricating oil necessary to keep the wheels of government services turning or, alternatively, as the cost of civilisation. But not all taxes fall into this class and those which do have to be compared with the reasoning behind government expenditures and its rationality. During the last 100 years, two different basic criteria of rationality in taxation have received support:

- the tax burden should be allocated according to benefit received; and
- this burden should be calculated according to the economy's ability to pay.

Two principles underpin these points. The absence of an equitable and effective tax collection system destabilises a country, as it deprives the administration of revenues with which to face its obligations. But at the same time, and this is the second principle, the people entrusted with administration of public money should keep a cap on public expenditures, rather than trying to cover runaway budgets through more taxes. 'Too many taxes kill the taxes,' Jacques Chirac used to say, prior to being elected president of France.

Whichever way one wants to look at it, there is no limit to government extravagance; and large deficits can have far-reaching consequences. In 1513, a Medici became Pope Leo X. He fought to keep Italy free of foreign domination and started to rebuild St Peter's Cathedral (it took 120 years to complete), but also extended his family's influence outside Florence and spent recklessly on his pleasures. His motto was: 'God has given us the papacy. Let us enjoy it.'

Enjoyment comes at a price. To raise money, the Church granted indulgences, or pardons for time in purgatory, for a sin that has been forgiven through penance. As more money was needed the value-added solution was indulgences that did away not only with past sins but also with future ones, and cancelled a priori their divine punishment. In 1517, however, an Augustinian monk in Germany dissented, and his dissension became known in history as Martin Luther's 85 Theses which almost wrecked the Catholic Church.

Tax laws enacted by parliaments are not free from indulgences or from exposure to economic wreckage. They may be skewed, or they may be downright counterproductive. This often happens when they distinguish between different forms or levels of financing, going overboard one way or another: for instance, financing a company through loans or equity capital. Interest paid upon borrowed or creditor capital is deductible as a business expense before the tax is computed. The effect is to encourage corporate financing through the use of borrowed funds, represented mainly by bonds, commercial paper and bank loans (which is *leveraging*); but, from the point of view of public policy and sound business operation, important advantages arise from a greater use of venture or equity capital, which is the company's own. A sound equity base sees to it that economic stability is increased, and in hard times the danger of forced liquidation and of receivership is reduced or avoided altogether. Current laws do not favour equity capital financing. The benefits to stockholders arising from trading in the equity are rather limited (however, so are the risks). The opposite is true when a company is leveraged through heavy loans.

Over the years, in the USA the balance has tilted slowly towards leveraging. In the first income tax law of 1913, interest could not be deducted on an amount of indebtedness greater than one half of the total indebtedness plus the capital stock. The Revenue Act of 1916 relaxed this limitation with the provision that interest could be deducted whenever the indebtedness on which the interest was paid did not exceed the sum of:

- the entire amount of the paid-up capital stock; and
- one-half of its interest bearing indebtedness then outstanding.

This was a minor modification of the 1913 income tax law, but it did not last long. Beginning with the 1918 law, all interest has been fully deductible except on debt that was incurred for the purpose of carrying tax-exempt securities. These restrictions reflected the fact that interest is a fixed charge which usually carries no option as to payment which can increase the number of failures.

Other sorts of skewness in tax laws came from double taxation, which is an example of inequality in tax structure which impacts greatly on the provision of equity capital. A company's net income is taxed once in the hands of the firm and again as dividends in the hands of stockholders. It is as if governments try to kill the goose that lays the golden egg rather than planning for the future.

A different but equally perverse type of double taxation is when two or more different governments require a company or a person to pay taxes for the same business and the same income. To a certain extent this is taken care of through the bilateral double taxation agreements which proliferated after the Second World War but, as already stated, which hold no water in connection with Internet commerce. To partly compensate for overtaxing, governments also support certain phases of business activity for which they care more. This has usually taken the form of a subsidy, which may be:

- direct, in cases such as the land-grant to railroads and early canal companies;
- indirect, as evidenced by protective tariffs, or by assuming the risks on capital investment in various categories of housing.

The Internet has been a beneficiary of the direct subsidiary policy. Arpanet (Advanced Research Projects Agency, or ARPA), its first home, was designed and implemented at the end of the 1960s as a military system, linking sites any-to-any in an efficient and reliable approach based on packet switching. A dozen years down the line, however, the Pentagon made a present of Arpanet to the American universities and the Internet took off.

Judging retrospectively the money spent on Arpanet, and what it has achieved, we see that this was a good investment of taxpayers' money. Another first-class investment, particularly in America, have been laws which permit the avoidance of inheritance taxes by giving generously to Foundations and other not-for-profit organisations. One of the reasons why Rockefeller, Ford and Carnegie-type foundations do not exist in other countries is that the law is myopic regarding the huge benefits derived from non-profits.

The sense of the reference made in the preceding paragraph is that in practically all countries today the tax system needs a breath of fresh air, and a lot more clarity in the way public money is used. There should be in place means and safeguards for achieving private action along lines deemed necessary in the public interest. In the general case, this is done through special tax privileges, such as:

- accelerated amortisation of facilities essential for national defence or other reasons; and
- tax relief for I-commerce over a number of years, until an equitable global solution can be elaborated.

This fails to take the proverbial long hard look. The questions to ask are: do taxes encourage or hinder business activity? Do taxes impede or encourage the free choice of a trade or occupation? These are highly important queries because they help in framing tax criteria. Other crucial questions include: do taxes promote or handicap investment and employment? Do taxes aid the attainment or resource allocation consistent with public preferences? Or do they interfere with the pattern of private spending which would otherwise prevail?

For instance, to answer whether or not a certain excise tax makes sense, one has to know how equitably the revenue burden is distributed. While one may consider the rationality of a novel individual tax, a bigger question is how this new tax fits with or duplicates other existing taxes. Such questions must be faced at the level of the entire tax system, and this is very rarely done.

In conclusion, the principle is that taxation, as a process, is necessary to pay for common services, but this is not always true of individual taxes. At the same time vested interests see to it that it is not easy to do a thorough tax overhaul. When in March 2000 the French government correctly decided to streamline tax collection, it found its hands full with a revolt of its tax agents and had to backtrack. As already mentioned, some taxes were costing the administration more money to collect than was received; but they paid for unnecessary administrative jobs.

5   BASIC CONCEPTS IN TAXING INTERNET COMMERCE: SALES TAXES AND STABLE ESTABLISHMENT

A hands-off policy from taxing Internet commerce has been often compared to tax cuts benefiting the public at large. Can we predict the likely effects of such a policy? Not long ago, in a meeting on this particular subject, one of the participants suggested that hands-off taxation of I-commerce is similar to the early 1980s tax cuts by Ronald Reagan which ended by increasing the US deficit; shortly afterwards, the Reagan deficit transformed America's public agenda.

This was a dissenting view, the majority of participants at this meeting being against taxing I-commerce. The pro-hands-off policy people said that while Reagan's tax cuts gave Americans a political appetite for them, they also forced lawmakers to think hard about controlling public spending. Lawmakers finally saw that they could not support more pork barrel policies, at a time when people wanted lower taxes, and Congress has had to place a halt on spending, also because the bond markets were reluctant to absorb more government debt.

For this and other reasons, supply-side policies have given proof that they work, and hands-off taxation of Internet commerce is a supply-side solution *par excellence*. Supply-side economics run contrary to the policies of socialist governments in Western Europe which are characterised by 'tax and tax, spend and spend other people's money'. Coupled with an arteriosclerosis in social structures and stiff, if not downright punishing, labour laws, this has led to:

- 12 per cent or more unemployment (as against less than 4 per cent in the USA); and
- a curious resistance to this level being reduced to below 10 per cent.

It is no less true, nevertheless, that local and regional governments must have an income. Should this be derived through more income taxes or sales taxes, and therefore taxes on Internet commerce? There is no single answer to this query.

A sales tax covers almost all commodities which are widely consumed. In the USA, Delaware, Montana, New Hampshire and Oregon have no state tax levy. Alaska, too, does not have a state tax, but some cities in the state do have a city tax. North Dakota, Vermont and West Virginia have a 3 per cent state tax; Connecticut charges 7.5 per cent and New York 8 per cent (the highest in the country).

No matter what their level may be, VAT and sales taxes raise marginal costs in merchandising and hence tend to reduce the propensity to consume. A sales tax is paid by consumers without distinction of income level and ability to pay; but it also hits the manufacturers and vendors because it raises the cost of the product or of the service, making a sale somewhat less likely.

Since the beginning, sales taxes have been controversial. One of the primary virtues claimed for the sales tax was that it would raise money. This is no different from the argument about income tax at large. The sales tax affects almost all persons as buyers or sellers of productive services, on the broadest level. Therefore, in theory at least, since the people involved are the same either way, it makes little difference whether technically the burden is passed:

- forwards through higher prices, or
- backwards through lower monetary incomes.

In practice, however, there are different effects on consumers and vendors and changes in sales tax or VAT level see to it that these effects are shifting. Something similar is true with excise taxes. One of the basic differences between sales taxes and excise taxes is that the latter apply only to selected commodities while the sales taxes apply to all, or a very large number of goods at a certain rate. This being said, it must be admitted that the distinction between a general sales tax and a wide range of excise taxes is not very clear.

Is the borderline between sales taxes and excise taxes ill-defined? The excise tax on petrol and other motor fuels deserves attention because of the manner in which most such revenues are spent. Theoretically, receipts from petrol excise taxes are used primarily in improving highways and streets; therefore, such taxes are partially justified as benefit levies. Practically, these excise taxes are used to cover holes in the government's budget which are often totally unrelated to motor traffic. *If* gasoline tax and other fuel taxes were used to improve the roads system, *then* what the motorist pays as excise tax might be regarded as a sort of substitute for a price charged for the use of roads.

In a way, the purchaser of petrol would have been buying, through the petrol tax, mileage on government roads. The fact that this is only remotely the case should be kept in mind in any discussion about Internet sales taxes. I bring the reader's attention to this issue because not long ago, in an Internet meeting, I heard that I-commerce taxes (when they come) should be earmarked for improvements in the Internet's infrastructure. This argument is fake, and it forgets two basic issues.

1 The infrastructure of the Internet is luckily a private company business; there is not another posts and telecommunications bureaucracy which takes care of it.
2 Tax money earmarked for a certain purpose is rarely spent on that purpose. Usually it pays the salaries of people who are sitting at desks rather than working on improvement of a given service.

A generalisation that may be made about the overall incidence of a general sales tax is that it will decrease the incomes of productive agents relative to the prices of finished goods. This proposition holds good whether the tax is retail or wholesale, local, state or federal. What about purchasing something from out-of-state companies resident in states where there is no sales tax? In principle, a great variety of products can be bought through mail order without paying state tax; some states, however have sought aggressively to reduce such tax-free trades, with a varying degree of success.

Regarding the purchase of cars by their residents from a sales-tax-free state, where savings can be considerable, states with a sales tax closed the loophole by imposing a registration fee usually equal to the corresponding sales tax. As for the mail order loophole, most states attacked it by requiring out-of-state companies to collect sales tax if they have a *business presence* in the state where the sale is made.

Business presence is usually interpreted as a *stable establishment*, but the way this is defined is, to say the least, very lax. It does not necessarily need to be an office: it may be a salesman, a delivery service, or even a catalogue pick-up service. Still there are ways to circumvent this definition because most speciality companies do not fit even the poorest definition of the business presence terms.

This brings our discussion back to the challenges posed by the very notion of a stable establishment, and the difficulties associated with its definition. As briefly discussed in the introduction, a stable establishment is a concept developed to help define the local presence of entities engaging in sales activities. An SE is largely connected to bricks and mortar. Is the Internet server a stable establishment? The answer is 'yes' and 'no' at the same time. For sales tax purposes, a server cannot be taken to be a bricks-and-mortar SE by any stretch of the imagination (see also section 7); but legislators might extend the concept to include virtual companies in the SE definition, in which case the server could become part of it.

In conclusion, online transborder trade changes the concept underpinning an SE. A company may have a stable establishment in one country and not in others, but it trades over the Internet in many countries. This is precisely why the reference to US sales tax practices and the controversy arising from the heterogeneity of different species, which are all called sales taxes, are so important to every person and every company, whether one is for or against taxing I-commerce.

6 INTERNET COMMERCE CALLS FOR THOROUGHLY REVAMPING WHAT IS AND WHAT IS NOT A SOUND TAXATION PRACTICE

Crossborder sales over the Internet are not the only reason why the old definition of a stable establishment does not hold any more. Quite apart from electronic commerce, identification of an SE becomes most complex with *virtual companies*, because they may have no bricks and mortar at all. *Nomadic computing*, and trades done through portables, add another layer of uncertainty to the old, crumbling SE definition.

There are, in addition, other challenges. Bilateral agreements protect from double taxation (see section 4) but, as explained, there is no way to apply double taxation agreements on the Internet when snap, online buy and sell decisions are made. Hence, should Internet commerce be taxed? Who should be doing the taxing? How? And how much?

If there is an Internet commerce tax, how are the proceeds to be shared? With whom? For what reason? Here it is no longer a question of bilateral but of *multilateral* agreements which are pie in the sky. Not only the magnitude of the problem but also the conflicting interests that would come into them discourage any attempt to solve the Gordian knot. Figure 7.2 shows what this involves in a trading sense, with particular emphasis on complex interconnections.

To better appreciate what is at stake, let us leave aside for a moment Internet commerce, and look only at the challenge of multilateral agreements for business taxation reasons. Euroland should have

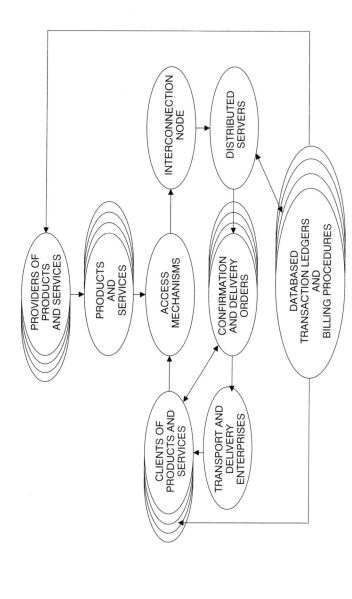

Figure 7.2 Internet commerce is a complex web with no easy answer to who, when and how much is liable for sales taxes

streamlined its tax laws and tax rules by now, eliminating double and triple taxes as well as adding other provisions aimed at clarifying the tax laws of member states in the European Union. This has not been done yet, but it is generally agreed that it will be a three-step process which – in my opinion – starts from the wrong end.

1 Identification of harmful tax regimes (read: tax havens), where these exist.
2 Rolling them back in a reasonable time (the end of 2002 is being discussed, which is an unrealistic timeframe).
3 Preventing new negative tax provision, weeding out conflicting current laws and toughening the more lenient rules.

Any person who uses his head to think, rather than his feet, would have started from number 3, precisely because this is the toughest. If we do not set goals and establish standards, the definition of 'harmful tax regimes' is a totally subjective business, which is hardly worth the time and money spent on it.

Which are the tax regimes to be eliminated? Can these principles (if any) be applied to Internet commerce? Based on ongoing discussions at the EU executive, here is the answer to the first of these two queries: those laws and rules favouring non-residents; providing ring-fencing; making no rational economic sense (!!!); resulting in big deviation from international standards (which standards?); violating transparency; ending in favouritism towards some taxpayers. This list reads like 'motherhood and apple-pie', but there is no substance below the surface.

As an example of what would be required for ironing out those taxes labelled as 'harmful', take the first item in the above list. Ireland offers very interesting non-tax possibilities for non-residents, and the same is true of Switzerland for some income not subject to the blanket 35 per cent imposition: for example, capital gains for foreigners, non-resident in Switzerland. But neither Ireland (a member of the EU) nor Switzerland is about to turn away a population whose presence in the country presents so many other benefits.

What about ring-fencing? Many things can be done with a holding company in Spain. In fact, holding companies tend to be tax-proof instruments because usually they make it possible to optimise tax benefits specified by law in countries other than the one in which they are registered. Try to take them out of the system, and you have a job which cannot be finished even in the long life of Methuselah.

The commission which is studying these supposedly unwanted tax breaks in the EU and elsewhere is said to have compiled a list of some 285 harmful items of which 66 are, reportedly, the worst offenders. It is generally thought that these existing tax measures are essentially huge loopholes exploited as special tax regimes by multinationals: for example, taxing at the lowest available tax rate, and taking a cost-plus basis for taxing, rather than income.

Statements such as weeding out 'harmful tax laws' by *general consent*, made by supposedly serious people, are laughable. Everyone knows that these tax loopholes were purposely created by governments to attract multinational companies and therefore create employment. One of the jokes going around the world is that worse than being exploited by a multinational is not being exploited by one or more of them.

The revamping of 'harmful' tax laws, however, is not for tomorrow. Commissions and special studies are the best way to increase employment (at least among local friends) while delaying any action as far as possible. Any entity can play in this game. The OECD has come out with a long list of tax havens in the world, anywhere, for any purpose. Even the thought that this will be of any use in chopping their heads off is another joke.

Poor Holland, if this chopping-off ever happens. It is going to get a shock because, from what is being discussed, the Netherlands is today the nerve centre of international legal tax optimisation (read: minimisation). Tax havens, and they are plenty, are no secret to anybody who knows how to read, and how to count. It is unnecessary to make another list. And after all, what is the point? Are they going to bombard them, or send a UN-sponsored multinational occupying force?

People who are more serious than those engaging in the aforementioned wasteful exercises suggest that when studying the European Union's investment structure and taxation it is necessary not only to look at these from a legal viewpoint, but also to examine the technological perspective. This is particularly important in connection with Internet commerce. With the Internet it becomes more difficult for governments to identify the taxable person and taxable company and his (its) income. 'The art of taxation is not to kill the goose which lays the golden egg,' Colbert, the finance minister of Louis XIV, once suggested. Attention should also be paid to the method of taxation. Other things being equal, direct taxes would be easier to apply than indirect taxes (such as capital appreciation) if the different governments could find a common equitable base. Even if there is a general line of agreement among governments, and that is by no means certain, treating issues which relate to double taxation would be a very tough job. The same is true of intended favours, such as capital gains free of tax if done by an individual through zero bonds for instance, as is the case in Germany, Austria, Holland, and other countries.

Then again, no matter how clear may be the writing of taxation laws and rules (and taxes rarely fit that billing), the sense of what is stipulated will not become beyond doubt until the law is tested in court. Let me take as an example a recent case. It concerns the fact that, according to the Third Circuit Court of Appeals in the USA, banks may deduct loan costs in the year the loan is made.

The Court of Appeals held that a bank may deduct from Federal taxes the full amount of expenses which it incurs for researching, marketing and originating loans – as *loans origination expenses* – in the year the loan is made. This case, *PNC Bancorp* v. *Commissioner of Internal Revenue*, involved two banks acquired by PNC which had treated loan origination expenses as deductible for Federal tax purposes in the year they were incurred: they did so on the basis that such expenses are ordinary and necessary, pursuant to Section 162 of the Internal Revenue Code. However, the Internal Revenue Service (IRS) disallowed the deductions and declared that loan origination expenses must be capitalised and amortised over the life of the applicable loan.

In 1998, the US Tax Court held that loan origination expenses must be capitalised by PNC pursuant to Section 263 of IRC. PNC appealed to the Court of Appeals which reversed the Tax Court's decision and held that loan origination expenses are a routine part of a bank's daily business. Therefore, they are deductible under Section 162, and do not come within the purview of Section 263.

In spite of this ruling, this issue is not necessarily resolved as the IRS could seek a ruling with a different taxpayer in another circuit court of appeals, trying to create a contrarian jurisprudence; or it could file a petition seeking a decision from the US Supreme Court. Where is the EU legal system permitting the testing of I-commerce tax legislation to create a body of jurisprudence?

The point I wish to make with these references is that it is not enough to write transnational laws and rules regarding I-commerce and its taxation, supposing this job is really feasible. It is just as important to put in place a legal infrastructure which can interpret these laws in a homogeneous way, although this would be irrelevant if the court sat in the USA, Brazil, Britain, Germany, the Philippines or Nigeria. This will take, at best, a generation or two.

7   CAN INTERNET COMPANIES CAPITALISE ON NATIONAL AND INTERNATIONAL TAX LOOPHOLES?

In no country today are proposals to tax the Internet popular with companies; and they are anathema to the general public. The opposite is true about the reaction of government bureaucrats; but politicians have their own ideas. In the year 2000 in America, both presidential candidates and the majority of candidates for Congress queued up to explain how they would stop the taxman plunging his greasy hands into cyberspace. But are they sincere in this?

The argument of those who belong to the tax-and-tax school is that if Internet commerce grows anything like as fast as predicted, failing to tax it could do serious damage to the finances of state and local governments. In the last analysis, as we have already seen, all governments depend on sales taxes for a great deal of their revenues. Yet it is no less true that the growth provided by the new economy is best embodied by the moratorium on sales taxes on Internet commerce. A tremendous amount of money that would otherwise have ended up in the coffers of omnipotent bureaucrats has been preserved in high-tech companies and contributed to their success, as well as directly benefiting consumers. There is also the Internet's direct contribution to efficiency to be considered: a mouseclick is sufficient to carry one's capital around the globe. Those who think that the wisest policy is that of hands-off taxation of Internet commerce believe that not only will the heavy-handed taxman's intrusion into cyberspace be harmful to the prosperous new economy, but also because of globalisation the legal basis to tax is not there (let alone the total lack of standardisation about what should be taxable and what not).

This is by no means a theoretical argument. It is one which goes to the root of the new wave of economic theories promoted by deregulation, globalisation and technology. Evidence currently available suggests that internationally lower taxes motivate companies to generate higher profits, improving by so much their ability to survive. Higher profits can be earned when more cash is invested, which in turn builds the base for more rapid growth. Rapid growth has proved to be the best way to create and protect jobs, in a way which has turned out to be more lasting.

Higher incomes and better profits are also good for the government's treasury. As long as the economy grows, the government's coffers fill up without increasing the threshold of taxation which ends by being most counterproductive or, alternatively, leads towards exploiting tax loopholes wherever they exist.

There is a horde of tax loopholes in every jurisdiction. An example are the different investments featuring tax-free income. In the USA, for instance, since the beginning of Federal income taxes in 1913 (see section 3), an exception has been made regarding income from local municipal bonds. The Federal government does not tax the bonds of states and the states do not tax US Treasury bonds.

Other investments exempt from current income taxation are deferred annuities, different insurance policies, pension plans, return-on-capital, utility dividends, and All-Savers Certificates issued by local banks and thrifts. The same is true of tax-free exchanges in real estate, engineered by Real Estate Investment Trusts (REITs). REITs tend to pay almost 100 per cent of their dividends in tax-free returns on capital distributions.

Tax havens offered by REITs and All-Savers Certificates are interesting examples. While today the concept underpinning them is not universal, in the future it might expand to other countries as a way of bypassing Internet banking taxes. In the USA, the Economic Recovery Act of 1981 created a tax shelter for interest paid on bank deposits. In other countries this interest is subject to a withholding tax.

What about similar legal loopholes in connection with Internet commerce? In my opinion the nearest thing to it is the inability of different European Union governments to define – even less agree on – what constitutes a stable establishment. Let me start with the simplest possible example from the old economy. If an Italian company puts some espresso vending machines in Germany, is this an SE? The answer is evidently: no! Precisely in the same way a client of Internet commerce is not an SE. Hence, he or she should pay no tax. By contrast, an Internet Service Provider (ISP) is an SE. The ISP should pay tax, but where it resides.

As we saw in section 5, the server *might* also be an SE. It all depends on what the server is doing and on whether virtual companies are legislated as old economy firms. This is still an issue in search of definition, and such a definition is not forthcoming. Let me ask another question. Is the Web site an SE? The answer is: no, because it has no fixed installation. By extension, the ISP on a Web site is not taxable. The ISP is taxable, under current laws, only where it has a stable establishment. We have spoken already of the SE as a possible tax haven.

Between the notions presented in the preceding paragraphs, and the realities based on the limited perspective of existing national laws, filter loopholes galore. The basic problem is that on the Internet few things have a stable presence. Companies need, however, to keep these legal loopholes permanently on the side of legality. To do so, they need to:

- study carefully what is and what is not taxable under different jurisdictions;
- track all operations anywhere for any purpose, with any client, from a tax viewpoint;
- have available both the pattern and the detail of all historical references to similar events; and
- not only keep a reliable documentation but also audit it regularly to assure its accuracy (see D.N. Chorafas, *Implementing and Auditing the Internal Control System*, Macmillan – now Palgrave, London, 2001).

More to the point, if Internet sales were taxed both the accounting and the auditing job would become at least an order of magnitude more complex than they are today. Take taxation at source as an example, as applied to Internet banking. Belgium and Holland have no withholding tax at source. Others have, but say that it is applicable only if used in the same country; otherwise it is not. For instance, the USA has 30 per cent *if* consumed in the USA, and zero otherwise. Still other countries do not make that distinction.

Over and above what the previous paragraphs have mentioned, the accountant must clearly define if the payment is for an *active* service or for a *passive* service. This will help to decide if there is added value tax (which is recoverable by the client company) or a sales tax that probably is not. If the sales tax is a state or federal tax it might be recoverable by non-residents, but the conditions vary from one country to the other. The conclusion is that a clean job on Internet sales obliges full transparency of city, state and national government legislation.

All this makes accounting for, and auditing of, Internet sales a very complicated enterprise. Among tier-1 companies in technology, many of these decisions and associated record keeping will be made by *agents* (see D.N. Chorafas, *Agent Technology Handbook*, McGraw-Hill, New York, 1998). The others will keep on doing them by hand at great cost and low efficiency. Transborder Internet taxes will also mean that there will be never-ending appointments with lawyers and philosophers, hosted by bureaucrats intent on building a better Internet tax mousetrap.

8 Getting our Company Ready for Shifts in Market Power

1 INTRODUCTION

A proverb says that lotteries are the taxation of the stupid. If so, mismanagement is the taxation of companies that cannot put their house in order, and where nobody is in charge. Taxation due to mismanagement is much more severe, and its results are far more destructive to the firm, than the most horrid taxation scheme devised by governments; even worse than those we have seen in Chapter 7.

Mismanagement has many faces. One of them is a dependence on catchwords for salvation. A modern catchword is technology. A basic fact the Board, the chief executive, the chief financial officer and their assistants must appreciate is that all by itself technology will not bring their company all the success in the world. But at the same time, failure to adapt to (and adopt) high technology can be fatal.

Part 1 has given plenty of evidence on the strategic role the Internet plays in *our* company's ability to survive and compete well into this twenty-first century. Not only alert business leaders but also governments have started to understand that technology shapes the future of business organisations, and therefore the welfare of citizens. The more policy makers are aware of this fact, the more they are likely to consider how technology could improve their economy and position them for leadership in a global scale.

Senior management of companies which read the trends which will most probably shape the future is keen to capitalise on the relationship between technology strategy and financial performance. What really matters most in the forward-looking management of investments in technology is insight and foresight.

1 *Insight* is at the heart of both the rise of technological and any other entrepreneurism.
2 *Foresight* makes the difference between dynamic firms poised for survival and those losing their clout.

To 'read the future', senior management must thoroughly examine the strategic aspects of technology, learning from industry leaders about changing patterns of innovation in every business channel. These include a wide array of issues: the way we understand the process of change and its market impact (see Chapter 1); the importance of flexible industrial structures which are able to turn on a dime; and the relationship between large and small firms when dealing in nearly equal terms through the Internet.

This chapter and Chapter 9 include many practical examples from information technology and logistics. We should be always keen to learn from the best companies in the industry. The text also addresses some of the problems large organisations find in their way when they try to master sprawling logistics problems, and it concludes with the need to establish boundary conditions. There are limits to any system, whether natural or man-made, and we should be aware of them.

2   PRODUCT LEAD TIMES, COST EFFICIENCY AND MANAGEMENT EFFECTIVENESS

Management is the art of making things happen through people. In the global market, effective management requires taking a longer-term view of every business situation, even if sometimes it resorts to short-term measures. Building and sustaining genuine partnerships is a long-term proposition. It is also a principle in merchandising as well as in banking. From this perspective, the job of logistics is to support business relationships in an effective manner. Four principles guide an efficient supply chain management:

- swamping product lead times;
- projecting demand and tuning supply to reduce stocks;
- improving quality and reducing errors; and
- increasing operational and cost-efficiency.

Costs matter, because they show up in the bottom line, and the bottom line is what, in the last analysis, interests firm's stakeholders. Owners provide capital in return for which they receive a claim to the company's residual income stream. Managers decide how the company for which they work is organised, financed and run. Customers and generally business partners decide with which company to deal, then order a supply of the company's products and services and pay for them. The customers' decisions are usually made on the basis of cost, quality and availability. The cost-efficiency of the business partner is a relatively new criterion which gains increasing importance.

Take merchandising as an example. FFR goes beyond the effective implementation of JIT inventory management (see also Chapter 9). In merchandising, it banishes stockholding from the retail floor to make room for customer walkways, as well as for new products and services. It also frees space at the wholesalers, and does the same on the factory floor where JIT is instrumental in improving the timing of deliverables.

From receiving an order to delivering the parts in the precise order in which they will be needed, we must observe a minutely calculated schedule. This is done through models and real-time computing. Operating upstream through online systems from retail stores, supermarkets and hypermarkets, impacts on the stock kept in warehouses. It also dictates what warehouses deliver to the sales points, according to each customer's needs. This is, in the last analysis, the whole sense of the supply chain.

Figure 8.1 presents a frame of reference which defines the solution space for efficient inventory procurement and usage. One of the axes in

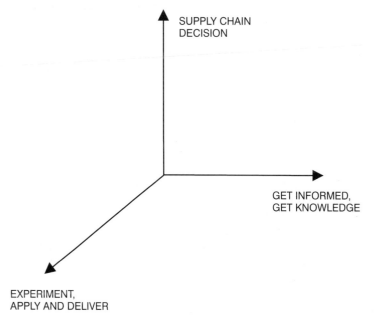

Figure 8.1   A frame of reference for well-managed inventory procurement and usage

this framework is the supply chain decision or decisions. Another refers to the quality and timeliness of information as well as to skills. The third axis of reference concerns the ability to apply optimisation through experimentation, which helps to deliver better results.

This frame of reference is relevant both to the individual firm and to the supply chain as a whole. To improve their performance, companies need to forge strong links with customers and suppliers, agree on two-way information exchange concerning requirements, and integrate their planning and scheduling chores. Indeed, such collaboration has become a mark of profitable organisations of the 1990s and is assisted, to a significant extent, by technology. ERP and other off-the shelf software can be instrumental in assisting the management of the supply chain, but by far the most important factor is the Board's decision to do a neat job and so fulfil organisational prerequisites which are always present.

Due to this synergy between top management decisions and tools, such as ERP, tier-1 companies are always keen to link their technology strategy to their overall corporate strategy. They are taking all necessary steps for a non-blocking process of development of better solutions in logistics by relating technology to markets, products and customers, and by placing emphasis on timely implementation of an improved methodology.

For return on investment reasons, well-managed companies evaluate the effectiveness of chosen solutions, but also the benefits derived from moving products and services to market at fast pace. There are other criteria senior management must bring into perspective as well.

In a world of increasing complexity and a significant amount of novelty in customer demands, one of our primary goals must be to make our products easier to use as well as more effective for our customers. In part, this means developing simpler interfaces, able to hide the most involved underlying features from users without diminishing the product's effectiveness. This is feasible and it can be achieved by getting closer to *our* customers and working harder to understand their wishes.

There is, however, a lot we need to put in place before we get to the point of having the best possible systems support. Sometimes optimised solutions are complex because they involve at the same time many variables relating to machines, languages and software engineering. They may also call for changes in problem definition to be done through modelling. A lot depends on:

- the conceptual approach to our problem;
- the validity of the technology we are employing; and
- the accuracy of the accounting system which we use.

The restructuring of our accounting system and of our logistical support must fully account for the fact that with the Internet *the network is the market*. Contrary to other markets, which our company has, quite likely, known better, the Internet market is steadily characterised by *exposed pricing*, and everyone sees everybody else's bid and reacts accordingly in real-time.

Not only must the product lead time be reduced to its bare bones, so that we can capitalise on innovation, but also costs must be swamped and pricing kept dynamic. An accounting system which does not provide senior management with the support necessary to meet this triple challenge is a liability to *our* company rather than an asset. There are other reasons why our accounting system may need the most urgent re-tuning.

As I never tire of repeating, *cost accounting* is one of the major developments characterising the twentieth century's sound management practice, yet not every company today masters it as should be the case. This is suicidal because every company has to cut costs (a process now taking place across industry boundaries). Without first-class cost accounting it is not possible to cut the fat.

Cost accounting can be instrumental in cost-efficiency. It also helps our firm in choosing a strategy of value differentiation. Cost accounting details are essential for another reason. In the domain of supply-chain relationships we are now seeing that the online co-ordination framework among business partners is elevated to first-class status. This may not require tremendous research investments in technology, but it calls for:

- great attention and concentration on cost and benefit associated to problems we wish to solve; and
- an accounting and logistics methodology which make it possible to reach satisfactory real-time solutions.

A key ingredient in this particular frame of reference is knowledge engineering. At least some of the knowledge-enriched models available today, more precisely experts and agents, address supply-chain operations and focus on *arbitration*. The need for arbitration arises whenever a resource is shared by independent contending users. Arbitration schemes must be able to provide a good degree of fairness, so that they reduce the resource allocation time, while presenting no conflicts of interest in resource utilisation. The key features of arbitration executed by, say, two agents will not necessarily be different from those prevailing with humans, provided the rules guiding the artefacts are realistic. Practical experience with online arbitration, as well as simulation and experimentation, helps to develop more complex models. It also suggests that by varying the arbiter parameters in conjunction with priorities and costs, an efficient allocation of available resources can be achieved.

Management will, however, be well advised to appreciate that, in a way similar to that of reaching human decisions, the large majority of models is an approximation of the real world. On the one hand, we want models to be realistic, but on the other hand, the more accurate the simulation model is the greater its complexity, and therefore the need for very skilled analysts, and high performance computing.

3   SUPPLY CHAIN RELATIONSHIPS AND REALISTIC TRADE-OFFS

Let me start this section with the following thoughts. While a great deal depends on technology, management is still an art rather than a scientific discipline. Even if we use models and analytical computational finance for prediction and optimisation, the results which we reach will not carry the same kind of robustness or confidence associated with similar work in the physical sciences. Many of the models to which reference is made are quite powerful and have the ability to give us answers quite rapidly, in the short term. However, the dependability of the competitive advantage which we gain can be increased through studies which are both fundamental and look at the longer term.

From their professional experience, logisticians and managers know that up to a point they have to be ready to compromise on the outcome of 'this' or 'that' analytical study to obtain a realistic trade-off. While the *what if* rules of knowledge engineering are much closer to the way the human mind works than inflexible Cobol programs, computers and simulation are tools, and not substitutes for human ingenuity. The same is true of information conveyed by the accounting system.

Realistic trade-offs acceptable to the counterparties are important because every business operates in an environment of increased competition. This happens every day, even every minute, on the Internet. A new accounting framework, as well as models, expert systems and computers, are vital tools to online negotiated solutions in both retailing and wholesaling. This is true in sectors of the economy as diverse as banking, insurance, electronics, electrical equipment, auto-motive, aerospace and medical industries. Some companies are afraid that migration from bricks and mortar to Web-brokered deals presents unknown factors they are not yet prepared to handle, and therefore might lead to economic disruptions to their detriment. Competitive solutions, however, are found by forging ahead, not by staying behind.

The art of compromising is not new. When committees meet and discuss a marketing or inventory strategy, many compromises need to be made until everyone agrees with the projected solution. While many committee members may say that the compromise itself is not exactly what they had wanted, the chosen solution is generally considered to be better than starting the negotiation process all over again.

Can we do such negotiating through knowledge artefacts, which some companies see as the future while others do not? As negotiating becomes more intense, and profit margins are trimmed, it makes sense to automate the less controversial parts of a negotiation. Modelling and experimentation can help not only in making better analytical estimates, but also in providing reasons for holding the line.

Insight and foresight promoted through experimentation, associated with logistics or other processes, are now key words in business competi-tiveness. In the final analysis, it is not only how many 'senses' we bring to the problems on hand: it is also how well all the computing and display mechanisms are integrated within *our* operating environment, and whether they point to action.

Over the years, this action-oriented activity has become more demanding as many logistics executives have added to their responsi-bilities planning for and controlling a greater variety of commodities and materials. They are also responsible for sourcing and purchasing with a view to cutting costs, while increasing user satisfaction. Answer-ing the whole range of these challenges effectively is a matter of survival for many industrial and merchandising companies. Supply-chain clients are more and more frequently telling even the mightiest of manufacturers:

- what kind of goods to make;
- in what shapes and colours; and
- how much to ship and when.

Survival in a supply chain which practically knows no geographic frontiers requires that the blueprints of agreements are based on a great deal of experimentation, therefore on technology. Armed with clever logisticians, high power computing algorithms and heuristics, the successful manufacturers and merchants are forcing their suppliers to rethink whom they sell to as well as the five 'hows':

- how they price their products;
- how they promote their market appeal;
- how they support their operations through sophisticated models;
- how they structure their own organisations to gain market edge; and
- how their accounting works to provide reliable cost information.

From the tiniest of private-label suppliers to giant firms, the shift in market power obliges manufacturers to overhaul themselves to cope with the demands of retailer hypermarkets. This shift in power will continue. Therefore, the more integrated become the surviving companies' logistics, the better they can face the challenges which continue to arise. Boards, CEOs and CFOs are well advised to take notice.

In conclusion, the whole set of relationships between business functions and supports needs rethinking. A bird's-eye view of what I am saying is presented in Figure 8.2. Hypotheses have to be made and tested in the real world: hence, under conditions of market reality. Scenarios must be developed and their conclusions evaluated under different, even contrasting, viewpoints. Every block in Figure 8.2 impacts upon the end results *our* company will obtain and therefore it should attract the undivided attention of senior management.

4   WHY SENIOR MANAGEMENT SHOULD CARE ABOUT AGENCY COSTS

Some years ago, Andersen Consulting made a study of its fast flow replenishment model for a group of leading European retailers. It did the same in America for Coca-Cola. In both cases, the results have shown that FFR makes a contribution to efficiency and has a good future, particularly in the grocery industry, but it also has dramatic organisational consequences in terms of the management of change (see Chapter 1). FFR's basic characteristics are:

- implicit dependence on shared information; and
- partnership between retailers and their suppliers.

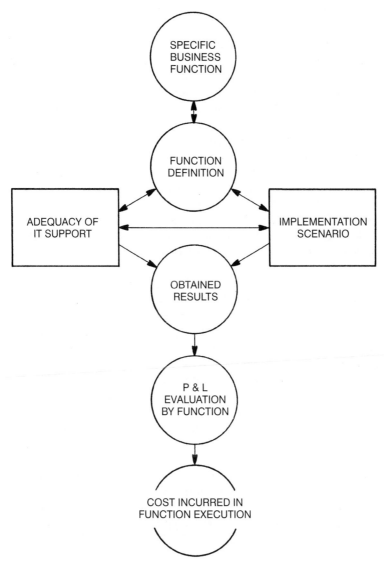

Figure 8.2 The interaction between business function and supporting information services

An FFR-oriented logistics system needs to take account of varying levels of demand and this requires realistic assumptions as well as powerful algorithms and heuristics approaches. Experimentation based on algorithms and heuristics requires lots of computer power: for example, Monte Carlo simulation is a job which has to be interactive and executed in real-time for each product under control.

A keyword is variation in patterns because of changing consumer habits or other reasons. Supermarkets, for instance, are busiest at the end of the week; soft drinks sell faster in summer; other lines of retail business have their own additional peaks of demand as well as lows in sales. There is no magic about meeting market requirements: valid answers call for attention to detail and steady testing.

Valid answers also need to pay attention to the concept behind *agency theory* developed by economists to explain the way in which businesses are organised, managers behave and frictions develop, as well as to identify the costs due to these frictions. Agency theory says that companies successfully competing in a given industry are those whose ownership structure allows them to minimise costs. Simplifying the model, these costs fall into two classes:

- development, production and distribution costs; and
- friction or agency costs, which at times can be significant.

Evidently, production and distribution costs are the cost of goods sold in the narrower sense: labour, materials and so on. But there are also costs arising from incentive conflicts within the firm and within the supply chain. A vast consolidation in retailing has produced giant enterprises that use sophisticated inventory management, finely tuned selections, and competitive pricing. Such policies can also lead to certain types of friction, which cost money. This happens all the time, both in classical bricks and mortar and in the Internet supply chain (see Part 1).

Boards and CEOs should be on the lookout to detect friction and eliminate it, because it slows down the company and adds unnecessary costs. Because a major source of friction is delays in execution, *our* firm's customers, distributors, and suppliers should be able to access online *our* information resources in order to:

- place orders;
- find out when shipments will arrive; and
- check payment status and other data.

An additional advantage is that direct access to databases by authorised companies and people allows our employees to shift from low-value repetitive work of an administrative nature to improving services that build stronger customer relationships.

On the Web where fierce price competition, consolidation, dwindling product differentiation and vanishing brand loyalty seem to be all but eliminating profits, improvements in efficiency and productivity are the key to survival. In an environment where information is instantaneous, traditional retailing barriers to information exchange are disappearing and buyers can immediately compare the offerings of sellers worldwide. Companies need to adapt to the Web's competitive realities, and this means developing strategies to combat the classical agency costs.

Accounting systems are not particularly tuned to reflect agency costs, yet these weigh on the profit and loss account and therefore they should be taken into consideration. We have to rethink cost accounting to map into it agency friction, and we should pay attention to the fact that every company has several groups of *stakeholders* (do not confuse these with shareholders) whose interests conflict: owners, managers, employees or business partners with a stake in their assets. For instance, bankers finance supply-chain associates using their assets as collateral.

Agency costs can be defined as in two ways: direct friction costs, and costs of reducing these conflicts. Part of agency cost is the value of output lost because of such conflicts, as well as delays, quality defects and other failures. Inasmuch as rapid prototyping, for example, is reducing friction between engineering and manufacturing – or between business partners – it is a means for reducing agency costs. Typically, as Figure 8.3 suggests, rapid prototyping helps in swamping agency costs because it:

- shrinks time-to-market; and
- weeds out deviations before it is too late.

Figure 8.3 brings into perspective the fact that prototyping acts as a dynamic link between a concept and the expected product. For this reason, real-time simulation can be of great help. Rapid product transition from development to production and marketing are good examples because they accentuate another factor critical to modern business: the need for an infrastructure which permits quantum leaps in administration. Analytical logistics models make it possible to work out a more efficient management process, by paring down waste. Saving waste saves both time and money, provided the proper culture is in place to capitalise on such savings.

Applying an integrative logistics approach means working more closely with customers and suppliers; in turn, this can be instrumental

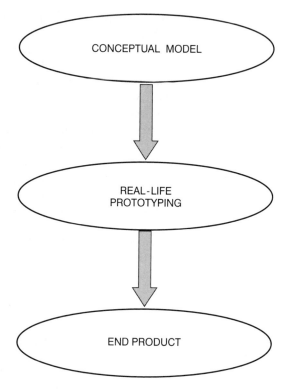

Figure 8.3   Rapid project development through the use of prototyping helps to reduce agency costs

in reinventing *our* firm. The days are gone when transport companies, for instance, simply moved goods. Companies which will lead the way in the early part of the twenty-first century understand that, by incorporating all elements of the supply chain, logistics maps the evolution of our business.

If an analytical and experimental approach to logistics is a powerful tool for manufacturing and retailing in one and the same country, it is even more essential when cross-country barriers fall. For instance, business moves further north and south with the North American Free Trade Agreement, and all over the old continent in the euroland.

The case of euroland brings to the foreground another source of energy costs: cultural and linguistic differences, and also differences in standards and in norms for quality assurance. Both JIT and FFR can be jammed by cultural and quality standards differences. Yet, to survive stiffening competition, manufacturers, distributors and their customers must rationalise where they hold stock, and reduce the costs associated with the delivery cycle.

'Big' can be profitable, particularly in warehousing, only when it is supported by the right technology. For example, it is calculated that a single large warehouse can provide the same service with a total inventory of only half that of four smaller ones, and will also be cheaper in an administrative sense, because of economies of scale. On the other hand, to be managed properly, big warehouses require sophisticated decision support models.

In other cases, the problem leading to agency costs may be not with warehousing but with marketing: for instance, with auctions. Let me take one example which recently came to my attention. It concerns a 1999 survey by the MIT Sloan School which estimated that the total volume of transactions conducted by auctions would probably reach $50 billion by 2002. The impediment is a certain level of dissatisfaction with current auctions because most are based only on price criteria.

Professor Sandy Jap, one of the lecturers at MIT's 'Logistics on the Internet – Auctions and Fulfilment' Symposium (27–8 March 2000) has found that some of the existing suppliers' relationships are hurt by *reverse auction* processes. Suppliers' suspicions tend to increase after the auction. Similarly, incumbents' satisfaction with the auction relationship tends to decrease after the auction. Therefore, Sandy Jap recommended that companies use auctions selectively, and concentrate on commodity items rather than on strategic materials.

Something can also be done to improve the efficiency of auctions by developing a more sophisticated set of criteria. To overcome the problems created by concentrating on only one criterion (which is usually price), Jeremie Gallien, also of the MIT Sloan School, has developed a smart B2B auction artefact for industrial procurement. The model is designed to take into account non-price features such as:

- capacity constraints; and
- logistics performance.

Using this model, suppliers can adjust their bid prices based on the quantity of products the buyer wants to purchase. They can also make conditional bids. Notice, however, that agency costs associated with dealing with business partners are not the only problem. Inordinate costs and legal risks big enough to be brought to the Board's attention come from the fact that in spite of all the rhetoric about globalisation there exist among countries significant differences in legislative and regulatory frameworks.

As I never tire of repeating, there is a heterogeneity of laws, rules and regulations, in addition to the fact that management cultures differ and there is a certain decoupling in regard to business practices. Under different legislation and regulations,

- what functions should be performed by the Board of Directors and by senior management; and
- what sort of legal responsibilities are associated with these functions and what is the penalty for non-compliance?

There is furthermore the issue of personal responsibilities. One of the most widespread notions of accountability is that since the Board acts on behalf of shareholders it must exercise the utmost caution in preserving the company's assets and in ensuring a rigorous management discipline. But the degree to which this is enforced varies widely from one country to another. It would take an extraordinary effort to make it more homogeneous.

5   SENIOR MANAGEMENT AND THE LEGAL RISKS FACING THE COMPANY

Adding to the background of the Board's responsibilities described in Chapter 1, let me bring to the reader's attention that in some countries the Board of Directors has the main, if not exclusive, function of supervising senior management to make sure that the latter fulfils its tasks effectively. But in other countries the Board has executive functions, which means a broader competence because it lays down the general framework for line management, and not only for the strategic plans.

Executive responsibilities at Board level are not synonymous with an attempt to micromanage a complex trading system, a system of lending activities, or any other line functions. At the heart of line responsibilities are major tactical moves and legal issues. Differences in legislation and regulation from country to country and from one jurisdiction to another within the same economic body, such as the European Union, make difficult a universal definition of legal risk confronting the Board of Directors and the line managers.

Nobody doubts, however, that the Board is accountable on legal matters. Even down to the fundamentals, one of the problems concerning an accurate definition of *legal risk* is that in many cases members of the Board lack a clear idea about the complexities involved in the legal aspects of a business, particularly of a public company operating across borders. Neither do Board members expect to be personally confronted with the intricacies of local legislation and the specifics of regulation, yet there is plenty of legal exposure confronting each member of the Board (D.N. Chorafas, *Membership of the Board of Directors*, Macmillan – now Palgrave, London, 1988).

Speaking from personal experience, legal risk can be managed, but to do so efficiently one has to master both the art of management and the law of the land. Starting at the bottom of the food chain in personal accountability, the Board must ensure that the firm's activities are planned and controlled in an effective manner and that appropriate policies are in place. This affects the choices made by directors and executive officers because it requires:

- forecasting coming developments and measuring their consequences;
- establishing a valid course of action and seeing that it is followed;
- organising all company efforts and the activities in an efficient manner; and
- obtaining full evidence that line management obtains concrete results without inordinate agency costs.

One of the most frequent snags in a company line is the failure to staff the organisation with individuals able to face current and coming challenges. This is compounded by the lack of on-the-job lifelong learning. Directors are not yet legally responsible in a direct way for the failure of upkeeping employee know-how, but if one interprets the writing on the wall this challenge is not far away. What is evident for the time being is the moral responsibility of caring for the company's human capital.

There are other responsibilities to take note of as well. Within the framework of Board oversight fall, for example, specific functions such as policies for R&D, product development, marketing, areas of operations, efficiency, cost control and awareness of how senior management performs its day-to-day activities. Efficiency is a double-sided sword. Both underperformance and extreme zeal against competition have many negatives.

Board members are not immune from senior management's violation of antitrust laws. In the USA, the Federal Trade Commission (FTC)

investigated whether MasterCard and Visa have been forcing merchants who accept their credit cards to use their less popular debit cards
as well, a practice that could dampen debit-card competition (*Business
Week*, 23 March 1998). References like this lead us way up the food
chain to the Board of Directors' responsibilities. Control used to mean
making sure that execution of business activities conformed to plans.
Now it involves much more than that; it has become a broad internal
control responsibility. On the surface, nothing has changed dramatically.
The application of the principles of management is just as important in
safeguarding the company's assets as in running the firm day-to-day, no
matter what the business or industry. Conceptual and analytical abil-
ities are necessary and the same is true of executive skills. But below the
surface have come into existence a great deal of special issues, many of
them sanctioned by the law.

In some of the G10 countries, insider trading did not become a criminal
offence until the mid-1980s. With the change in the letter of the law, the
legal responsibility of directors broadened. Stockholder activism has
added considerably more weight to legal accountability of Board members than used to be the case, particularly as the big stockholders are
now institutional investors with plenty of legal advice and legal support
within easy reach.

Legal experts suggest that in the final analysis legal risk can best be
judged in the context of the legislative, economic and social environment, and also through jurisprudence. Knowledge of all four constitutes a sound basis for controlling many of the factors entering legal
risk. Another test is that of the exposure each Board member takes in
connection to *reputational risk*, which is essentially an aggregate of
other risks, when one or more of them come to the public eye (as
Helmut Kohl seems to have learned, in the year 2000, the hard way).

Reputational risk increases exponentially not only when a company
gets involved in non-ethical or illegal practices, but also when its
governing body becomes bureaucratic, too hierarchical, wasteful,
inflexible and alienated from business reality. The Board as a body, and
each director individually, should look at reputational risk in the most
careful way. What about reputational risk connected with Internet business? A survey by SIIA, a trade association that protects the intellectual
property of the software and information industries, found that most of
the software auctions on the Net are illegitimate (*Electronic Design*, 20
March 2000).

Conducted over five days at three major Internet auction sites, this
study discovered that 60 per cent of the auctions involved illegal soft-

ware. Based on these findings, SIIA developed approaches that auction sites can take to do away with unauthorised activities. For instance, SIIA suggests Internet sites should ban the distribution of copyrighted software (this would prevent bootlegs from passing themselves off as legitimate), and all sites could review all auctions that transfer software prior to their posting.

There are, of course, limitations to the practicality of both procedures. Illegal software was not invented for Internet auctions. It is a 50-year-old problem and, because of it, copyright holders lose millions of dollars. As for customers, they can receive software that does not work, contains a virus or, at best, would not be eligible for any technical or upgrade support.

Where the Internet creates a new pirating problem or amplifies an already existing one, it is true that it both facilitates the sale of illegal software and provides a log through which its buyers and sellers can be tracked down. This is important because buyers and sellers of illegal software may be subject to civil or criminal liabilities.

6   TRANSPARENCY IS THE DIRECT RESPONSIBILITY OF THE CHIEF EXECUTIVE OFFICER

Quite often, this text has made reference to the important role played by a company's culture. As I had the opportunity to explain, by culture is meant the inner values and attitudes that guide a person, a company or a whole nation. A main component of culture is *virtue*, and at least one philosopher (Socrates, 470–399 BC) considered virtue to be knowledge which cannot be taught. But there are virtuous people.

The examples which we saw in section 3 suggest that to position itself against the shifts in market power a company must strengthen its internal control system. The first basic principle of an effective internal control is that accountability for it starts with the Chairman of the Board and the Board members; the next in line is the chief executive officer. Internal control and transparency correlate: sunshine is the best disinfectant, as Justice Louis Brandeis aptly said.

In a market more dynamic than ever, with so many unknowns because of globalisation deregulation and technology, transparency is a key word in sound management. Transparency at all levels enhances the internal control system's ability to reach every corner of operations, down to the single person and the single transaction. It needs no explaining that this principle of transparency also helps to produce a clear focus and edge (D.N. Chorafas, *Reliable Financial Reporting and*

Internal Control: A Global Implementation Guide, John Wiley, New York, 2000). However, some executives think that transparency goes against the general culture. Only in a few companies is senior management willing and able to see to it that transparency carries the day; yet management can catch a sophisticated crook only when it obliges everybody, a priori, to be transparent.

The Board should be sceptical about general statements that 'our employees are beyond reproach'. The financial battlefield is littered with cases of misappropriation, concealment, creative accounting, gambling with the company's and with other people's money, and other frills. Embezzlement looms large in the business landscape, yet is thought to be rare in the world of high finance because:

- its professionals make stupendous amounts of money; and
- if they want to have more there are legal ways to get it.

This is only half-true, as a number of court cases help to reveal. An example is the decision by Judge Robert W. Sweet who said to Tony Gebauer, a Morgan Bank star performer whose misdeeds eventually came to light: 'You are indeed a Lucifer, a fallen angel of the banking world. Although your employment at the top of your profession provided you with princely income, you spent like an emperor' (Ron Chernow, *The House of Morgan*, Touchstone/Simon & Schuster, New York, 1990).

Along with big loans, Gebauer had responsibility for the accounts of top Latin American businessmen. Technically, these were not personal accounts, but they were owned by the senior executives with whom Morgan was dealing; they were a way to befriend and please key people. For years, Gebauer diverted money from some of the bigger accounts residing in Panamanian holding companies, and this happened in a bank proud of its tough internal controls.

An industrial example of where internal controls have been wanting, and which led to the inevitable misappropriations, is that of Electrolux. On 4 January 2000, it was announced that the company had suffered a two-digit millions of dollars loss from unauthorised foreign exchange trading by one of its employees. Deception can hide all over the organisation and it is difficult to fully understand, let alone foresee, each crook's methods. But a policy of transparency, assisted by mining online an internal control database, can bring to light hidden deals, and provide hints on where to look for embezzlement.

With plenty of examples of unscrupulous use of company money in the background and the Board's slow response, the Basle Committee is justified when it states that the Board of Directors and the chief executive officer are responsible for establishing the culture needed to facilitate an effective function of internal control, and also for monitoring both exposure and accountability at all management levels. To perform this function effectively, the Board must look after the reliability and completeness of financial information, and internal control intelligence should be on hand to answer specific, clearly established objectives, including compliance with laws and regulations.

The Board of Directors and the CEO have an instrumental role in shaping a company's culture as well as in steering this culture towards strict ethical values, but they also have the responsibility of ensuring that the principle of transparency applies widely, and not only to financial matters. Many hidden technical deficiencies eventually explode, and they translate into financial woes.

Several issues should be transparent in technology management: the allocation of R&D money and effort, the direction of new projects, their ability to meet deadlines, assured quality of service, time-to-market considerations, cost control, and evidently the integrity of remediation. Though the Year 2000 (Y2K) problem is now behind us, let me take it as an example of this last reference.

As many companies discovered to their dismay, would-be fixes for Y2K introduced new bugs. Windowing deferred some problems until later, while some projects used Y2K fixes as an opportunity to insert Trojan horses into the company's software, and there were also cases of financial fraud. In fact some of the many mishaps with Y2K corrective action may not be evident for some time.

The Department of Defense had a self-inflicted Y2K misfix whose aftermath was a complete loss of ability to process satellite intelligence data for almost three hours at midnight GMT on the year turnover. Even after curing that, there was only a trickle of data from 5 satellites for several days afterwards. The Pentagon DefenseLINK site was disabled by a preventive mistake, while in a totally different domain many people received bills for cumulative interest since 1900.

The reason I bring up these references is that results of remedial technical action are rarely transparent to the Board and the CEO. This is particularly true of short cuts which seem advantageous in the short term. For instance, they help to reduce immediate costs and shorten timetables, but may well be counterproductive in the long term.

7   A CASE STUDY WITH WAL-MART DOCUMENTS THAT RETAIL IS DETAIL

According to a retail industry adage, 'Retail is Detail'. The same is true of many businesses. For big organisations, following up on detail means a massive amount of data pertaining to all sorts of activities, analysed and presented in a way that helps buyers and suppliers. Even if in the past the classical type of data processing has been of assistance in handling large data sets, present requirements of logistics go beyond past practices and beyond number crunching. They call for:

- discerning customer trends;
- managing merchandise assortment;
- using fast flow replenishment;
- tracking inventory; and
- evaluating profitability.

To answer overwhelming logistics requirements, Wal-Mart has created the world's largest commercial data warehouse, able to handle detail and develop a more intimate understanding of its customers. Since the mid-1990s its 24-terabyte database and decision support complex has provided management with both analytics and detail.

On the inventory management side, such a massive storage capacity meant that Wal-Mart could track merchandise volume and movement in each of its nearly 3000 stores and clubs in eight countries. It manages its stores as individual locations with specialised needs, providing a product assortment uniquely tailored to the preferences of the customers that each store serves. Market analysis personnel can identify site-specific opportunities at the neighbourhood retailing level, and suppliers can access this information to help the company's buyers manage inventory.

In this and other similar advanced applications, supply chain networking helps to promote good management. Wal-Mart is giving hugely valuable scan information to its suppliers, who are optimising the inventory going into its stores. By doing so, the hypermarket is unloading some of its costs but is also building up relationship management which can serve it in many ways, including more efficient business partnerships on the Internet.

Wal-Mart has been pursuing Internet commerce activities since 1996. Currently the company offers 25 000 different products for sale through its Web site, leveraging the presence of its thousands of stores to handle one of the difficult aspects of Internet commerce: product returns. This would not have been possible without the integrated database solution to which I made reference.

For instance, in apparel returns average 25 per cent due to size and colour variations. This mass of returned items is expensive. Capitalising on its technology, Wal-Mart lets customers return merchandise to any store rather than mailing it to a central warehouse. This is practicable because its information system means that any product sold anywhere by Wal-Mart shows up on a Master Item List.

There are multiple advantages from such practice. The customer finds it easier and less expensive to drive to the Wal-Mart store, rather than repackage and post the return item. Once there, he or she is fairly sure to buy something else. Such a policy also sees to it that any store can put any item back on the sales floor, regardless of whether that store typically sells the item or not. The information system, however, knows that the return was from a Web-based sale, and it does not penalise the accepting store for receiving the returned item.

Any-to-any seamless access to Wal-Mart's massive database also has other advantages. The company's 4000 suppliers behave as partners in the proper management of Wal-Mart's access to the warehouse and are jointly responsible for managing its inventory and shelf stock, down to the detail of the individual store level. This warehouse-based co-operation has greatly reduced assets locked up in inventory and made the giant retailer more responsive to changing market conditions.

The sort of sophisticated services I am describing are not practical for retail organisations which continue to use legacy systems that were developed many years ago in a relatively independent, non-integrated manner, and which still focus on individual functional areas, one-by-one: for instance, a marketing system here, an inventory systems there, an accounting system somewhere else. Today, practically all of these legacy solutions have compatibility problems because of different data models, definitions, updating cycles, and other technical factors. As a result, it is difficult to access seamlessly the kinds of data needed for a cross-functional view of the company's business, optimising inventories and emphasising client-oriented processes.

I insist on Wal-Mart's solution because it is a leading example of how a company redesigned its logistics to fit its business perspectives and answer the requirements of its business strategy. What kind of advantages will Wal-Mart get by introducing the electronic product code (see Chapter 6) and by using smart materials? An easy answer is that automatic identification will greatly strengthen the system I have just described in three different ways:

- receiving into the warehouse;
- tracking the merchandise in transit and in the store; and
- helping in checkout services, billing, returns and other client assistance.

Another benefit is that it will keep Wal-Mart ahead of the curve as its competitors are catching up with what has been achieved so far. No doubt another great benefit to Wal-Mart will be an enhanced understanding of its customers and their needs.

Even today, with its point-of-sale (POS) solution, the retailer captures transaction information from each outlet and stores it in its huge database system where it is analysed for *trends* and *patterns*. But information embedded in 1 kilobit chips attached to each item will offer much greater detail than the bar code (for instance, about business partners and quality of product). Using pattern analysis, Wal-Mart, and any other retailer adopting smart technology, will make much more focused decisions about:

- sources of supply;
- cost and quality criteria;
- fast flow replenishment capabilities;
- customer preferences and satisfaction;
- profit margins with mark-downs (and so on).

It will do so in *minutes*, upholding its hard-earned reputation for exceptional customer service that ranks Wal-Mart above its competition in the American consumer satisfaction index, as reported in *Fortune* magazine. Over the last dozen years Wal-Mart's goal has been that its customers should find the right items in stock when and where they want them. Smart materials will further promote this reputation.

As the examples of both the US Army (see Chapter 1) and Wal-Mart have shown, there is also the effect of large size to cope with. This requires knowledge engineering with expert systems and agents (D.N. Chorafas, *Agent Technology Handbook*, McGraw-Hill, New York, 1998), petabyte (a million bytes) databases, intelligent broadband networks, and high performance computing power. The job is possible but, as we saw through practical examples, there are prerequisites.

197

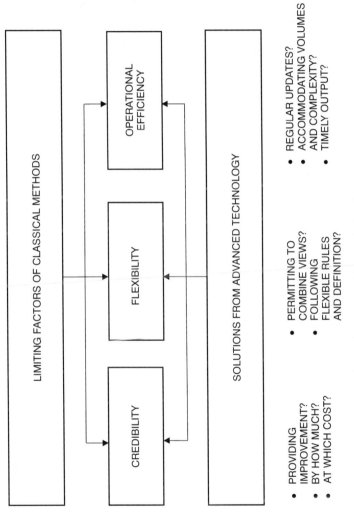

Figure 8.4 Limitations of past approaches to be corrected by new technology

In conclusion, from real-time mining of *petabyte* (millions of giga-bytes) databases to smart materials, new technology creates opportun-ities available to all companies, though only a few – the best – really take advantage of them. Figure 8.4 brings to the reader's attention this trans-formation which targets greater credibility, flexibility and operational efficiency, and also the way to greater profitability and therefore to corporate survival.

9 The Real Revolution in Computers and Communications is in Logistics

1 INTRODUCTION

To build a solid foundation for the twenty-first century we need know-ledge management solutions which will allow us to navigate throughout *our* organisation's information landscape in ways which help to radic-ally renew product design, production planning, quality assurance, inventory management and marketing strategies. Those people and companies will benefit the most from new technology who are able to:

- rethink their business;
- reinvent their strategies;
- redefine their policies; and
- revamp their information resources.

No other sector will need this restructuring more than *logistics*. The most persistent message from recent congresses and symposia stresses the necessity of rethinking the way technology affects the logistics system. Such effort must fully take into account the new realities, visu-alising future requirements and doing a commendable job in providing solutions which inevitably involve new processes affecting logistics management.

New processes can be instrumental in gaining competitive advan-tage. Key to Dell's business success is the company's made-to-order business model, which greatly limits inventory. In 2000, Dell turned over its tiny inventory 60 times a year – a ten-fold improvement from 1994 – while mass customisation also allows the company to make only the products it will sell.

New cost-effective approaches do not necessarily demand putting aside the experiences and traditions of the past in a wholesale manner. But they do oblige us to look anew at the way we use our resources – hence our logistical support – all the way from master plans and the type of investments we are making, to the nuts and bolts of the solutions we provide. Re-engineering affects:

- the operating processes and products we manage;
- the systems and procedures available to manage them; and
- the approaches which make it possible to continue to deliver, at an increased level of efficiency.

Even prosaic industrial enterprises can reap quantum efficiencies by applying the new, technology-empowered management principles of the twenty-first century. Competition forces Boards and CEOs to head down two tracks at the same time: renewal and continuity (a bifurcated approach that is very demanding, but feasible).

The most valuable asset of a commercial, financial or industrial organisation is the inventory in its knowledge base. It is also one of the hardest-to-manage corporate resources, as we will see in section 5. The majority of knowledge workers can be productive only when they are getting the information they need in an *ad hoc*, timely and accurate fashion. In the majority of cases this is still more difficult than it should be.

In most companies, information dissemination still involves creating and distributing paper documents or spending time on the telephone and in meetings with fellow employees to get logistics information that should be available interactively on request, as a matter of course. New digital solutions can be used to enable knowledge workers in a far more efficient manner than the best approaches we have known so far. Agents can be used to make this enabling proactive (D.N. Chorafas, *Agent Technology Handbook*, McGraw-Hill, New York, 1998).

2   IN THE MOST GENERAL SENSE, LOGISTICS IS THE ART OF COMPUTING

Logistics is sometimes defined as the organisation of supplies and services. This is, however, a narrow definition. The whole art of computing, including the calculation with fractions, was called *logistics* by the ancient Greeks. Plato distinguished between *practical* and *theoretical* logistics, just as he discriminated between practical and theoretical arithmetic (Gorgias, AD 451).

Theoretical logistics dealt particularly with the study of numbers in their mutual ratios, while theoretical arithmetic was concerned with the even and the odd, which was the basis of Pythagorean theory. By contrast, practical arithmetic concerned counting and calculation and therefore, to a considerable degree, was taken as synonymous with practical logistics.

It is indeed most interesting that the Pythagoreans, like the Babylonians, concerned themselves with the solution of systems of equations with more than one unknown. This today we call algebra, but in the days of old it was part of practical logistics. It is remarkable that, according to the same source, logistics and money correlated, and this might have been at the origin of geometry becoming an important branch of science: 'Through the fault of one of their numbers, the Pythagoreans lost their money. After this misfortune, it was decided to allow him (Pythagoras) to earn money with geometry – thus geometry came to be designated as "The Tradition of Pythagoras"' (B.L. Van der Waerden, *Science Awakening*, P. Noordhoff, Groningen, 1954).

Today, money and logistics correlate very strongly among themselves and with practical arithmetic. Materials planning, production scheduling, inventory control and supply chain management are all examples. In fact, as section 3 will demonstrate, logistics extend all the way to asset management. Linear programming and dynamic programming are tools of logistics. The same is true of JIT inventory management in manufacturing, and FFR in merchandising and sales. Internet supply chain management has been instrumental in promoting this major cultural change. In the past, no one worried excessively about production inventories, except maybe during annual stocktaking. Improvements to machining, presswork, assembly and finishing were piecemeal until about the late 1950s.

The 1960s were a period of transition. Many experts believe it was the reality of Japanese competition, in the early 1970s, which spurred Western car and truck plants to take seriously and examine in greater detail production economics and logistics. Competition drove tooling, presswork, machining, welding and assembly line technology to higher productivity levels but its really visible aftermath has been in inventory management.

Then came the 1980s when developments already under way were fine-tuned. The growing use of computers permitted the optimisation of logistics processes. The early 1990s saw the globalisation of plants, a wave of mergers and an efficient way to lower supplier prices. In the late 1990s came the Internet supply chain challenges which helped to make the business partners' inventory management tools highly transparent.

While in terms of scientific breakthroughs in the coming years we will see, in all likelihood, applications in biology combined with human vision modelling and other advanced projects which expand the capability to model in chemistry and in the material sciences, experts believe that nowhere will the breakthroughs be greater than in *integrated logistics*. One of the reasons is the need steadily to boost competitiveness by increasing the productivity of capital (not only human productivity) and cutting costs. At the New York Stock Exchange and NASDAQ, companies go through an *earnings confession* season four times per year. No management can afford to forget about efficiency and costs.

Indeed, many firms announce earnings disappointments, most commonly blaming weak pricing, operational problems, a rebound in so far depressed oil prices, undervalued exchange rates or weak foreign demand. These problems reflect an environment where capacity is ample, competition intense, and firms that make mistakes cannot hide behind price hikes. The capital market is not forgiving towards companies which fail in their earnings reports. Many experts look for this harsh but healthy environment to continue, and they expect that management will put skills, costs and logistics at the top of its priorities list.

Plenty of cases document how companies strong in logistics have become pacesetters in cost performance. They have turned to streamlined logistical solutions, largely based on mathematical analysis, that allow designs to go from concepts to manufacturing and sales in as little as a few weeks.

Sound solutions to the problems of logistics and good profitability correlate. Figure 9.1 presents statistics from eight computer companies (called A to H) which show that those with higher operating margins are able to truly swamp the costs of goods sold, while spending more money on sales and marketing. These companies are better performers than their competitors. Large, unwarranted inventories:

- add tremendously to cost of goods sold;
- reduce the return on investment ratios; and
- depress the quarterly profit figures.

In the mid-1990s, within a year, Compaq developed a just-in-time inventory management system which shrank stocks to under 30 days, from 69 days a year earlier. This contributed $1 billion to the $4 billion cash Compaq had at the end of December 1996. By January 1998, Compaq had trimmed more than a month off its dealers' inventories by doing more of the customisation it had already performed through new,

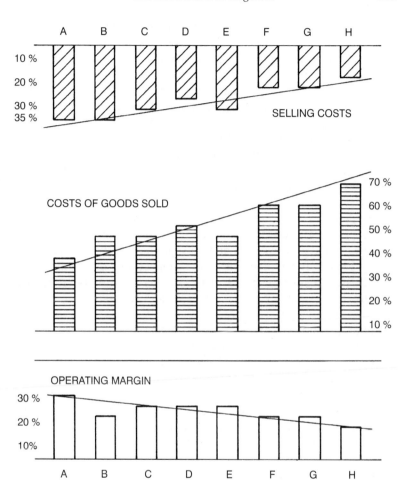

Figure 9.1 Companies with higher operating margins swamp costs of goods sold while spending on sales and marketing

more powerful JIT models and tools. This has been by no means the 'ultimate' solution: Dell significantly improved Compaq's model, and Cisco excels over Dell's inventory policy by a good margin.

Sound logistical solutions have prerequisites. Apart from management culture, this includes support by computers, communications and software, as well through database mining and knowledge engineering artefacts. The goal is to improve a company's focus on streamlined logistics. A parallel goal in manufacturing is concurrent handling of engineering design. Toughening competition, economic changes and the swamping of costs have made not only industrial organisations but also financial services providers and merchandising concerns aware of the need to steadily tune up their logistics.

Market competitiveness, productivity improvements, cost control, and better profit figures are the incentives. There are no 'safe havens' from competition, and this underpins the attention that needs to be paid to logistics. In a survival of the fittest environment, it is much harder to be successful than it once was; hence the need for more effective approaches. Even the best competitive edge is usually short lived, but those companies are faring better that are able to rapidly improve their performance.

The winners in an Internet supply chain (which is more competitive than ever) are those who are flexible in customising products, while keeping production, inventory and distribution costs low. This is one of the key reasons for so much interest in supply chain management. Not only do the foremost companies ensure quality in customer service, but they also keep a close eye on their competitors' logistics practices, both within their own industry and outside it.

Another winning characteristic is that of reducing substantial proportions of cost by re-examining the *value chain*, and shrinking product cycle times for main business products and processes, as well as developing and using sharper tools. This requires not just incremental progress, but a fundamental revaluation of policies, procedures and models for logistical support. However, a new, more competitive culture will not come about without top management initiatives, and it will not take hold until new, more powerful methods and tools are available to *our* organisation.

The appreciation of what has been discussed in this section leads to a careful rethinking of what constitutes the best investments in logistics, differentiating them from those which do not fit the profitability bill. Steady improvement in organisational performance can increase the market edge, just as sophisticated information technology can play an instrumental role in effective logistical support.

3   IS MODERN LOGISTICS AN ART OR A SCIENCE?

Since antiquity, logistics has been the art and science of supplying armies and fleets, then the biggest assemblies of human planning efforts, with the sophisticated supporting services required to carry on their mission. Today, logistics not only underpins the industrialisation of production and distribution, but is also the key to the efficient co-ordination and administration of practically all human activities.

Many historians believe that Alexander the Great would have been unable to move into and conquer the heart of Asia if it was not for the support Greek logisticians provided him with. Today multinational companies and global supermarket chains command more people and materials than Alexander the Great ever did in his far-away expeditions, and they need first-class logistics very dearly. Business depends on logistics as much as the army needs generals. In turn, this requires a well-balanced and optimised decision system for ensuring:

- the right people manage the right goods;
- materials and information are in the right place at the right time; and
- there is tangible evidence that all this happens at the right cost.

One reason for the leadership acquired in the 1980s by Japanese car manufacturers has been that they were pioneers of modern logistics. They were the first to answer such critical queries as how to run just in time inventories, how to do fast flow replenishment, and where is the best place for a warehouse to serve shops and outlets spread over whole continents.

In year 2001, the specific criteria for successful business operations are different, but logistics and supply chain management are always on top of the list of solutions which are increasingly influenced by technology. Technology has radically revamped whole areas of the American economy, particularly those industries whose customer base is not only in the USA but world-wide. Virtually any firm today realises the importance of becoming Web-enabled in all of its operations, dynamically maintaining its supply chain. Supply chain partners in Web-enabled solutions are companies that provide the requisite software, hardware and operating expertise on the spot.

Logistics has become a largely online exercise, with buyers and sellers in electronic market places exchanging information, setting prices, holding auctions and doing reverse auctions. They perform all the activities of negotiating, buying and selling products interactively and in rapid succession (as we saw in Part 1), and they expect their business partners to do the same.

The list of online players is growing, and things that used to be clear in regard to the planning and execution of business deals are not so clear any more. Enlightened spirits have always challenged what to others might seem 'obvious', but to them is a wasteful practice. In his seminal book, *My Years with General Motors* (Sidgwick & Jackson, London, 1965), Alfred Sloan makes several references to inventory control, pointing out how an ongoing practice may well prove to be spoilage, particularly when times turn tough:

> The worst of the emergency problems was the inventory... Uncontrolled purchases of raw and semi-finished materials by the division managers had reached a total of $209 million by October of 1920, exceeding the Executive and Finance committee's maximum allotment by $59 million and far exceeding the amount that could immediately be used in the plants.

Sloan was a master of choosing the right people for the right job. He assigned John L. Pratt, a civil engineer, to solve the poor inventory management problem because he believed that Pratt had 'a great capability for handling large issues with plainness and simplicity. He could get to the point.' In this mission Pratt worked together with Donaldson Brown, an expert accountant and ingenious cost controller.

In the crisis of 1920, the first step of the Inventories Committee (headed by Pratt) was to send out, under the signature of the president of GM, a letter instructing all general managers to buy nothing until the Inventories Committee could review the situation with each individual general manager and decide on:

- what material would be received; and
- what would not be received.

This work was largely done by Pratt who sat down with the general managers in their own offices and went over in detail each division's inventory situation. Sloan acted without any loss of time because he appreciated that the more a bad situation in logistics is allowed to persist, the more difficult it is to solve it successfully.

Many business schools, and some business magazines, which have recently got into the habit of criticising Alfred Sloan's model as 'obsolete', are wrong in their judgement. Such criticisms are often hollow and they are usually made by the unable, who have been asked by the unwilling to do the unnecessary.

What is true about Sloan's principles is precisely the opposite of what this cavalier disregard of basic management theory wants people to believe. Sloan's model of management has been the father of the flexible and dynamic approach to the solution of business challenges; a solution which we are so proud to have in the Internet age.

The best test of a good manager is adaptability to the ever-evolving business conditions. The next best test is his or her ability to evaluate alternatives, and with that the skill to keep costs under control. Alert business executives know this and they do not allow logistics to get out of hand. They also appreciate that earnings per share and days supply in inventory correlate negatively with each other. This is shown in Figure 9.2 which comes from the 1999 annual report of Dell Computers.

Managing this negative correlation is more complex if we account for the fact that even among the world's most developed technology firms, continuing advancement makes inventories obsolete. Yet no company can put the need to satisfy customer demand on the backburner. This is true of any industry characterised by continuing improvements in technology, which result in:

- frequent introduction of new products;
- short product life cycles for each one of them; and
- continual improvement in product price/performance.

While any Board may believe that its company's inventory management model is offering it an inherent competitive advantage over its competitors, product transitions present some of the greatest challenges and risks for any firm. A failure to effectively manage product transition directly affects:

- the demand for *our* products;
- the money locked up in inventories; and
- the profitability of *our* operations.

Therefore, from a logistical standpoint, an increasingly sophisticated business model must give senior management the ability to operate with reduced levels of materials, components and finished goods inventories. A company's financial success is in large part due to its asset management practices, including its virtuosity in achieving rapid inventory turn around.

This statement extends the definition of logistics to *asset management*, within the context of a production- and distribution-oriented accounting. It also extends asset management to the supply chain because a company's manufacturing process requires a high volume of quality components that are procured from third-party suppliers.

208

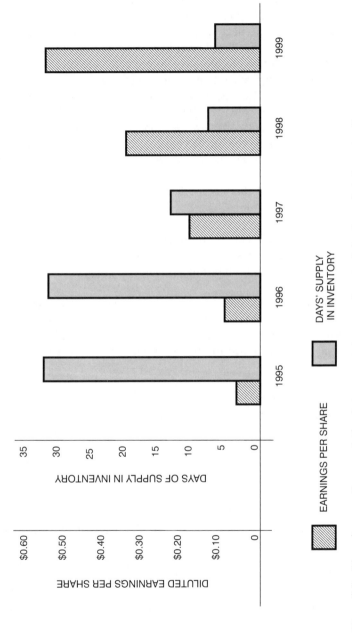

Figure 9.2 There is a negative correlation between earnings per share and days' supply in inventory*
*Statistics from Dell Computer's 1999 Annual Report

Reliance on suppliers can be expressed both in absolute terms and in relative terms of industry supply conditions. This generally involves several risks, including the possibility of:

- defective parts, which can adversely affect the reliability and reputation of *our* company's products;
- reduced control over delivery schedules, which has negative impact on manufacturing efficiencies; and
- increases in component costs, which have a direct effect on *our* company's profitability.

In an environment where supply chains are king, and virtual enterprises flourish (see section 4), a company must have direct control over supplier relationships, ensuring that each of these relationships is advantageous due to performance, quality, support, delivery, capacity and price considerations. If these sources are unable to sustain a timely and reliable supply chain, then *our* company would experience manufacturing delays or inefficiencies, adversely affecting the results of operations, while increasing the market risk.

In conclusion, Internet supply chain relationships cannot be treated as a mystery wrapped in an enigma. Quality histories of supply relationships should be carefully preserved in our company's database or, more precisely, its corporate memory facility. This is one of the themes of section 5 which focuses attention on the efficient exploitation of corporate knowledge and what this means in terms of management information and its prerequisites, such as storage capacity and advanced tools for database analytics.

4 LOGISTICS, VIRTUAL COMPANIES AND INTERNET COMMERCE

Rather than evolving into a structure more or less similar to that of the Industrial Revolution, which characterised the last 100 years, the virtual companies of the Internet age keep enormous flexibility by incorporating new information technology, increasing their range of options in terms of organisation, and placing particular emphasis on real-time modelling and speed of transmission. An example of what these new factors can do for business is given by Wal-Mart (see Chapter 8 and section 7 in this chapter). The world's largest merchandiser has inventory turnover four times faster than most of its competitors.

Management quality makes the difference. Technology provides all industries, from aircraft design to finance, with the twin cutting edge of modelling and speed in execution. But, as I never tire of repeating, the effective implementation of new technology requires a significant cultural change. This includes both co-involvement by senior management and restructuring through a transition from the Sloan model of a multidivision, multinational hierarchy that predominates today to networked, independent business units that use development and marketing alliances of various sorts.

As the examples we saw in section 3 demonstrate, those companies gain real advantage that are adaptable and flexible, addressing new market opportunities and using new technologies effectively. Advanced information systems also seem to accelerate the trend among organisations to do more outsourcing, by using partnership facilities provided through electronic markets. Let me, however, first define what is the sense of a *virtual company*.

The concept of a virtual business organisation has evolved with the new economy, and it is characterised by the usage of complementary resources existing in a number of co-operating firms *as if* these resources were under single management. On the contrary, such resources are left in the place they currently belong, but are integrated, so to speak, on the fly to support a particular product and/or market effort for as long as this is viable.

Well-run virtual companies and real companies have several things in common. One of them is that their products and services, along with their other assets, are bright stars in the market's constellation, as shown in Figure 9.3. Where virtual companies differ quite substantially from more classical companies is in their prevailing management culture and organisational structure; both should be characterised by steady evolution. Virtual companies must be supported by virtual office systems based on agents, to help expand the boundaries defined by organisational lines. Agents can speed business processes and facilitate commerce, through interaction with a broader range of business factors, than is possible under traditional approaches.

Accounting is one of the most important business factors affected by the change to which I have made reference. In my experience, setting up and operating an accounting system for a virtual company is almost of an order of magnitude more difficult than the corresponding accounting solution for an old economy company. Legacy software with Cobol-type programs, and the obsolete concepts underpinning them, would not do. The accounting system must use knowledge engineering in

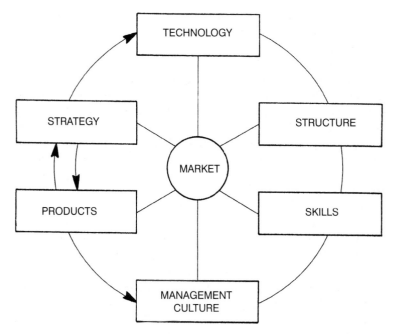

Figure 9.3   Market positioning works both ways, affecting many critical elements

order to:

- be very flexible and adaptable as business partners change, and new business partners are added with different accounting standards from our own; and
- be able to retain a great deal of detail about old partnerships, reintegrating past accounting data with new when past partners co-operate together once again.

Furthermore, because in a dynamic market intra- and intercompany resource availability can change from minute to minute, advantages are accruing to parties able to rapidly arbitrage resource availabilities, and therefore leverage their assets. Virtual organisations use advanced information technology to improve their cognitive capability, thus providing themselves with an advantage in spite of constraints existing with globalisation.

As we have seen through practical examples in Part 1, to a very substantial extent virtual companies capitalise on Internet commerce in a way quite similar to that of the best managed real companies. This is as true of co-operative purchasing agreements (see Chapters 3 and 4) as it is of using the Web for sales. Chapter 5 gave examples with financial institutions. Dell is an example in the computer industry. Through sales via www.dell.com, by the end of fiscal year 1999 it had reached $14 million per day in sales, and I-commerce accounted for 25 per cent of its revenue in the fourth quarter of that same year. In an intensive use of Web facilities, as of mid-1999 Dell was hosting more than 15 000 Premier Pages, unique sites within dell.com that are tailored to the specific needs of individual corporate and institutional customers. However, without a first-class logistics system and the dynamic accounting infrastructure Dell has developed to serve its Web commerce, the Internet drive would have been largely theoretical, if not downright counterproductive.

Many virtual companies capitalise in a similar way on Internet resources. They appreciate that Web pages offer services such as approved product configurations, global pricing, paperless purchase orders, real-time order tracking, invoicing and purchasing history, among other efficiency tools. They also understand that each one of these tools requires first-class logistics and accounting supports.

In Dell's case, its online *virtual account executive* provides high-level services to small businesses. The Internet connection helps to furnish all its customers, from the largest corporate client to the individual home-PC buyer, with a virtual help desk featuring natural language search. Let me add that Dell is by no means the only company making lots of money through I-commerce.

As we have already seen, Cisco Systems handles about 85 per cent of all its orders over the Net and its employees never even touch more than half of them. In fact, among the majors Cisco is the nearest thing to a big virtual firm. It develops product, manufacturing and testing specifications. But, using the Internet, it owns only two of the 20 plants (or 10 per cent) of those producing its network switches and routers. To a significant extent, this is how a virtual enterprise operates.

Smart procurement policies and practices are another characteristic of well-managed virtual and real firms. Many develop their own sophisticated tools. Others are buying their tools online. One of them is jointly developed as a prototype system by the National Institute for Standards and Technology (NIST) and Enterprise Integration technologies. Known as SmartProcurement, this software employs autonomous agents over the Internet and other networks. Procurement information can be located throughout the Web in heterogeneous databases. The agents enable purchasers to increase their reach, make a focused selection and interactively execute procurement.

A SmartProcurement process is initiated by a request for quotation (RFQ) made by either an agent or a human user. As vendors for the item are being sought, a purchasing agent acquires a list of other agents who have been registered (for instance, with CommerceNet) to represent different vendors.

The RFQ is sent to those targeted agents, who then decide whether or not to bid. Bids are returned to the purchasing agent, who accumulates them before the set deadline. Subsequently, the buyer selects from the group of bids being submitted, and the winning vendor agent is automatically notified. In the meantime, however, every one of the vendor agents has to develop and maintain accounting files, including bid data and standard costs.

From procurement to manufacturing and sales, the examples given in this section can be mapped into a flexible pyramid of function like the one in Figure 9.4. The infrastructural level is the network. Over this

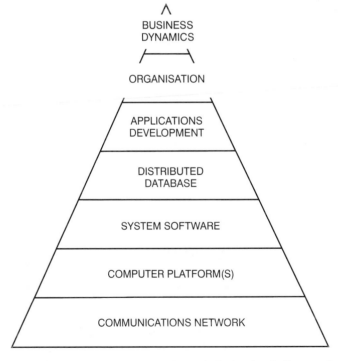

Figure 9.4   A layered architecture is advisable in facing the challenges of online trading and procurement

come service layers whose functions culminate in the support of the company's business dynamics. How well this is done, and how flexible the whole system is, are the determining factors in deciding the success or failure of the company and its business.

5   CHALLENGES POSED BY INVENTORYING CORPORATE KNOWLEDGE

By the year 2001, both the more classical transactional database and the modern *corporate memory facility* (CMF: see D.N. Chorafas, *Risk Management in Financial Institutions*, Butterworths, London, 1990) have become an integral part of practical logistics. Top-tier companies realise that their business success, growth, productivity and profitability depends on *shared knowledge*, not just on datamining and exchanging information on past transactions. Yet few organisations have done fundamental studies to establish how they can capitalise on a store of knowledge. Xerox is one of them, and it has found that:

- 46 per cent of corporate knowledge is still captured by documents in paper form.

The problem is that this knowledge is scattered all over the firm, and is often difficult to find. It is even more difficult, if not downright impossible, to exploit. Furthermore,

- 42 per cent of corporate knowledge resides in the heads of individual employees.

This is inaccessible to their colleagues, and it will leave the company as these people change employment or simply retire. Under current conditions such knowledge cannot be recovered.

- Only 12 per cent of a company's knowledge is captured in a shareable electronic memory facility.

The majority of this 12 per cent is handled through expert systems. The best managed companies believe this part is destined to grow over the coming years, at least among those firms who take seriously the issue of keeping precious corporate resources safe. Furthermore, while the knowledge base of an organisation is used mainly to represent scientific, engineering, financial and trading experience, a globalised business increasingly involves interdisciplinary fields and management decisions on a wide variety of topics. Some of these topics have become recurrent and this sees to it that knowledge artefacts are critical to accessing *and* assessing knowledge *when*, *where* and *how* it is needed.

Another major change affecting the company's management information system is taking place during the first decade of the twenty-first century. Datamining makes available online tens or hundreds of terabytes of information, but the analysis of this stored world of knowledge becomes increasingly complex as we are dealing with massive data sets (see also section 6). Effective usage of computer power requires primary, secondary and tertiary storage systems able to manage these massive data sets as they become of *petabyte* capacity.

For instance, massive data sets are held by AT&T which keeps track of *billing information* for 250 million calls each day. This results in 18 petabytes of billing data per year, which is an unprecedented storage capacity of mainly accounting information which has to be explored not at a leisurely pace but in real-time. Similar challenges are posed in merchandising concerns for logistics management, as we saw with the Wal-Mart case study in Chapter 8.

Today, such colossal database requirements are characteristic of selected industries, not of all industries. But the trend points towards them becoming much more widespread. After all, only ten years ago terabyte storage was the reserved area of only some big banks, while today it is becoming fairly common. One of the interesting aspects of this rapid growth of online storage needs is that it leads many companies to outsourcing part of their database in an effort to keep costs under control. Today, in the USA, on average database bandwidth requirements increase by about 40 per cent per year; but among new economy companies the growth is 100–120 per cent per year.

As is to be expected, this rapid growth in databasing has created major problems for data centres, and a new industry of *storage on demand* is being born. For example, Storage Networks, a US company, has developed 50 data centres coast-to-coast, each capable of storing 100 terabytes. This network of *50 petabytes* is expected to represent a capital investment of about $1 billion.

Customers outsourcing part of their database requirements look for savings not only in storage cost but also in salaries of system engineers, who command $100 000 per year or more. They also look at outsourcing some of their storage needs in the expectation that during the coming years the demand for databasing will increase further, as advances in Internet infrastructure lead to greater databasing bandwidth, and as the need for having a top-tier CMF in-house will be increasingly felt.

In the background of this reference to a steadily and rapidly growing database bandwidth lies the fact that the management of corporate knowledge, advances in Internet infrastructure and datamining are connected, as shown in Figure 9.5. They share the challenge of broadband communications and petabytes in storage. How much database bandwidth will be required during the next five years depends on:

- interactive analytics;
- other applications;
- protocols being chosen; and
- the physical layer (nodes and links)

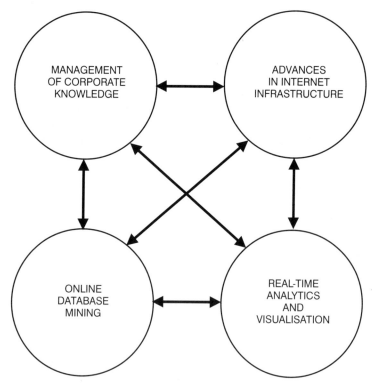

Figure 9.5   The four major reasons promoting database bandwidth impact on one another

and also on design criteria for information systems, such as efficiency, flexibility, scalability and quality of service. It is also sensible to bring to the reader's attention the fact that in terms of both network design and database design, there is significant difference between *raw bandwidth* and *useful bandwidth*. The latter is smaller than the former and this difference influences the fact that in communications we now plan for terabit per second (TPS) capacity, and (eventually) beyond; while in databasing terabyte storage capacity has become commonplace, and petabytes is the next step.

As far as sophisticated applications are concerned, there is an even greater challenge which cannot be faced without much more powerful models than those currently available. In the background of the new analytics is not only the search for management *intent*, but also the need to unearth relations which are not transparent to simpler, classical, linear models.

The AT&T billing information example, to which I made reference, demonstrates that careful evaluation and analysis of information contained in massive data sets becomes an important requirement for competitiveness. Therefore, research now focuses on determining the diameter and the pattern of *directed multigraphs*: for example, the maximum of intermediate acquaintances required to link:

- any 2 phone numbers;
- any 2 business partners;
- any 2 credit risk profiles;
- any 2 traders or investment officers.

A good example is a directed multigraph concerning investment decisions, including all necessary conditions, credit rating, growth potential, management drive, prevailing constraints, volatility in prices and other considerations. For instance, transborder investments may involve a family of crucial variables, such as currencies, equity indices and interest rates, which change all the time.

A directed multigraph can represent practically any kind of complex interaction scheme, linking variables as well as algorithms represented by trunks and nodes in the graph. The way to bet is that such links will be dynamically changing. Analytical results show that complex pattern analysis will replace correlation coefficients in non-linearities and other environments where linear models are no longer useful. Let us keep this in mind when we talk about the challenges currently present in accounting and logistics.

6 WAREHOUSING POLICIES, INVENTORY CONTROL AND MASSIVE DATA SETS

Amazon.com is spending a large amount of money on advertising to attract customers, but also holds a formidable cost edge over rivals such as Barnes & Noble (B&N). When not long ago Amazon.com was posting an annual sales rate of $1.2 billion, this was equal to about 235 Barnes & Noble bricks-and-mortar superstores. Because of the efficiencies of selling over the Net, Amazon has spent only $56 million on fixed assets, such as computers and warehouses, whereas B&N has spent $472 million on its 100 or so stores, which amounts to 843 per cent more money. The fact that Amazon's investment in new warehouses can support $15 billion in sales is another major 'plus' from Internet commerce. Financial analysts say this is one of the reasons why its $21.2 billion market capitalisation is of more than an order of magnitude greater than the $1.8 billion of B&N.

Warehousing and inventory management constitute a major challenge for both wholesalers and retailers. Supermarket chains and their suppliers have been at the sharp end of the logistics process which engulfs both manufacturing and distribution industries. A good example comes from the frozen food business where faulty delivery patterns cause overstocking and cost big money. Miscalculations leave shelves empty, and empty shelves are disappointing for customers. Also, delays and other mistakes take the chill off frozen foods and are therefore disastrous for the bottom line.

As far as the frozen food industry is concerned, changes in terms of delivery delays can have dramatic implications for any company. Longer delays are associated with firms whose monitoring and control system is less than perfect, and 'perfect' is a moving target. Distributors who are operating by classical ratios and rule of thumb are unable to face the business challenges which loom in the market.

Can we address the problems posed by integrated logistics in a way which makes sense in a highly competitive environment? Can we do so by building the system which we need in one stroke? The answer to the first query is quite definitely 'Yes!', but it is negative to the second question. An efficient warehousing and inventory management solution cannot and should not be done monolithically, even if bog systems are not small systems which have outgrown their former boundaries.

Figure 9.6 presents a better solution than most currently available. It advises on the wisdom of adopting a transition policy which rests on a grand design. After having established the larger perspective of the big

1. MAKING FULL INVENTORY OF ACTIVITIES

2. PROJECTING THE BIG PICTURE

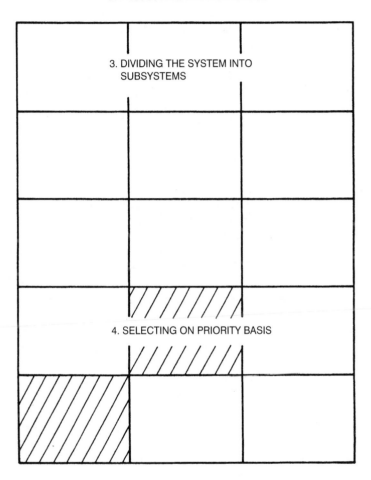

3. DIVIDING THE SYSTEM INTO SUBSYSTEMS

4. SELECTING ON PRIORITY BASIS

5. EXECUTING THE PRIORITY SUBSYSTEMS

6. CONTROLLING THE QUALITY OF WORK

7. PROGRESSING TOWARDS COMPLETION OF TOTAL SYSTEM

Figure 9.6   Establishing a transition policy within the framework of an enterprise architecture

system, which includes the goals to be attained when the whole is in place, it splits the grand design into manageable parts, assigns priorities and follows a building block approach.

Importing this type of solution into the broader business environment requires a properly thought-out methodology and effective usage of it for the purposes of applications building. It also calls for the development and use of knowledge engineering artefacts, as discussed in the preceding sections. One of the building blocks in Figure 9.6 will be analytical accounting, another cost control, and still others will interface with:

- online complex transaction processing; and
- the distributor's growing data management needs.

One can already see a significant number of associated accounting applications along the lines being discussed, not only because of synergy between procurement, warehousing and inventory control, but also because each one of these applications needs sophisticated data management with credit and debit balances. Accounting accuracy is indispensable while the commercial world is progressing towards greater complexity in modelling, with quantitative formulas and number crunching routines which until recently were primarily used in the technical world.

As we will see in Chapter 10, there are also real-time data filtering and data fusion problems, with a number of similarities between merchandising, banking and other industries. In the financial world, for instance, institutions which act as market makers have tremendous quantities of incoming data, representing a world-wide market. An important question then is: 'Can we make sense out of massive data in a way which is fast enough and accurate enough?' As we have seen, such a challenge is already present at AT&T and other big communications companies. However, it is fast spreading into other industry sectors, finance being an example.

The answer to many problems associated with complex trading and investment decisions is to be found in the management of *massive data sets*, a concept introduced in section 5. The message is that new mathematical techniques are necessary, and they are being developed to handle massive data whose importance in decision support is a phenomenon of the last five years. In principle, massive data sets contain collections of information whose size is measured in millions of gigabytes or terabytes. Examples include the databases of big multinational corporations, from money-centre banks to global manufacturing and service companies.

The careful reader will remember that AT&T keeps track of billing information for roughly 250 million phone calls each day. Every record includes: the caller's number, the number of the person or company called, time of day, duration of call, pricing information, discounts, and so on. Practically nothing can be discarded.

While individually meaningless, the information elements contained in the 18 million gigabytes (18 petabytes) to which I made reference fit together to form a *pattern* which is a huge mathematical structure. It represents the interconnectedness of the 300 million phone numbers known to AT&T's computers. The scope of datamining is torturing the information elements to reveal their secrets.

Torturing (or patterning) massive data sets is no easy job. It requires not only supercomputers but also a great deal of ingenuity. A multi-graph developed by AT&T involved 123 million connections among 53 million numbers. The largest cluster was found to contain at least 30 numbers. Defined in company jargon as a *clique*, this cluster of phone numbers is a grouping of all the names who call each other on the same day.

Complex derivative instruments, particularly products of structured financing, with their underliers, pricing algorithms, exposure limits, bilateral agreements around the globe and secondary markets have similarly complex patterns. Because decisions without risk patterning are more or less blind, careful analysis of information contained in massive data sets has become an increasingly important requirement in the capital markets.

1 In the case of global phone companies it helps with both pricing and infrastructure planning and financing.
2 For warehousing and merchandising firms, the exploitation of massive data sets holds the key to successful marketing.
3 In finance, trading commitment can end in disaster without the visibility provided through patterns.

Pattern analysis in these non-linear environments is aimed at answering questions such as: what's the user profile of *our* supposedly best clients? Is current pricing rewarding this user profile? Are we taking too many risks with certain major counterparties? Which pairs of counterparties deal with each other most often? Such concepts are the result of the diffusion of financial products in the new environment of bank intermediation, as well as of social behaviour at large.

One challenge of pattern analysis connected to massive data sets is to find new mathematical tools able to hold their own when faced with a very large quantity of data. Another challenge is to develop metrics which are generally understood and appreciated. (for instance, determining the diameter of multigraphs). An example is the maximum number of intermediate acquaintances required to link:

- any 2 phone numbers;
- any 2 parties in a supply chain;
- any 2 derivatives traders;
- any 2 investors; or
- any 2 financial products.

This is only an intermediate objective, not the ultimate one. Once the 'any two' challenge has been met, the next goal would be 'any three' and then 'any n'. Not only analytical models but also accounting standards and tools must follow this progression because, in the final analysis, globalisation presents senior management with increasingly complex situations, and there is a pressing need to analyse and understand them, as well as to foretell their effect on risk and on the bottom line.

7   WHY SOPHISTICATED LOGISTICS SOLUTIONS MEAN MARKET CLOUT

The examples presented in sections 4 to 6 helped us to appreciate the fact that sophisticated logistics represent a major competitive advantage which tier-1 companies cannot afford to forgo. This is true all the way down to the distribution end, where thousands of suppliers (large and small) are feeling the effects of a vast consolidation under way in retailing. In category after category of merchandising, giant power retailers are using advanced mathematical models to:

- optimise inventory management;
- finely tune product selections; and
- establish competitive pricing policies.

All three issues are instrumental in crowding out weaker players who cannot live up to the challenge. The winners are those companies which are better positioned than others to determine exactly what the customer wants to buy, and then provide it at an affordable price and in timely fashion. Triumphing over the less well organised firms are superpower retailers such as Wal-Mart (see also Chapter 8).

By means of online database mining, retailers can monitor sales through a wealth of statistics. They also exploit in real-time data streams created at the checkout counter. Mathematical models for fast flow replenishment help to restock the shelves before a product is sold out. Tomorrow, smart technology will actuate an even more dynamic data flow and put into play models for fast flow replenishment without human intervention. Working upstream and downstream using the Internet supply chain, smart technology will:

- reach from the checkout counter the giant warehouses at the source of the chain;
- help in controlling stock loss and pilferage through automatic identification of each item; and
- improve product availability at the racks of retail stores through more efficient inventory management.

As envisioned by an ongoing Internet supply chain project at MIT, smart materials will be endowed with an electronic product code (ePC) carried on radio-frequency tags. These are little more than silicon microchips embedded between sheets of paper lined with conductive ink. Such chips will be identifiable to grids of computer-based readers in warehouses and retail outlets. The readers will themselves be linked to the Internet and therefore to the global supply chain.

What I am saying is not a futuristic projection bordering on science fiction, but a step beyond what is done today. For instance, as a matter-of-course application, Wal-Mart records every sale in thousands of its stores in the USA in large database computers used for honing its market strategies. Database mining is instrumental not only in helping management to master the company's marshalling yards channelling goods to its stores, but also in promoting its global sales effort.

Capitalising on its just in time inventory management and its high quality logistics operations, Dell Computer designed its newest factory with no room allocated for inventory storage. Through the efficient use of high technology, just prior to its merger with Daimler, Chrysler increased production without building factories. Model-based marketing campaigns, just in time inventory and fast flow replenishment are not just manufacturing success stories which differentiate winners from losers: they are global examples of thousands of new business practices made possible by the effective use of state-of-the-art technology and its tools.

Unearthing what makes the customers tick and which are going to be the market's future requirements is no crystal ball business. Along with management drive, it takes a great deal of high-powered computation running sophisticated models to serve the real-time needs of huge mass merchants and their markets, and therefore to serve the public. The heroes in this battlefield are rocket scientists and computer experts.

The principles of integrated logistics embrace the advanced functions of market performance, all the way to the storage and handling of goods and raw materials. This reference evidently includes interfacing with business partners. From proper handling of customer requirements to purchasing operations and relations with suppliers, the new logistics is vital in the battle to make industry and commerce:

- leaner in personnel requirements;
- lighter in terms of carrying costs; and
- more responsive to market needs.

Thanks to better logistics support, whose effects reach all the way to price tags, consumers are flocking to new retailing channels which, as a result, increase their market clout. They patronise warehouse clubs and the tightly focused firms known as *category killers*, which are taking over sales of everything from toys to tyres. Some experts estimate that such speciality stores, along with warehouse clubs, have a share of appliance sales of over 30 per cent, and this share is growing.

Through knowledge robots, sophisticated models, intelligent networks, global databases and computer power, today's topmost retailers are steadily squeezing costs out of the system for distributing consumer goods. Wal-Mart holds its operating and selling expenses to 15 per cent of sales, as against 28 per cent for Sears Roebuck and other retailers who have been slow in revamping their culture and their technology.

Costs matter, and a rigorous cost control not only helps to improve profitability, but it also assists in improving market share, as much of those savings are passed on to consumers. The super-efficient warehouse clubs provide a good example. A McKinsey study found that they offer 26 per cent lower prices than those found at traditional supermarkets. This is one of technology's contributions towards keeping inflation in check.

Companies which are ahead of the curve exercise steady pressure in an industry-wide sense. Cost pressure from power retailers is forcing manufacturers to become leaner and more low profile, and the growing importance of retailer hypermarkets tends to favour big suppliers at the expense of the smaller, particularly those unable to keep up with steady cost control and with technology. It is usually the more technologically advanced manufacturers that have the capacity to produce on time the huge quantities required by hypermarkets. Only a supplier with multiple product lines can offer big retailers an efficient way to buy many different products, provided it has the appropriate logistics support.

Seen from a different perspective, what I am saying is not a matter of size but of management ability. Whether a company is big or small, the winners in the retail game are in command of online computer-based experimentation and network hook-ups, so that the right products hit the shelves at the right time. Because inflexible manufacturers drop out and more efficient companies move in, hypermarkets know that they can steadily cut costs. They also appreciate that if they pass on the sav-

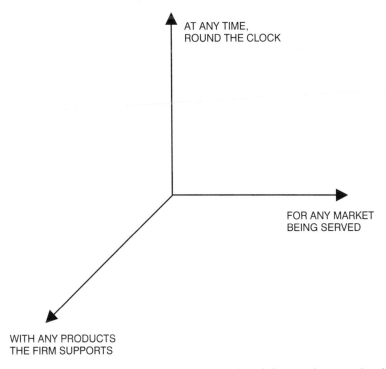

Figure 9.7 The solution space for integrated logistics can be served only through high performance computing power

ings, they will be able to deliver to their customers better conditions and deals their competitors cannot easily match.

In conclusion, the integrated logistics which a national or multinational marketing company makes available to itself must address any market and any product at any time, not just some of them, some of the time. Figure 9.7 identifies the solution space by following these three axes of reference. Limited approaches will not respond to the growing needs of a demanding market, because those who rest on their laurels or take nearsighted shortcuts forget that, as Mies van der Rohe aptly said: 'God is in the detail.'

10 How Time-Constrained Applications and Data Filtration Impact on Accounting and Logistics

1 INTRODUCTION

Time-constrained applications are often conducted at scales of size and complexity whose ramifications are poorly understood prior to analysis and establishment of the critical variables. Therefore, many projects are undertaken without an adequate definition and follow-up of what underlines each one of the applications they target. Under these conditions, it is difficult to reduce the risk of unknown factors or the likelihood of computer-related failures.

Nobody can forgo technological advances and survive in the longer term. This is true for a wide range of implementations, varying from the global risk management necessary to keep a financial institution out of trouble to anti-submarine warfare and next-generation medical imaging. State-of-the art signal and image processing is at the heart of a wide range of sophisticated applications. It also constitutes an excellent example of time-constrained usage of software, computers and communications.

The concepts the preceding two paragraphs have presented have been traditionally associated with high technology, its markets and its products, but they are now migrating from the corporate environment and entering the consumer market in a big way. There are reasons for this transition: take the automobile industry as an example.

MIT's Centre for Transportation Studies has addressed the dual effect of disruptive demographics and Internet commerce. In redefining the automobile consumer, it has come up with the intriguing conclusion that present-day car buyers are increasingly older: fifty-plus, healthier, wealthier and wiser than their parents' generation. These consumers have clout: they compose 20 per cent of the population, but have more than 40 per cent of the disposable income. To meet their needs, says Joseph F. Coughlin, the director of the Centre for Transportation Studies, cars must be designed to accommodate drivers with reduced vision, decreased strength and flexibility, and diminished attention and perception. Older automobile consumers want personalised services, and regular follow-up for maintenance and for performance monitoring. Market requirements change.

This is not what the motor vehicle market used to be. James B. Rice, Jr, director of the MIT Integrated Supply Chain Management Program, adds that unlike what some believe, supply chain management is very complex. Within the firm, it spans product development, procurement, production, distribution, after-sales support and recycling, which is *reverse logistics*. It is increasingly important to include the raw material source of *our* firm's supplier, and consumption (the customers who make or break a product).

'The four flows of the supply chain – materials, information, funds, and knowledge – are not simply linear,' says Rice. 'Together, they look like a bowl of spaghetti' (*MIT Report*, July/August 2000). Supply chain integration requires connecting and co-ordinating these four flows. It also calls for developing the appropriate infrastructure which can support them in the longer run. Data filtration is part of this process.

The problem is not only timely and accurate data but also the need to provide distilled information in an orderly fashion. This can be achieved through real-time data filtration. One of the challenges is that a synopsis of data streams or, alternatively, what passes through a classical filter, is not necessarily what is required for a golden horde of logistics and accounting issues. Data filtration must become flexible and adaptable. Many problems in the way of doing so are organisational; others are technical and have to do with the manner in which we use our company's information technology.

2   ACCOUNTING PRACTICES, DATA FILTRATION AND DYNAMIC PATTERNING

Data filtration is a generic name used to describe a variety of processes characterised by delivering information *after* appropriate massaging. Because the distinction between filtration (or filtering) and other handling procedures, such as data collection, retrieval, routing, datamining, classification and imaging, is not necessarily as clear as it should be, I will take a few paragraphs to explain these issues.

As a start, a great deal of the challenge lies in the fact that highly competitive, management-oriented applications require real-time data capture and processing. Increasingly our attention focuses on continuous streams of *high frequency* data. *Patterns* must be developed and visualised practically in real-time. Without high speed filtering, however, the resulting information is weak because it contains lots of noise. When this happens, the information we get is neither accurate nor comprehensive.

Noise is any unwanted input. Even chamber music is noise when one wants to sleep. In business, noise connected to information elements is situational, and it often (though not always) regards data unnecessary at the present time, or irrelevant to the decision which has to be made. Besides this, one person's noise is another person's knowledge. Filtration takes care of such noise, permitting us to focus on a given issue in a more efficient manner than the massive data sets usually associated with computing. The problem lies in accounting for the criteria of filtration. Filtered data responds to management information requirements, and not to the complete transcription required by the accounting journal.

This is shown in Figure 10.1 which suggests there is a bifurcation in the requirements of two functions: general accounting and management accounting. In a way, the latter resembles military situations in field environments where large streams of data must be processed in real-time signal and image for handling purposes. Timely execution of signal processing can mean the difference between life and death. For many civilian applications, in banking and in manufacturing, high speed processing of complex models is also an important consideration for

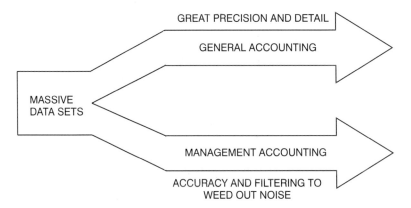

Figure 10.1   There is a bifurcation in accounting requirements according to the chosen implementation domain

profit and loss reasons. Because they involve an increasing amount of advanced signal and image handling, several financial and business processing applications have become time-constrained in nature. The required performance sets them apart from what traditional business statistics and leisurely verbal reporting procedures can offer; now the emphasis is on *analytics*. Signal and image processing applications pose challenges such as profiling, patterning, *visibilisation* (the ability to perceive the very big and the very small) and *visistraction* (the ability to 'see' notions, concepts and ideas). Their handling leads to complex software requirements. Real-time interactive computing assisted by agents distinguishes these applications from others of a more classical number-crunching nature.

Solutions to the problems I have just outlined should evidently consider the synergy between technology (software, computers and communications) on the one hand, and its users on the other. Over several decades there has been a confusion in performance requirements between signal/image processing and classical scientific computing.

As Figure 10.2 suggests, data transmission rate and high performance computing correlate. Some applications, such as signal and image processing, require machines of two or three orders of magnitude faster than

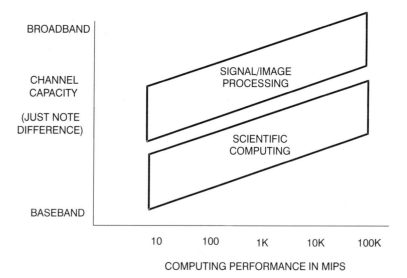

Figure 10.2   Performance requirements and processing characteristics of time-sensitive applications are distinct from those of number crunching

those needed for more traditional scientific applications. In business, too, a growing number of implementation areas have become most demanding in high-performance computing and broadband communications systems.

Company after company in different industry sectors is finding out that research undertaken to help understand filtration problems better has a substantial payoff with regard to future business. Properly tuned filtering procedures help to revise downwards the cost of real-time implementation in complex environments. The impact of what I just said starts being felt in all branches of industry, military as well as civilian (the latter ranging from manufacturing to banking).

One of the reasons why the degree of required timeliness and accuracy from different filtering processes is difficult to identify and address in a consistent manner lies in the hidden features of many application domains. Another key reason is the greater sensitivity required in the filtering process itself. Among the basic characteristics to keep in mind are that:

- the more complex filtration systems are usually designed for *unstructured* or *semistructured* information environments and their dataflows;
- while the better established filtration processes usually address themselves to the more classical applications that involve *structured* data.

The concept of a structured and an unstructured information environment is not a subject of this text. Typically, structured information not only conforms to a given format but also consists of relatively simple and known data types, each with well-defined meaning and fairly stable, even static, behaviour. This is nowhere to be found in an unstructured information environment, where vagueness and uncertainty dominate, *ad hoc* information requirements are the rule, and there is a very significant need for flexibility.

In principle, structured information environments exist in a business enterprise at the bottom of the organisational pyramid. This is shown in Figure 10.3. By contrast, an organisation's higher-up levels are characterised by semistructured and unstructured information environments, which call for appropriate filtering processes and impose their own modelling characteristics. Filtration, modelling and patterning are key words on which rests an advanced mode of information processing, in any organisation. Image recognition is a specific implementation example

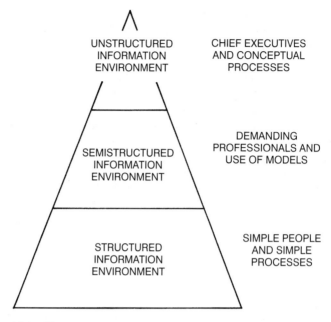

Figure 10.3 The structure of an information environment correlates with its intended usage

which, as a time-constrained application, requires high performance computing and sophisticated software.

People accustomed to working with mainframes tend to think that filtering incoming data streams or accessing the content of databases is primarily an input/output problem. That is the wrong concept. The right notion is that *filtering* aims to decrease not only the noise in data streams but also the amount of entropy, by means of mathematical processes. Whether they are applied to science or to the business world, the solutions we use in filtration have a similarity to one another. In engineering, we have been classically using physical filters. In business, the important issue is real-time logical filters rather than physical filters.

Let me explain another term, which is equally important in engineering and in business. *Entropy* is a measure of the information content of a message. Typically, it is evaluated in terms of its uncertainty, which tends to increase with time rather than the other way around. One of the business applications with filtering, which is intended to decrease the existing level of entropy, is the case of data bought from information providers such as Reuters and Bloomberg.

Measures taken for the reduction of entropy and decisions concerning data filtration in a business environment correlate. A difficulty experienced with the development and use of a filtration system is that of determining how well the algorithms and heuristics developed for filters are performing in practical business cases, and particularly in reducing the amount of entropy, and helping to create patterns and profiles. This dual job involves several challenges. Business filters must be specific to a certain situation, and effective in meeting chosen goals. General purpose filtration is what is practised by dictatorial regimes, not by business people. Neither is this a matter of a one-off solution. At any point in time, certain descriptors in a profile may perform well in matching relevant information elements, while others do not. We must be able to tell the difference.

One way to keep appraised of the effectiveness of our artefacts is to provide a feedback on how well an algorithm is matched against the sought-after profile. Feedback permits the setting aside of some filter elements, specifically those descriptors which are not performing in profiling, thereby allowing us to improve the deliverables.

In conclusion, the challenge with dynamic patterning in the business world is not to weed out input data streams a priori, but to do a first-class filtering job on them. 'We measure everything that moves, and we measure everything that does not move,' said a senior vice president of AT&T in a meeting which followed the launch of the carrier's successful credit card. His response was in answer to the query: 'What's the secret of the success of the Connect card?' Feedback conforming to well-chosen criteria is fundamental to the improvement of any process. Unless the underlying pattern is unearthed, a data stream may become inconsequential.

3   THE MESSAGE CONVEYED BY A PATTERN OF REAL-TIME FINANCIAL DATA

Both for analytical purposes and for reasons of adaptation, the design of a system addressing itself to filtering and patterning must be flexible, so that selections and changes in the way a particular data filter operates can effectively be made without discontinuities in operation. For instance, there may be a need for *ad hoc* changes to the descriptors, to provide a better match to a new type of financial reports we are after. Algorithms that result in documents that are well rated by their users could receive increased weight; by contrast, those whose popularity waned should be downgraded or weeded out.

This is a strategy we follow most often in engineering projects worth their salt. Many people fail to appreciate that engineering is not a static process. There is variation both in the factors we deal with, and in expected outcomes. Both end product specifications and the materials we use evolve over time. Also, optimisation requires discarding past models that have started to fade, or vastly improving upon them.

Compared to the creative genius of engineering, manufacturing seems to be a highly repetitive activity, but here too there is variation and evolution in requirements. Over and above that come the marketing needs. The whole concept of optimisation in logistics lies in this simple fact. In this whole complex of activities, models and algorithms are never static; as dynamic conditions change, our concepts and our models must be adapted to them or changed altogether.

To achieve its goal, a filtering process must be carried out interactively in accordance with specific criteria which help to retain only what is essential. Such criteria are themselves subject to a steady process of adaptation and change. Filtration is vital inasmuch as data (for instance, market data) is often voluminous, snowing under information elements which are rich in content and valuable in making decisions.

Data filtration is more important with the Internet than in connection with any private business-to-business network. When carried out on a level playing field its goal is often *customer focus*. Companies must be committed to helping their clients to become more agile in their decisions. This can be done, for instance, by implementing models that will position them in a fast-paced business environment. Customer focus is the best strategy for continued benefits from end-to-end systems. Patterning is also necessary for controlling the state of a system itself, including design and operating changes.

Among the key variables we find time and again in a business model are competitive position, manufacturing capacity, marketing network, distribution system, supply chain arrangements and their evolution. The recognition of evolving patterns in any one of these factors is crucial for financial management and accounting reasons, including derivatives activity, regulatory developments, future investments, or potential acquisitions.

Design, production and marketing are not the only important domains. Plenty remains to be done in other areas, where data filtration plays a key role. Since the quality of management is critical to credit quality, bankers, treasurers and investors try to get an understanding of a company's plans for the future (D.N. Chorafas, *Managing Credit Risk*, Volume 1, *Analysing, Rating and Pricing the Probability of Default*, Euromoney, London, 2000). This requires patterning of financial and operating data. A financial pattern is a presentation which helps management to identify risks and opportunities that could affect credit quality sometime in the future. Patterns underpin statistical forecasts and projections as useful indicators of a company's ability for meeting the market(s') demand.

A similar statement is valid at a more complex level, concerning the pattern of the economy as whole, and its specific sectors. For instance, the pattern of growth and profitability of the banking sector and its products is instrumental in representing the status of the economy. The pattern of financial instruments in a *mature economy* is substantially different from those of a *developing economy*. This difference in patterns serves as a guide in strategic choices which must be made by senior management of credit institutions, and the selection of banking products most favoured at a given state of economic development.

However, sometimes the underlying pattern is most difficult to decipher because of entropy, noise or other factors. For example, there is a strategic weakness among big credit institutions resulting from mergers and acquisitions. This concerns their ability to capture and add value to transaction-generated client information, which may be revealing of personal preferences and/or trends. Such failure is a negative because financial institutions need more clout than simply being bigger than their competitors: they have to be wizards in exploiting their customer base, but few of them do so in an effective manner.

Today anyone in a position to capture client information, whether from banking transactions, loans, credit cards, insurance policies or Web sites, employs specialised contractors to derive value from these data streams. A popular field of activity is that of redefining the banking products to be promoted. Unless credit institutions leverage the revenue potential of their client base at least as well as their competitors are doing, they risk becoming a sort of faceless back office.

These and many other references help to show that keeping ahead of the competition requires lots of skill, but skill is often lost as a consequence of mergers. Deutsche Bank's $9 billion acquisition of Bankers Trust was followed by high profile defections by the 'stars' the German bank had paid so much to acquire. Citibank's and Traveller's merger left Citigroup with a $1 billion headache in the form of some 150 000 different types of account which had to be effectively managed. This had to be done through an information system run on 28 different computer platforms yet, as senior management found out after the merger, many of these platforms did not talk to one another.

Pattern analysis is also necessary for cost-cutting, but the bad practice of using average costs, and missing information, blurs the pattern of expenses. Until otherwise proven through hard data, mergers usually lead to higher costs. Cost ratios in both Swiss banking and UK insurance have grown rather than fallen despite what was seen as significant consolidation. Royal & Sun Alliance, for instance, has delivered only a fraction of the cost savings that were used to justify the merger.

A retrograde information technology is another impediment to real-time analysis of data streams, and the establishment of characteristic patterns. As I never tire of repeating, the problem in the twenty-first century is not just poor information technology investments but also, if not primarily, the fact that such investments are disconnected from the business strategy. An important challenge is to rapidly realign IT investments when business changes, whether this is part of a plan or is done unexpectedly. Top industry leaders see this fast adaptation as their salient problem; however, lesser men and women do not care about such discontinuities.

Every Board and every CEO should be aware of the need to achieve a low latency level in keeping IT investments and strategies aligned. *Zero latency* allows an organisation to direct its product development, marketing and technology money more efficiently.

According to some estimates, between 5 and 10 per cent of the Fortune 500 companies already have planning mechanisms and architectural processes in place which allow them to readily re-engineer their information technology, and to do so faster than their competitors. There is another 20 per cent that understands the need to take such action, and either is, or is getting active in, rethinking their IT processes, business strategies and flexible information technology planning solutions. But the majority of companies have not yet woken up to the challenges posed by the Internet age.

4 BETTER ACCOUNTING PROCEDURES REQUIRE SIMULATION AT THE ENDUSER END

Using sophisticated technology such as collaboration filtering, vendors can provide themselves with on-target information, including recommendations for different products. Eventually new product designers will be able to analyse market data online, asking businesses and consumers what they want to see available, at what price, with what sort of characteristics. This will enable companies to sell first, then produce.

Both organisational infrastructure and technological support are necessary to properly implement the filtration process described in the preceding paragraph, as well as in sections 2 and 3. Throwing money at the problem by buying more equipment is no solution at all. Data filtration and patterning is not done in the abstract, but in relation to specific criteria which have critical data stream requirements and database retrieval needs.

These needs have to be served through appropriate, knowledge-enriched software for *database mining* and for *simulation*. Simulation is a working analogy. (See D.N. Chorafas, *Systems and Simulation*, Academic Press, New York, 1965.) When we find systems which are analogous to one another, we can use one to predict the behaviour of the other. The growing use of simulation is becoming a very effective management link, enhancing communications between:

- consumers and industrial or merchandising companies; and
- researchers, engineers, manufacturing and marketing experts.

Similarly, motor vehicle companies now request their suppliers to provide not only data sheets but also simulators of their components. For reasons of experimentation and optimisation, they emulate the whole solution of a power train and/or car body by incorporating the supply chain simulators. Co-simulation environments see to it that multiple mathematical models can run simultaneously, and co-simulators are also important in promoting multidisciplinary research and development. Simulators do not need to be complex. Simplification in modelling can take many forms, from leaving out secondary factors, to limiting the range of variation. Setting limits allows us to benefit from possible linearities existing within these limits, and therefore it helps to make simulation more accessible to smaller companies with lesser skills.

A good approach is breaking down a problem into smaller constituent parts. Producing light versions of existing products and processes eases the modelling job but it also requires the combination of partial results with different options. In turn, this calls for understanding what makes something complex. This is a rewarding exercise in analysis. Simulation has two major component parts:

- mathematical models mapping the real-life product or process; and
- rich databases which can be mined online, interactively.

Systems concepts fairly similar to those of filtering processes which have been described in the preceding sections apply to database mining operations. The latter exploit in real-time multimedia information resources accumulated over a period of years. The basic notion is that of *torturing* the database until it confesses its secrets. To be effective as database mining instruments, the tools we use must be sophisticated and able to identify and exploit an emerging pattern.

Knowledge artefacts play an important role in this process. Take financial transactions as an example, and say we wish to apply AT&T's strategy of tracking events and non-events. Agents are mining the distributed databases of *our* bank's transaction universe, identifying costs, risk and value embedded in each transaction. Other agents search for non-events: transactions which should normally be expected to happen but which do not may be explained by the client executing them through a different institution. As Figure 10.4 shows, the pattern of events and non-events can be nicely plotted in a 3-dimensional space

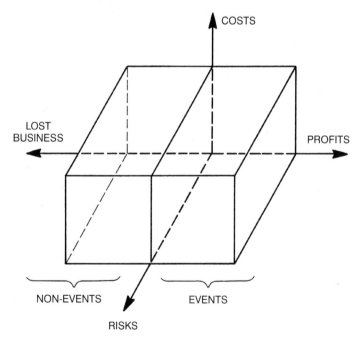

Figure 10.4   Any financial transaction has costs and risks, but also profits (a different model prevails with non-events)

graph. Alert management can detect that pattern, and immediately take appropriate action.

Whether used with an incoming data stream or in connection with database mining, filters and simulators present users with the opportunity to analyse the data and/or multimedia objects most relevant to their immediate needs. Through the proper artefacts, they can do so while avoiding burdening themselves with large volumes of irrelevant information. The questions to ask then are:

- how accurately should the end-user requirements be expressed;
- how can filters be specified, developed and/or acquired; and
- how can their usage take place in a time-sensitive form?

The answer is to build personalised models, each addressing a specific user need, in full understanding of the fact that it is not easy for each individual user to specify precise interests at any and every moment, unless he or she has been trained to do so. Furthermore, the models we develop must be flexible, adaptable and able to learn on the job (which is possible). Fuzzy engineering can help (see D.N. Chorafas, *Chaos Theory in the Financial Markets*, Probus, Chicago, 1994). It is advisable to keep in mind that the nature and precision requirements of information filtering and patterning differ among individual users, while at the same time critical application-oriented factors are changing. The user's interests are often related to a dynamic set of goals, address specific information types, and have other characteristics which evolve over time.

The careful reader will not fail to notice that there are reasons why so much attention is paid to data filtration, patterning and simulation in a book on Internet supply chains and their impact on accounting and logistics. The world of smart materials which is around the corner will produce a tremendous amount of data. Chapters 8 and 9 have brought this fact to the reader's attention through the discussion on massive data sets.

If companies and their senior executives are to avoid data indigestion, they have no other choice than to filter, massage and pattern such large amounts of information. This is by no means a manual job, and neither is it possible through Cobol programs and mainframes. The only way is mobile agents – a whole family of them – along with simulators, filters and pattern analysers.

Checking for patterns is necessary but not enough to model the enduser's specific interests in acquiring knowledge and information at any moment. Semantic and contextual references must also be used and they should be appropriately encoded, enabling the effective filtering of information flows and databased references. The user's own definition of what he or she considers to be the right filter encourages a conceptualisation of factors which must be present in database search, and can serve as an indicator of his or her evolving professional interests in real-time experimentation.

Key words which have been employed in the past for information selection and retrieval processes are not enough to satisfy developing job requirements, since they particularly apply to a structured environment and are derived from past events. By contrast, we now address databasing and dataflow problems which are semistructured, or even not structured at all.

In the final analysis, different users have different requirements in connection with database mining. Even the same user may have a variety of needs to satisfy in terms of information at different times, when he signs on to his company's database or to public databases. In a business environment, crucial queries often associated with datamining include the following.

1   Which characteristics describe, and/or permit the monitoring of customer behaviour, or buying patterns?
2   What is it important to know about customer habits, or about profit and loss from a given customer?
3   How does a product behave in each of the markets to which it is addressed, and what is its market penetration, or its profit margin?
4   What risk are we taking with a given financial instrument? How does this compare to other instruments we know better?

These and other queries cannot be answered in a structured form because the market, the counterparty's behaviour, the cash flow, the P&L figures and the risk factors we are confronted with steadily change, and also because the same question will not be asked again in exactly the same manner. Indeed, a given business challenge will probably not present itself the same way next time around.

5   STEPS IN DEVELOPING A BETTER APPROACH TO PATTERN RECOGNITION

Not only is business getting increasingly globalised, but also the databases, simulators, filtration processes and tools for analysis of patterns are becoming more complex. Purchasing alliances on the Internet (see Chapter 3) are a good example of the need for ERP software and database access across a variety of corporate landscapes, usually involving heterogeneous platforms and incompatible data structures.

The GM/Fiat cross-holding agreement of early 2000 has implications all the way from engineering design and manufacturing to marketing. Experts think it will impact on both the European and South American markets of the two firms. Although GM and Fiat have a strong presence in these markets, the potential for joint development of platform and powertrain strategies, especially in the small- and medium-car sectors, will make them an even more potent force in products where:

- profit margins are already squeezed to a minimum; and
- economies of scale are the only route to profitability.

This poses stringent information technology and organisation prerequisites. If GM and Fiat use the same number to specify two different items in inventory and these are synonyms, the computer will interpret these codes as belonging to the same item. It can also happen in reverse. If the same component has two different numbers, one in GM and another in Fiat, this will be interpreted by the computer as two different pieces, messing up schedules.

One of the major hurdles with mergers, alliances and cross-holdings is the huge time lag in stretching our inventory coding problems and control procedures. Few companies realise that item-by-item classification plays a pivotal role in streamlining inventory management procedures and in providing the basis for an effective logistics support. I write this based on personal experience in classification and identification of assets, from everything entering the inventory of raw materials, semi-finished goods and ready products, to factories, machinery, accounts, statistics, records and everything else which helps the hand of management. This experience comes from rigorous identification and classification projects with Osram (a German global lamp manufacturing company) and Italcementi (the leader in cement production and sales in Italy). Today, a company's classification and identification system should run in real-time in full knowledge of the fact that the use of online classification solutions acts as a sponge on computer power. Even in preparatory organisational work focusing on classification, there are difficulties in fully characterising classes of real-world objects. These arise from different sources. Materials classes generally *do not have crisp definitions*. Hence, they are often defined in a fuzzy manner, unless a rigorous classification effort is made, including part designs.

From personal experience I can add that it is not always obvious whether a certain configuration is or is not a given object. At best, we can assign it a degree of membership in a class of objects, while accounting for the fact that the space of configurations of object parts has many degrees of freedom, even if the parts themselves are as simple as pieces consisting of straight line segments.

To characterise the class of a given object we must define its membership function over a high-dimensional space. This involves *semantic* issues, which have to be handled in a way which can provide insight and foresight for further action. Such problems cannot be handled shot-by-shot. We must work within the confines of a master classification plan.

Ironically, the classification job is made more difficult because of a characteristic of many industrial, business and financial applications: their semantic richness, and the fact they often require support by unstructured messages, annotations, special communications, and so on. What I have said so far about seamless cross-database access and the classification/identification needs correlation.

Co-operative efforts are not the only ones encountering the organisational challenges I have just described. Many experts believe mergers and acquisitions (M&A) often end up at a loss, as a form of musical chairs takes place. But M&A experts usually forget another very important factor, namely classification problems, and, therefore, hurdles in inventory management.

The merger of Daimler with Chrysler is an example. Before having sorted out its many technical problems, DaimlerChrysler entered into a strategic alliance with Mitsubishi Motors, which transformed the German–American group into a global firm with engineering, manufacturing and purchasing in the three big automotive markets: North America, Europe and Japan. On the positive side, the latter move provided the company with instant access to Mitsubishi's direct injection technology and small car platforms. But engineering co-ordination and inventory management pose daunting problems.

Part and parcel of the bad news is that all on its own a piece of paper signed when an alliance is concluded is by no stretch of the imagination enough to provide business benefits or solve technical problems. What is definitely needed is data filtration and database mining in a cross-alliance pattern, combining:

- usually heterogeneous enterprise resource planning systems;
- fairly complex, multi-lingual Internet supply chain requirements; and
- advance management information solutions, at whose kernel is pattern recognition.

Historically, the unique and demanding needs of signal and image processing applications have dictated the use of dedicated pattern or image recognition systems designed from special-purpose components. Technology and its powerful commodity microprocessors did away with such a need, but we have to return to the fundamentals in order to solve management information problems. A knowledge-enriched system for image recognition should be able to emulate the concepts of perpetual saliency for parts, properties and relations. Humans base themselves on introspection to handle the requirements posed by this process. Sophisticated software does the same, because it is made by humans and for human use, but sophisticated software has organisational, classification and identification prerequisites which few companies really appreciate.

Managerial requirements come over and above this technical perspective. Filtering must satisfy priorities, schedules and control activities which go beyond computing property, bringing into perspective relations among parts, and the configuration of materials supplies in industrial concerns which have so far kept their policies and their means of managing their largely paper-based supply chain parochial and close to their chest.

6   MARKET DATA FILTERS ARE A PREREQUISITE TO SOUND MANAGEMENT PRACTICE

Filtering does not change the size or the nature of an information element. Its purpose is to effectively remove undesirable or not immediately appreciable information, for presentation reasons. As we saw in section 2 this unwanted component can be noise affecting the whole information process, or only that particular presentation. It may also concern a specific mission to which the filter is being applied.

As a general principle in systems design, the richer is the information channel we use the greater the need for filtering. *Market data feeds* are today a widespread product snowing under volumes of information both relevant and irrelevant to their users. Designed by information providers to operate within an environment of information oversupply, market data fees must be managed at the user end: filtering systems necessarily address themselves to large amounts of data but focused needs; they are indispensable in applications dealing with gigabytes and terabytes of data, text, documents and multimedia generally.

Whether one or more media is involved, filtering applications must typically handle streams of incoming information either being broadcast by remote sources or sent directly to *our* firm. As the previous sections underlined, they must also address the database mining requirements for engineering, manufacturing, marketing, financial or other reasons.

One of the better designed applications I was exposed to has built a market data filter employing high performance computers to upgrade and modernise financial data analysis in real-time. This job was previously done in batch and it was ineffectual. A parallel computer contributed both greater performance and the possibility of converting some of the earlier batch routines into real-time processing. More sophisticated modules saw to it that *ad hoc* queries could be dynamically changed.

Knowledge robots residing in the network's nodes work in tandem with processes which are served by an agent resident in each enduser's workstation. As shown in Figure 10.5, agents communicate among themselves and with databased objects through services supported by the intelligent information network. The parallel computer is just one of the network's servers.

In this application, the data fed by information providers and the credit institution's own system have been integrated into a networked server to permit the real-time exploitation of concurrent dataflows. The latter include securities prices, financial market news, political and other items. A similar implementation can take place in inventory management, supporting a supply chain and involving many business partners who use the Internet as their communications channel.

At the time that it was designed, the application I am describing was enriched with algorithms, heuristics and expert systems. Users commented that the adopted solution was a significant improvement over the batch practices which it replaced. With the earlier batch processing method, the bank's branches had to ask for information, required by them or their clients, at least one day in advance. This was extracted during the night run and sent to them the next day. By then it was obsolete, if not downright useless.

It is clear that if I had to redo this application today, in the post-PC era, I would have incorporated a great deal of business logic as well as an interactive logistics solution into it. The new system would have capitalised on $100 hand-held devices enriched with agents and using

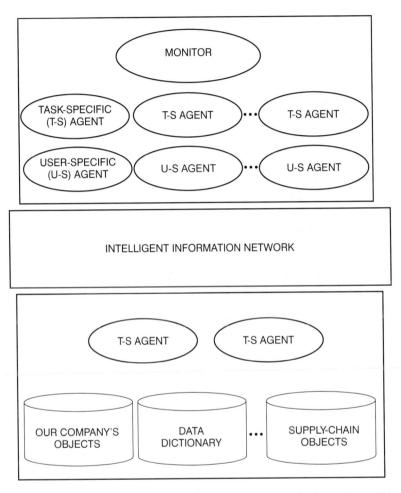

Figure 10.5 User-specific and task-specific agents work in tandem with processes which run under a monitor

object-centric software. In parallel with market data feeds and database filtering, all employees of the institution would have been trained in improving their productivity by using this system.

It is superfluous perhaps to state that now we have interactive networks and real-time responses are expected by analysts and investors, batched data is a totally uncompetitive system. The reason why I make this statement is that many institutions still persist in using batch. In June 1999, one of the largest European insurance companies at my seminar in Rome made the case that its mainframe-based system implemented in the 1960s is supreme, and that top management perceives no reason to change it. In fact, it has not been changed at all.

This is not a one-off example. Unfortunately for the companies which fall into that category of retrograde technology, it can be seen astonishingly frequently. The consequence is a loss of competitiveness, and with it a loss of independence. Executives who focus on the future rather than on the past have what it takes to appreciate that a competitive solution must definitely feature real-time response through:

- time-constrained handling of input data; and
- immediate execution of enduser commands.

An added value of the implementation I outlined in this section has been the *timestamp*, which works in a split second. Time stamping at subsecond level is being supported because of dynamic market feed requirements. During the October 1987 stock market crash, for example, many of the quotes provided online were so rapidly obsolete that they ended by confusing rather than informing traders on market movements. The October 1987 stock market crash is outstanding because it was a 14 standard deviations event. If we wish to test for outliers, as an increasing number of institutions do, then we must have a dependable time distribution of prices.

Neither are stock market data streams the only ones whose variables we analyse because we are interested in them for analytical reasons. Within the perspectives of the outlined application, a hash function performed bit operations on the currency keys. A further improvement has been the incorporation of modules which provide memory-based reasoning (D.N. Chorafas and H. Steinmann, *Supercomputers*, McGraw-Hill, New York, 1990).

A value-added characteristic of this market data filter is that it accounts for quality-of-service (QOS) criteria, tracked also in real-time. Such functionality proved important in realising specific service improvements. QOS requirements are expressed both at the time of service subscription and dynamically in connection to enduser requests. The specs have been based on the selection of parameter values such as:

- connection establishment;
- availability and reliability;
- effective throughput;

- acceptable transit delay; and
- residual error rate, if any.

Costs, too, are followed by transaction and by query because senior management firms believe that costs matter. The same is true of the evolution of QOS criteria in executing operational procedures. An adaptive performance tracking mechanism provides for remote measurement and dynamic updates of service parameters. Agents resident at the audit department steadily analyse crucial ratios to bring deviations to the auditors' attention for further in-depth investigation.

In conclusion, filtering plays a most significant role in the new economy. Collaborative filtering and recommendation engines on the Web have helped Internet commerce practitioners significantly improve on-line sales.

Major benefits have been derived by incorporating algorithms that create sophisticated customer profiles, analyse customer buying patterns, examine price sensitivities, and do other intelligence-enriched chores. Algorithms and heuristics embedded in such applications are used to adjust prices, focus on product lines, and improve marketing performance (*The MIT Report*, February 2001).

11 Operational Risk with Supply Chain: Privacy and Security

1 INTRODUCTION

Privacy and security are moving targets. They are also knotty problems for which there are no easy solutions. When it comes to the Internet, end-to-end security is practically a contradiction in terms, because the Web is a medium developed to provide wide access to information, while security means being able to restrict access on a selective basis. In terms of security, the Internet still has major problems and, in all likelihood, it will continue to do so. Visa noted at the Year 2000 GSM conference in Cannes, France, that 50 per cent of its total fraud related to the Internet.

Many security breaches do originate with hackers, who often hack for fun; but there is also a major element associated with crime. Crime and punishment, of course, is big business. In the USA revenues for the security industry, including everything from home burglar alarms to guard services for business and industry, as well as for correctional facilities, have risen by 46 per cent from 1995 to 2000, to $57 billion.

While statistics tend to indicate crime in America has fallen in the second half of the 1990s, spending on combating crime is up, including spending on Internet security. Some studies show that most of the crimes against property are committed by males under the age of 25. This is also the population which contributes to insecurity on the Web. By 2005, there will be some 20 per cent more teenagers in the USA than in 1995, which is likely to lead to a rising crime rate, even if there was no new game in town such as the Internet.

The explosive growth of the Internet and of I-commerce is increasing concerns both about breaches of privacy and about different types of fraud on the Web. Security and protection are more complex than ever before, because we increasingly deal with *virtual money* online. Asked 'What does one do with virtual money?', Walter Wriston, the former CEO of Citibank, was to suggest: 'One pays his bills.' But then he added: 'The problem with this kind of money is the *security* of the networks.

There exist too many 16-year-olds with gold chains around the neck, who break into the data system.'

Wriston has correctly pointed out that it is possible to work on more secure solutions through an ingenious use of organisational approaches, not only of hardware and software. But technology changes so fast that it would be stupid to say which one of today's systems provides the best protection in the future. The 'winner' will not stay long at the top because crooks, too, are ingenious and they learn how to use advanced technology.

Worried about hackers and internal snoops, network managers often seal off access to certain areas of the company and use firewalls to protect the databases. But open Internet standards were not designed with rigorous, integrative secrecy measures in mind. As a result, they wind up sporting a host of incompatible software, while security and protection are lightweight. The world has become so transparent, in an information sense, that nothing can be properly secured anymore, or secured in a lasting way.

2 THE EFFECTS OF INSECURITY ON ELECTRONIC COMMERCE

Security is and remains the Internet's Achilles heel. Recent reports indicate that security problems are far from being solved. About 80 per cent of 100 businesses surveyed by Netsolve reported at least one major network attack per month. A joint survey by the FBI and Computer Security Institute found that the cost of security breaches to 163 large American companies and the US government has been about $125 million in losses in 1998 alone (Merrill Lynch, *Theme and Profile Investing*, September 1999).

Experts are of the opinion that the business-to-consumer segment of Internet commerce may be hampered by concerns about security of payments, potentially fraudulent merchants, privacy of personal data, and similar reasons adding to the cost of accessing online merchants. The largest segments of B2C traffic are intangibles such as financial services, entertainment, travel and software. In this connection, factors such as:

- openness
- global reach
- lack of physical contact

make Internet commerce vulnerable to fraud, and increase certain costs for online merchants (as compared with traditional stores). Furthermore, given that the credit card is the dominant online payment method, both Internet commerce merchants and consumers are exposed to potentially high levels of fraud resulting from stolen cards or illegally obtained card numbers. New techniques are being developed to deal with credit card fraud but could raise costs by as much as 6 per cent, and what is more, such techniques are not foolproof; the 'perfect' encryption has not yet been invented.

The 30 August 1999 attack on Microsoft's Hotmail e-mail service brought a significant amount of attention to this theme of insecurity. Hotmail was hit by a security flaw that permitted unauthorised access to the private messages of its 50 million users. This followed the breaking of a common computer code used to encrypt financial transactions on the Internet.

The examples of insecurity to which I refer help to demonstrate that security is the main barrier to electronic commerce on Internet or, for that matter, on any other network accessible by hackers and crooks. Many efforts and plenty of proposals have been devoted to securing Internet communications, but it is difficult to find an ideal solution. Among current (misnamed) approaches are:

- Secure Electronic Payment Protocol, or SEPP (supported by MasterCard, IBM, and Netscape); and
- Secure Transaction Technology, or STT (backed by Visa and Microsoft).

Visa and MasterCard have also agreed to consolidate their standards into a single payment system called Secure Electronic Transactions (SET). For any practical purpose, however, the technology so far developed by Visa and MasterCard that outlines how credit-card transactions must be handled by merchants and banks leaves much to be desired, while new devices are always in the testing phase.

In the old continent, the Conditional Access for Europe (CAFE) program aims to provide payment systems that protect the privacy of the user. This is another example where the goals of accuracy and security are oversold. Among other sponsors, CAFE has involved France Telecom and Siemens, and it aims to realise a sort of 'electronic wallet' for payments, and more secure access to information services through identification.

This is a project which tries to kill two birds with one stone, and hits neither. Like the other silly business of the smart card for payments, it is also pie in the sky. Back in 1997 when CAFE had several supporters there was talk about possible extensions of the wallet including electronic passports, drivers' licences or house keys (*Fibre Systems*, May/June 1997). Practically all of them proved to be illusions.

Other hit and run initiatives of last five years include the Secure Electronic Marketplace for Europe (SEMPER), a consortium co-ordinated by IBM, with the goal of developing secure electronic commerce over existing networks, especially the Internet. There was also the Secure Operating System Smart Card (SOSCARD), which targeted the exploitation of cryptography in conjunction with smart cards. This was an initiative with close links to the CAFE project.

Still another research effort which aimed to bring greater security to electronic commerce has been that of *micropayments*. Micropayments are transactions in which the value of what is purchased is less than the cost of the transaction. Several attempts have been made to define low-cost transaction mechanisms, such as Millicent, PayWord and MicroMint. Micropayments are still a number of years away from anything tangible, and many experts doubt if they will ever come.

What all these research projects have in common (apart from the fact they have led nowhere) is their failure to appreciate that security is a global operational problem, not a matter of silly acronyms. Indeed, since the 1999 New Capital Adequacy Framework by the Basle Committee on Banking Supervision (see D.N. Chorafas, *New Regulation of the Financial Industry*, Macmillan – now Palgrave, London, 2000), greater security in financial transactions is in the mind of all clear-eyed bankers, but rigorous solutions are not yet here. This is important as operational risk is no more taking a backseat to market risk and credit risk.

The last couple of years have witnessed a growing interest in operational risk, with both financial institutions and vendors of risk control solutions searching for a sound methodology and cost-effective tools, able to bend the curve of growing insecurity (D.N. Chorafas, *Managing Operational Risk. Risk Reduction Strategies for Investment Banks and Commercial Banks*, Euromoney, London, 2001). Any research into security risk in the realm of operational exposure must approach this issue from several angles:

- outlining several distinct stages in the development of operational risk management;
- looking at best practices including: methodology, tools and market place trends;
- presenting an overview of the security/protection universe, and where the pitfalls lie today.

This approach must be enriched by case studies that illustrate the various stages of operational risk infrastructure, its implementation, and the successes and failures being encountered. Any security study must keep in mind that demonstrated robust solutions can have significant impact on financial services and in the industry at large, but each of these solutions has vulnerabilities and costs, not just rewards.

The beaten path should be avoided: for instance, self-satisfaction with the suggestion that all that is needed for secure communication is some sort of encryption (see section 6); 'a good means for authentication'; this or that type of firewall; or some vendor's 'secure' access control wave for site, page and field.

These are partial and therefore half-baked approaches which mean little or nothing. A sound solution always begins with knowing ourselves and our weaknesses, then studying what is needed for integration with business partners' security in the supply chain, including access control, firewalls and logging. Then, apart from using the best available software, our solution must integrate with:

- the corporate systems infrastructure, including internal control, validation and auditing procedures (D.N. Chorafas, *Implementing and Auditing the Internal Control System*, Macmillan – now Palgrave, London, 2001);
- the Internet system itself all the way to Web server security and beyond.

There is no lack of new security solutions. The problem is that they come and go. Only a few of them find a customer base and stay around. One of the newest is what is being called by its developers 'the world's smallest combination lock'. This device is a minuscule microelectro-mechanical system (MEMS) developed at Sandia National Laboratories, Albuquerque, New Mexico. Its goal is to assist in building a virtually impenetrable computer firewall that even the best hackers cannot defeat. The Recordable Locking Device consists of a series of notched gears that move into the unlocked position only when the right code is entered. Part of the strength of this device is that it is so small that it takes a microscope to see it, but only time will tell if it really provides a secure solution.

Sandia's approach is a departure from past practices. Computer firewalls have always been dependent on software, which means they are subject to manipulation. By contrast, this device is hardware. Its designers say an intruder has one chance in a million of picking exactly the right code, compared to a one in 10 000 chance with most software firewalls.

After one failed try, this new device mechanically shuts down and cannot be reset and reopened except by the owner. Only experience will show if it is really unbreakable by unwanted users.

In conclusion, until a truly reliable solution is found, concerns continue to linger about security, particularly among those companies and those consumers who are new to the Web or who need to make major purchases. Because both businesses and the public are still not convinced about security, in spite of all (light-hearted) promises by vendors and credit-card companies, it is a sign of bad judgement to be pushing online payments regardless of the level of risk.

3 AN EFFECTIVE SOLUTION TO SECURITY NEEDS SKILL AND UNDERSTANDING

The real problem with security, some experts say, is reluctance by companies to take hold of all aspects associated with security on the Internet, as opposed to implementing some security devices all by themselves. The basis of this wrong policy is that many people and companies think that in its current form, the Internet provides security, even if it is not perfect. My advice is that business firms should themselves seek to identify security risks, in order to manage them in the context of B2B; they should not wait for software suppliers to make the Internet completely secure, because this is not going to happen.

However, as far as B2C and C2B trades are concerned, even this argument misses the point. The myriad of Internet's private users does not have the skill and know-how to understand *how* and *why* their I-commerce activities create risk. Neither are they willing and able to put up the much-needed financial resources for secure Internet banking and secure Internet commerce.

As practically every person involved in security knows, good practice involves a level of investment balanced against the value of what must be secured, along with a well-thought-out strategy as well as a correct implementation policy. Only big companies can make this type of investment, and big companies will not be forthcoming until there is a very significant market (which will happen when the Internet is secure).

At the core of the challenge which comes up with this vicious cycle lies the fact that anyone with a PC and a modem is able to act as an Internet hacker, or even launch an effective denial-of-service attack against pretty much anyone else on the Web. This is a daily event.

MCI Communications has been receiving roughly four security complaints a day from its Internet customers (*Communications of the ACM*, March 1998; ACM: Association of Computing Machinery).

At the Monte Carlo Investment Forum (30–31 March 2000) it was stated that today three out of four Bulgarian kids try to attack Western PCs. This is probably an exaggeration, but it is also a vivid example of the new El Dorado, which is the way many younger people in former East Europe look at the Internet. Neither are kids in other countries passive bystanders, which leads to the fact that every year we hear of the cracking of a formerly unbreakable algorithm, such as RSA.

Let us face it: what we consider safe today will be broken tomorrow. That is why in the introduction I said that security is a moving target. Nobody really knows how to handle the Internet security challenge effectively, in spite of so many statements made to the contrary by otherwise dependable companies and people.

Persons and firms who want to do something about improving security appreciate that in a number of cases the laws of the land cannot cope with hacking. Bell Labs recounts the story of a Dutch hacker who broke into its computer system. Although he attempted to destroy its system, this hacker could not be prosecuted because hacking is not illegal under Dutch law.

As hackers have, so to speak, a free rein, there is a fairly widespread fear that legislation and regulation cannot keep pace with technology and its users or misusers. One reason why the Web is difficult to police is that tens of thousands of new sites come live every week. Even if the appropriate legislation and regulation were in place, if one cannot enforce them in a global sense, the result is false assurances to people and companies.

Ironically, another major security challenge is the rapid development of products and services to promote online sales. During the last few years, new products have been rolling out so fast that even if developers are careful in their design, security gaps happen that were not anticipated at the drafting board, and they escape attention all the way to the marketing and field service.

A further Internet security risk is generated by the fact that many companies are using the system to transmit sensitive internal information. This has created new types of security risk. 'The Internet was never designed with security in mind,' says John Hamre, US deputy Defense Secretary, in an interview in London with the *Financial Times*. 'The very openness of this technology, which leads to its dynamism, is what creates a risk' (*Financial Times*, 20 March 1998).

The dangers of outsiders gaining unauthorised access to computer systems were driven home to the Pentagon on many occasions. One of the better known happened in February 1998 when two teenage hackers in California mounted a sophisticated attack on the Defense Department's computer systems. This raid was not part of any plan; instead, the raid was the plan.

Civilian attacks are a legend, including the mysterious origin of the 'I Love You' virus which seems to have originated in the Philippines. The risks of disruption to civilian life were highlighted when, in March 1997, a teenager in Massachusetts was charged with an attack which shut down parts of a regional airport, although the prosecuting attorney said the boy 'didn't have a clue as to what he was doing.'

John Hamre suggested in the *Financial Times* interview that almost all attempts to hack into the Pentagon were by what he called a 'culture of voyeurism and modest vandalism rather than a national security problem'. However, he also added that the need for security was growing as almost all businesses are switching to electronic transmission of data via the Internet rather than private, proprietary networks. Both banks and utility companies provide an example of this trend.

Since the financial industry is a favoured target of hackers, in May 2000 the OCC issued guidance to national banks on how to prevent, detect and respond to intrusions into bank computers and other operational risks associated with security. This guidance notes that the risk and prevalence of computer intrusions is increasing as information systems become more and more interconnected, and as credit institutions make greater use of Internet banking services and other remote access.

The OCC's guidance declared that senior management and the Board of Directors of a bank are *responsible* for overseeing the development and implementation of a *security strategic plan*, key elements of which should include an intrusion risk assessment study, risk mitigation controls, intrusion response policies and procedures, and testing processes. The plan should also set forth many of the necessary components of these systems.

The regulators' guidance further suggests that national banks are required to report intrusions and other computer crimes to the OCC and law enforcement, by filing a Suspicious Activity Report. Management should also ensure that information networks are tested regularly, with the nature, extent, tools being used and frequency of tests being proportionate to the risks of intrusion from external and internal sources.

The same OCC directive specifies that management should ensure that an objective, qualified source conducts a penetration test of Internet banking systems at least annually. It also encourages information sharing among institutions in an effort to detect and respond to intrusions and vulnerabilities on a collective basis, as well as to exchange experiences which can strengthen the security measures taken by each individual bank.

On 2 August 2000, in London, Barclays Bank suffered a security breach which helps to document how sound is the American regulators' advice about regular check-ups of possible security vulnerabilities. The lack of security of any system is, to a large extent, the aftermath of the law of unintended consequences, or Murphy's law: 'Anything that can go wrong, will.'

4   THE REGULATORS ADDRESS THE CHALLENGE OF IMPROVING PERSONAL PRIVACY

Part of the enigma about the lack of security among formerly secure systems lies in the fact that both privacy and security need to be improved on a steady basis. In mid-May 2000, the US FTC issued privacy regulations (effective in July 2001) that could significantly curb the business of selling names, addresses, Social Security numbers and other personal details. The new regulations give consumers the chance to block such deals.

These FTC regulations are part of the financial services overhaul approved by the US Congress in the autumn of 1999, and concern so-called *credit header* information. Credit header includes personal details at the top of every credit report. In issuing the new privacy protection rules, the FTC declared that any personal information gathered by a financial institution is financial data subject to protection under the new rules. This rule, which follows on from European legislation, puts an end to the unrestricted sales of most sensitive types of information that constitute personal records. Institutions, including insurers, banks, retailers and any other firms that issue credit, will have to give consumers a chance to say *no* before allowing credit bureaux to resell personal data.

People care about their privacy. Financial institutions and other businesses will now have to tell customers about information practices that have been going on in secret for years. There is also a related legal decision on a similar issue. This case has been left undecided, by default. It comes from the US Supreme Court which declined to hear an appeal in a case that overturned a federal rule prohibiting a regulated industry from using certain customer information unless the customer *opted-in* to that use.

This case concerned a Federal Communications Commission (FCC) regulation that prohibited phone companies from using information about individual customers' calling patterns to market additional products, without an express opt-in from the customer agreeing to such use of pattern data. US West (a telephone company) objected to this ruling and it sued the FCC. The company argued that the regulation infringed its First Amendment right to free speech. It did so, US West said, because it prevented it from using that customer's data to market to customers who had not opted in.

The US Court of Appeals for the 10th Circuit found the FCC rule unconstitutional and therefore quashed it. The constitutional analysis of competing governmental interests in protecting consumer privacy and protecting 'free commercial speech', as set forth in the 10th Circuit's opinion, could provide a framework for the evolving debate concerning privacy of consumers' financial information. However, since the Supreme Court declined to hear this appeal, the constitutionality of opt-in imposed by regulation or by statute remains unresolved.

The issues underlining personal privacy as opposed to free commercial speech has also been raised in the US Congress, but no specific legislation has been enacted. What has been enacted, however, is the Gramm Leach Bliley Act of 1999 that establishes standards for safeguarding the security, confidentiality and integrity of customer information possessed by commercial firms.

The regulators have built upon the Gramm Leach Bliley Act provisions. In late June 2000 the Federal Reserve, OCC, Federal Deposit Insurance Corporation (FDIC) and Office of Thrift Supervision (OTS) jointly proposed a rule pursuant to sections 501 and 505(b) of the Gramm Leach Bliley Act. This would implement standards as safety and soundness *guidelines* rather than as regulations.

The proposed Rule would require financial institutions, under the supervision and ongoing oversight of their Board of Directors, to create a data security program to assess the risks that could pose a threat to customer information. Financial institutions would also be required to adopt a written plan containing policies and procedures to both manage and control those risks. The plan promoted by the regulator guidelines would include safeguards which reflect the size and complexity of the institution, and the nature and scope of its activities. As a part of its risk management programme, an institution would be expected to assess, among other things:

- access rights to customer information and controls on that access;
- access restrictions at locations where the customer information may be stored;
- encryption of customer information when the information is in storage; and
- contract provisions and oversight mechanisms to protect customer information maintained or processed by third party service providers.

Institutions would also be required to adjust their privacy protection plans periodically to reflect technological changes, the respective level of sensitivity of customer information, and internal or external threats to information security. They should test their security programs as well, and provide adequate employee training with respect to these issues. Furthermore, they are expected to exercise due diligence in managing and monitoring outsourcing arrangements to ensure that third party service providers have effective customer information security programs.

The FTC, SEC and state insurance regulators are also issuing customer information privacy and security standards for the institutions they supervise. As a *Business Week* article (20 March 2000) was to suggest, 'Clearly, privacy policies are backbreakers to write. But it seems the hardest part about them for any company is coming up with a privacy philosophy that they will stick to.' And, I would add, that is reliable enough to provide real protection. Furthermore, privacy policies governing buying habits, credit records, drug prescriptions, and similar data from transactions on the Internet are one thing; but when data is captured and maintained electronically, privacy problems can take forms so far unknown and therefore difficult to track, let alone legislate.

The problem of ensuring personal privacy becomes very complex because sometimes established rules contradict one another. To boost Internet commerce, in 1999 countries such as Germany and the city-state of Singapore have passed legislation that gives electronic signatures legal weight (see section 6). The USA passed similar laws in 2000, and many other jurisdictions are considering doing likewise. Those in favour think these new laws will make it possible for consumers to do exciting new things, such as request money or doing Individual Retirement Account (IRA) distributions over the Net, while those against believe that such rules will dent personal privacy.

5   THE CONFLICT BETWEEN PERSONAL PRIVACY AND SECURITY

One should in no way be surprised that the relative lack of privacy and security bears negatively on Internet commerce and Internet banking. Business is built on confidence and confidence wanes as private users become aware of the likelihood that their personal data is insecure, their credit card numbers may be pirated, and the credit institutions' databases are the prey of all sorts of crooks. In a 1998 survey, 78 per cent of those interviewed said they would use the Web more if privacy were guaranteed (*Business Week*, 16 March 1998). In another survey, 50 per cent of the computer users polled said that government should pass laws on whether personal data can be collected and used on the Internet.

Fears that snoops can peek into one's private life and track what one is doing at every moment would restrict the number of people using the Web. In that second survey, some 57 per cent of poll respondents who used the Internet said that site policies able to guarantee the security of their personal data affect their decision to make online purchases in a significant way.

At root, however, a policy of strict security and the mechanics of an open society contradict one another. Today, anybody using a cellular phone can be tracked by the police to within 100 metres at most. This distance is significantly reduced in some countries, becoming only half a metre in Japan. 'We have been selling privacy for security for some time,' said one of the experts interviewed in connection with this research.

In late 1999 in the USA, the federal government announced new technological standards for cellular phones that will broadly expand the ability of law-enforcement agents to monitor conversations. Agents can monitor cell phone calls after obtaining a search warrant, but under the new FCC rules they will also be able to determine the general location of a cell phone user by identifying which cellular antenna the phone company employed to transmit the call under surveillance (*Communications of the ACM*, Vol. 42, No. 10, October 1999). Other new rules permit agents to identify all callers on a conference call, whether cellular or conventional, and enable agents to determine whether suspects are making use of such features as call forwarding and call waiting.

This FCC ruling has been a setback for civil liberties groups and privacy advocates. But senior officials at the Justice Department applauded it, saying it would be a powerful new tool for combating crime. When privacy and security collide, one of them must be given the upper hand. Our society has not yet made up its mind which this should be.

Industry executives suggest that while the new rules to which I made reference went beyond what is authorised today by law, they would comply with them. They could hardly do otherwise since they themselves do the monitoring. At major US corporations, in 1998, there was a 43 per cent chance (up sharply from 35 per cent in 1997) that employers monitored workers' e-mail files, voice mail, computer files, phone calls or other work-related activities, according to the AMA (*Communications of the ACM*, Vol. 42, No. 6, June 1999).

Polling 1054 human resource managers, the New York-based AMA said the sample mirrored its corporate membership of 10 000 entities that among themselves employ one-quarter of the American workforce. The financial industry conducted the most monitoring, with 68 per cent of companies involved in some form of snooping, followed by business and professional service providers at 51 per cent, and wholesalers and retailers at 47 per cent. Most monitoring was performed by spot checks.

Global surveillance is by no means short of tools. Real-time tracking and pattern analysis are emerging techniques expected to take over as the shortcomings of other, more classical approaches become increasingly evident. One of the lecturers at the Monte Carlo Investment Forum said that in Monaco and London your picture is taken 20–30 times per day, and it is databased.

There is also an evolution in security methodology. Classical approaches to security have been either token-based or knowledge-based. Examples of the former are passports, identity cards, credit cards and keys. The latter are based on something one knows, and therefore allows one to make a personal identification (for instance, a password or personal identification number).

To put it mildly, PINs are today obsolete and render a substandard service. Many companies are in search of a better alternative. One of them is combining fingerprint recognition with smart cards by putting the fingerprint pattern directly on to a smart card for subsequent comparison and recognition. This poses both social and privacy problems. Civil liberty groups suggest that the fingerprint information must be kept strictly on the card to prevent a *de facto* fingerprint database being produced. This is a very ineffectual argument, first because storing on a smart card is also databasing (and the same is true of all types of biometric technologies), and second because smart cards can be stolen.

Face, facial thermograms, voice prints and retinal pattern are examples other than the more common fingerprints and hand geometry which might be used for identification purposes at the expense of privacy.

The use of any biometrics is a matter of privacy violation which involves feature-extractor, pattern analysis and databasing, whether the latter is or is not authorised. It is a major social problem.

Why not to stick to cryptography as *the* solution to both privacy and security problems? The answer is: 'Because it is unreliable, even if many people think that cryptography is a sort of a magic word for protection.' It is wrong to stick to one and only one approach, and cryptography is by no means free of failures.

Using not only the brute force of computing but also information about the radiation and power consumption of a device when it executes a cryptographic algorithm as well as its timing, code breakers have been able to crack open would-be secure tokens. By forcing faults during operation, it is possible to break any algorithm. Such approaches have been known as *failure analysis*, or side-channel attacks.

Attacks on supposedly secure algorithms are based on how systems respond to legitimate errors, including codes stored on smart cards. At times it is not necessary to break the code itself but rather the way it is used. Both secret services and crooks have demonstrated that it is possible to break the security of a system, without even cracking its cryptography.

This procedure is not new, and it eventually leads to breaking the code. That is what Alan Turing did during the Second World War with Enigma, the German super-secret military code. Cryptoanalysts have analysed many systems by breaking the pseudo-random number generators used to supply cryptographic keys. The cryptographic algorithms might be 'secure', but the key-generation procedures are not; they are the weak link in the chain.

Cryptographic solutions might be at greater risk of attack, and crooks could have a ball, if they are based on industry standards, and are specified in a manner simplifying the interconnection of supply chain systems to that of our own company. This helps to mitigate technical risk, but standards-based asymmetrical approaches are vulnerable even if they use different keys for encrypting and decrypting data.

Vulnerability of pure algorithmic solutions has led to research into biometrics-based solutions, as already discussed in this section. As we have seen, however, at heart the name of the game is privacy as against security. Choices are difficult and, to a very substantial extent, they are political rather than technical. Queries bringing up personal protection issues range from: 'Is this the person who he/she claims to be?' to 'Is this the person *our* agency is after?' Associated with these queries are others aiming to identify fraud, which go well beyond the stricter sense of privacy.

6   DIGITAL SIGNATURES AND DIGITAL CERTIFICATES

From a security viewpoint, the very strengths of the Internet – its wide-spanning communications capability, any-to-any connectivity and powerful search engines – are a matter of worry. These otherwise great qualities enable abuses by unscrupulous companies and individuals. The fact that much of modern business greatly depends on database mining intensifies the security problem.

Problems connected with security are not only associated with outright fraud, but also include other issues of a more subtle nature. By all indications, untruthful advertising is increasing and so are different types of *unwanted* information filtering (see also Chapter 10). Experts believe that most characteristics of Internet voting are not well understood, even if there is a rush to implement them. New challenges have also come from non-proprietary software offered free of cost, and a list of other issues whose control is still elusive. For instance, different aspects of anonymity serve a purpose, but also foster abuses in a wide-ranging network landscape. As we have also seen, privacy issues relating to encryption and surveillance have not yet found fully satisfactory solutions. There is even a certain amount of identity theft.

Network-tapping raises many issues, while the required infrastructure for digital certificates brings up integrity problems. The only way industry can even begin to develop a uniform code for security is to embrace standards for *digital signatures*. Section 5 brought to the reader's attention the risks associated with these standards, and there is yet another interesting question: 'Which standards?'

Let us first look at signatures at large. Each person has a unique style of handwriting, therefore his classical-type signature is considered part of biometric identification. Because no two signatures of the same person are exactly identical, methods have been developed to ascertain their accuracy by looking at variables in pattern. Two of these methods dominate in connection with classical signatures:

- a *static*, based on shape which is the more traditional; and
- a *dynamic*, which adds to shape trajectory features such as pressure, acceleration or velocity.

The exercise of classical-type signatures is not feasible with Internet commerce; hence the *digital signature* concept which allows us to verify the identity of the sender. Although a digitally signed Internet commerce deal is still not 100 per cent safe, one at least thinks that it might be reasonably sure if it comes from a trusted source (more on this later).

In simplified form, a digital signature is a string of bits computed from data being signed, along with the private key of an entity. The value differentiation in security is made by the methodology being chosen. Characteristics which contribute to the safety of a piece of signed mobile code are:

- the ability to verify its authenticity; and
- an assurance that it cannot be forged;

In other words, it should somehow be impossible to claim that a given signature is for any other data. Also, there should be an assurance that the signed data cannot be changed because under normal conditions the signature will no longer verify it as authentic.

The object of *digital certificates* is to guarantee that a particular control was indeed generated by the person one thinks created it, and that it has been transmitted without modification. Nevertheless, all by itself the digital certificate offers no guarantee that the code is safe or well-written, though it does provide an opportunity to decide whether or not one can trust its originator.

In principle, adhering to a policy of allowing only digitally signed transactions into the network will also increase our level of trust. Under this principle, the use of digital signatures lets mobile codes become trusted, and therefore run with fewer restrictions. Also, if one has questions about the trustworthiness of the particular person or company shown as the owner of the certificate, one can investigate. An Authenticode certificate that appears on screen will contain a link to the originator's Web site; theoretically, this provides an opportunity to get a closer look at what the sender is really up to.

As this brief exposition suggests, a digital certificate should be seen as a digitally signed statement from a trusted entity, which says that the public key of another entity has a particular value. Typically, a digital certificate is issued by a *certification authority* (CA); therefore both the certificates and the authority behind them are indispensable building blocks of Internet commerce. Let us look at this scenario: when two parties meet for the first time over the Internet to transact, they do not necessarily trust each other. Trust can be improved by placing confidence in a mutually appreciated third party, who certifies them both.

Since there is no quick and dirty way to authenticate identities online without some authority and its certificates, there has been a call for such a service. In the UK there is already such a system in place. In the USA, government-published standards, such as the Orange Book (more formally known as the Department of Defense Trusted Computer System Evaluation Criteria) serve as a guideline for security, because they provide a rather rigorous method for control.

Indeed, some task-specific CA solutions are already familiar at least to some companies: the Federal Reserve Bank is an example. They are used to control access to information and certify the sender of a document. Trials on the Internet aim to promote more widespread uses, such as e-mail certified and time-stamped by national post offices, bringing the PTTs (old telcos and post offices) back into the picture but also allowing a person to get some measure of assurance.

What the previous paragraphs have been suggesting requires both legislation and regulation, and first-class software. Vendors are forthcoming with solutions. Microsoft enables digital signatures through Authenticode, which permits ActiveX controls and other routines to be digitally signed. However, the disadvantage of this and similar offerings is that they place the burden of making security decisions on end users.

An alternative is a server-based solution involving a firewall or other server-based products such as Trend Micro's InterScan WebProtect and Computer Associates' Unicenter TNG, which call for keeping in Internet service the palaeolithic mainframes. Sun Microsystems' approach to digitally signing Java applets is more modern. It requires all Java code and related files to be collected into a Java Archive (JAR) file. A digital signature is then applied to the JAR file.

Sun Microsystems also uses a graphic user interface (GUI) utility, known as Jarsigner, which signs JAR files and verifies the signatures and integrity. It employs key and certificate information from a keystore to generate digital signatures for JAR files. As the reader will appreciate there exist alternatives, but none is 100 per cent foolproof, or even approximates that level of assurance.

7   RULES, REGULATIONS AND CONFLICTING LAWS GOVERNING DIGITAL SIGNATURES

The fact that legislators in many countries are rushing through laws formalising encryption-based technology used for electronic commerce has led to a lack of uniform international policies. Experts believe that this rush, and the fact that crossborder consultation among governments is wanting, will eventually hamper rather than promote the growth of I-commerce and I-banking.

Legal experts also suggest that, at times, laws and regulations leave little room for the private sector to set its own rules, while they tend to put forward limits which may even exclude emerging technologies, because they reduce the margin of flexibility. For instance, enacted in August 1997, Germany's digital-signature law imposes stringent licensing terms on certification authorities. It requires users to be physically present with identification in order to be allocated a digital certificate, and significantly reduces, if not eliminates, the possibility of Internet-delivered certificates.

The Italian law, also passed in August 1997, typically transplants existing regulations governing public notaries into the digital environment. Since September 1997, Malaysian law requires that CAs must be licensed by the country's government, and companies issuing certificates must be registered in the country. Malaysia became the first Asian country to pass a digital signature law.

In mid-June 2000, in the USA, the Electronic Signatures in Global and National Commerce Act (S.761) passed the House of Representatives by a vote of 426 to 4, and the Senate on a vote of 87 to 0. Thereafter, President Clinton signed into law the Act using new digital technology, in recognition of the need for federal legislation to establish a uniform standard for engaging in electronic commerce nation-wide.

Experts suggest the S.761 legislation has been particularly necessary as many Web sites now offer consumers cheque and savings accounts, credit cards, loan offerings, and insurance products. They also transfer funds, receive and pay bills, trade securities and allow the possibility of viewing accounts from either home or office.

With the new legislation, financial service providers will be able to deliver online a wider range of products and services to consumers. A consumer could:

- apply for a mortgage to buy a home with an online lender; and
- elect to conduct the transaction electronically, including receiving federal and state disclosures online.

Electronic signatures are the cornerstone of these transactions. They are attached to, or logically associated with, a contract or other record. They are adopted and executed by a person who intends to sign the record. A basic notion in the process I am describing is that of *electronic records*, which include notices and disclosures or any writing communicated online. But privacy and security problems are not solved with the new law.

It is a false belief that security can be legislated. Both in America and in other countries, legislators typically fail to pay full attention to a core issue: defence against an attack on digital signatures, as well as on real and assumed rules, must be engineered. This is now known as *security engineering*, but the ideas on how to go about it are not so clear. We need to increase ten-fold our knowledge on how to make sure security is not broken, even in the presence of a determined and technologically sophisticated adversary, and that it is *we*, not the adversary, who hold the high ground in analysing the behavioural pattern of other entities. These other entities, for instance, may do everything in their power to break the code. Some experts even think that defending against yet unknown attacks is impossible, although the risk can be mitigated with good system design, not just cryptographic algorithms. In other terms, better security is not a product, but *a process*, and the whole system we call the Internet must be upgraded for greater security.

By contrast, current legislation takes a product view. The US initiative on digital signatures implies a general *rule of validity*: a signature, contract, or other record related to any transaction or affecting interstate or foreign commerce, may not be denied legal effect or enforceability solely because it is in electronic form. The focus is on the product. Besides, the new legislation only affects laws imposing writing or signing requirements. It does not impact on:

- consumer protection laws;
- content or timing of disclosures required by law; or
- requirements by a federal regulatory agency.

Consumer rights are taken into account. As a special protection measure implied by S.761, electronic records may be used to satisfy any law which requires that records be provided to consumers in writing, only *if* the consumer has affirmatively consented to the use of the electronic records and has not withdrawn such consent. Furthermore, prior to obtaining consent, the electronic record provider must deliver a clear and conspicuous statement informing the consumer of:

- rights or options to have the record provided or made available in paper form;
- the right to withdraw consent and any associated conditions or consequences; and

- the vendor's obligation to provide the record(s) during the course of the parties' relationship.

The vendor must also inform the consumer about procedures he or she must use to withdraw consent, as well regarding hardware and software requirements for access to, and retention of, electronic records. Also, if there is a change in the hardware and software requirements needed to access or retain the electronic records that creates a material risk, the consumer will not be able to access or retain subsequent electronic records.

Consumers must consent, or confirm their consent, electronically, in a manner that reasonably demonstrates acceptance of information in electronic form. Federal pre-emption of state law is another significant clause of S.761. My question is one of global validity of such clauses. Because the Internet is a borderless medium, it cannot accept a patch-work of state rules regarding the electronic delivery or disclosures of signatures.

Globalisation through I-commerce and Internet banking promotes the need for a uniform transborder law on security and protection which applies to transactions no matter where they originate or where they are executed. Like the US law affecting interstate commerce which is designed to satisfy both federal and state legal disclosure and/or signature requirements, there should be a clear and unambiguous uniform global law about electronic signatures applying in all jurisdiction for all trades done on the Internet, whether B2B, B2C, C2B or C2C, and it should focus on processes, not only on products.

CONCLUSION

In all classical tragedy from Aeschyllos to Shakespeare and from Sophocles to Schiller, the tragic failure of the leading figure has been his failure to change. This is seen in the destiny to Oedipus as well as in that of Hamlet. Every great classical tragedy moves its audience not because the latter has been deceived as by tempting illusion, but because it is led to recognize the perils of immobility.

Presenting the reader with the rewards and risks of Internet commerce has been a deliberate choice. No matter the turbulences of Nasdaq and of high technology stocks in other exchanges during 2000 and the early part of 2001, the Internet is the *agent of change* in our society – and it is here to stay.

True enough, by February 2001 after the market punished the technology, media, telecommunications sector for its excess valuation, some investment analysts suggested that for 2001 their clients should follow the new 'B2B', namely *back to basics*. That quality and consistency of earnings became once again the keys to successful portfolio performance is not surprising; they should have been so all the way.

Like in the 1890s in the United States a severe financial crisis put in question the wisdom of building railroads, by early March 2001 it became fashionable to view the on-line business-to-consumer market as a wreck. The share prices of some of the market leaders have been down by anything up to 95 per cent from their peaks of just one year earlier. Among them lie former star performers in equities, struggling to survive.

Past the initial euphoria and subsequent dismay, however, one might discover some bellwether stocks that largely set the B2C tone like: Amazon, eBay, and Yahoo! which have become remarkable businesses by ordinary measure. In the 1890s, incidently, the US railroad industry also revived and this led to its subsequent boom which carried all the way to the fortunes created in steel and automobiles.

Industrial success is neither a 'right' nor a 'matter of course'. Good organisation is a prerequisite to sound business and ultimately, as with all capital spending, the strength of technology investments depends on their contribution to the bottom line. In its fourth quarter 2000 earnings announcement by General Electric claimed it would generate $1.5 billion of operating margin benefit thanks to the Internet and digitization. With cost savings of that magnitude, new investments in high technology do not look like a problem.

Appendix of Participating Organisations

The following organisations, through their senior executives and system specialists, participated in the recent research projects that led to the contents of this book and its documentation.

AUSTRIA

National Bank of Austria

Dr Martin OHMS
Finance Market Analysis Department

3, Otto Wagner Platz
Postfach 61
A-1011 Vienna

Association of Austrian Banks and Bankers

Dr Fritz DIWOK
Secretary General

11, Boersengasse
1013 Vienna

Bank Austria

Dr Peter FISCHER
Senior General Manager, Treasury Division

Peter GABRIEL
Deputy General Manager, Trading

2, Am Hof
1010 Vienna

Creditanstalt

Dr Wolfgang LICHTL
Market Risk Management

Julius Tandler Platz 3
A-1090 Vienna

Wiener Betriebs- and Baugesellschaft mbH

Dr Josef FRITZ
General Manager

1, Anschützstrasse
1153 Vienna

GERMANY

Deutsche Bundesbank

Hans-Dietrich PETERS
Director

Hans Werner VOTH
Director

Wilhelm-Epstein Strasse 14
60431 Frankfurt am Main

Federal Banking Supervisory Office

Hans-Joachim DOHR
Director Dept. I

Jochen KAYSER
Risk Model Examination

Ludger HANENBERG
Internal Controls

71-101 Gardeschützenweg
12203 Berlin

European Central Bank

Mauro GRANDE
Director

29 Kaiserstrasse
29th Floor
60216 Frankfurt am Main

Deutsches Aktieninstitut

Dr Rüdiger Von ROSEN
President

Biebergasse 6 bis 10
60313 Frankfurt am Main

Commerzbank

Peter BÜRGER
Senior Vice President, Strategy and Controlling

Markus RUMPEL
Senior Vice President, Credit Risk Management

Kaiserplatz
60261 Frankfurt am Main

Deutsche Bank

Professor Manfred TIMMERMANN
Head of Controlling

Hans VOIT
Head of Process Management, Controlling Department

12, Taunusanlage
60325 Frankfurt am Main

Dresdner Bank

Dr Marita BALKS
Investment Bank, Risk Control

Dr Hermann HAAF
Mathematical Models for Risk Control

Claas Carsten KOHL
Financial Engineer

1, Jürgen Ponto Platz
60301 Frankfurt am Main

GMD First – Research Institute for Computer Architecture, Software Technology and Graphics

Prof. Dr Ing. Wolfgang K. GILOI
General Manager

5, Rudower Chaussee
D-1199 Berlin

FRANCE

Banque de France

Pierre JAILLET
Director, Monetary Studies and Statistics

Yvan ORONNAL
Manager, Monetary Analyses and Statistics

G. TOURNEMIRE, Analyst, Monetary Studies

39, rue Croix des Petits Champs
75001 Paris

Secretariat Général de la Commission Bancaire – Banque de France

Didier PENY
Director, Control of Big Banks and International Banks

73, rue de Richelieu
75002 Paris

F. VISNOWSKY
Manager of International Affairs
Supervisory Policy and Research Division

Benjamin SAHEL
Market Risk Control

115, Rue Réaumur
75049 Paris Cedex 01

Ministry of Finance and the Economy, Conseil National de la Comptabilité

Alain LE BARS
Director International Relations and Cooperation

6, rue Louise WEISS
75703 Paris Cedex 13

HUNGARY

Hungarian Banking and Capital Market Supervision

Dr Janos KUN
Head, Department of Regulation and Analyses

Dr Erika VÖRÖS
Senior Economist, Department of Regulation and Analyses

Dr Géza NYIRY
Head, Section of Information Audit

Csalogany u. 9-11
H-1027 Budapest

Hungarian Academy of Sciences

Prof. Dr Tibor VAMOS
Chairman, Computer and Automation Research Institute

Nador U. 7
1051 Budapest

ICELAND

The National Bank of Iceland Ltd

Gunnar T. ANDERSEN
Managing Director
International Banking & Treasury

Laugavegur 77
155 Reykjavik

ITALY

Banca d'Italia

Eugene GAIOTTI
Research Department, Monetary and Financial Division

Ing. Dario FOCARELLI
Research Department

91, via Nazionale
00184 Rome

Istituto Bancario San Paolo di Torino

Dr Paolo CHIULENTI
Director of Budgeting

Roberto COSTA
Director of Private Banking

Pino RAVELLI
Director Bergamo Region

27, via G. Camozzi
24121 Bergamo

LUXEMBOURG

Banque Générale de Luxembourg

Prof. Dr Yves WAGNER
Director of Asset and Risk Management

Hans Jörg PARIS, International Risk Manager

27, avenue Monterey
L-2951 Luxembourg

Clearstream

André LUSSI
President and CEO

3-5 Place Winston Churchill
L-2964 Luxembourg

POLAND

Securities and Exchange Commission

Beata STELMACH
Secretary of the Commission

1, Pl Powstancow Warszawy
00-950 Warsaw

SWEDEN

Skandinaviska Enskilda Banken

Bernt GYLLENSWÄRD
Head of Group Audit

Box 16067
10322 Stockholm

Irdem AB

Gian MEDRI
Former Director of Research at Nordbanken

19, Flintlasvagen
S-19154 Sollentuna

SWITZERLAND

Swiss National Bank

Dr Werner HERMANN
Head of International Monetary Relations

Dr Christian WALTER
Representative to the Basle Committee

Robert FLURI
Assistant Director, Statistics Section

15 Börsenstrasse
Zurich

Federal Banking Commission

Dr Susanne BRANDENBERGER
Risk Management

Renate LISCHER
Representative to Risk Management Subgroup, Basle Committee

Marktgasse 37
3001 Bern

Bank for International Settlements

Mr Claude SIVY
Head of Internal Audit

Herbie POENISCH
Senior Economist, Monetary and Economic Department

2, Centralplatz
4002 Basle

Bank Leu AG

Dr Urs MORGENTHALER
Member of Management
Director of Risk Control

32, Bahnhofstrasse
Zurich

Bank J. Vontobel and Vontobel Holding

Heinz FRAUCHIGER
Chief, Internal Audit Department

Tödistrasse 23
CH-8022 Zurich

Union Bank of Switzerland

Dr Heinrich STEINMANN
Member of the Executive Board (Retired)

Claridenstrasse
8021 Zurich

UNITED KINGDOM

Bank of England, and Financial Services Authority

Richard BRITTON
Director, Complex Groups Division, CGD Policy Department

Threadneedle Street
London EC2R 8AH

British Bankers Association

Paul CHISNALL
Assistant Director

Pinners Hall
105-108 Old Broad Street
London EC2N 1EX

Accounting Standards Board

A.V.C. COOK
Technical Director

Sandra THOMPSON
Project Director

Holborn Hall
100 Gray's Inn Road
London WC1X 8AL

Barclays Bank Plc

Brandon DAVIES
Treasurer, Global Corporate Banking

Alan BROWN
Director, Group Risk

54 Lombard Street
London EC3P 3AH

Abbey National Treasury Services plc

John HASSON
Director of Information Technology & Treasury Operations

Abbey House
215-229 Baker Street
London NW1 6XL

ABN-AMRO Investment Bank N.V.

David WOODS
Chief Operations Officer, Global Equity Directorate

199 Bishopsgate
London EC2M 3TY

Bankgesellschaft Berlin

Stephen F. MYERS
Head of Market Risk

1 Crown Court
Cheapside, London

Standard & Poor's

David T. BEERS
Managing Director, Sovereign Ratings

Garden House
18, Finsbury Circus
London EC2M 7BP

Moody's Investor Services

Samuel S. THEODORE
Managing Director, European Banks

David FROHRIEP
Communications Manager, Europe

2, Minster Court
Mincing Lane
London EC3R 7XB

Fitch IBCA

Charles PRESCOTT
Group Managing Director, Banks

David ANDREWS
Managing Director, Financial Institutions

Trevor PITMAN
Managing Director, Corporations

Richard FOX
Director, International Public Finance

Eldon House
2, Eldon Street
London EC2M 7UA

Merrill Lynch International

Erik BANKS
Managing Director of Risk Management

Ropemaker Place
London EC2Y 9LY

The Auditing Practices Board

Jonathan E.C. GRANT
Technical Director

Steve LEONARD
Internal Controls Project Manager

P.O. Box 433
Moorgate Place
London EC2P 2BJ

International Accounting Standards Committee

Ms Liesel KNORR
Technical Director

166 Fleet Street
London EC4A 2DY

MeesPierson ICS

Arjan P. VERKERK
Director, Market Risk

Camomile Court
23 Camomile Street
London EC3A 7PP

Charles Schwab

Dan HATTRUP
International Investment Specialist

Crosby Court
38 Bishopsgate
London EC2N 4AJ

City University Business School

Professor Elias DINENIS
Head, Department of Investment
Risk Management & Insurance

Prof. Dr John HAGNIOANNIDES
Department of Finance

Frobisher Crescent
Barbican Centre
London EC2Y 8BH

UNITED STATES

Federal Reserve System, Board of Governors

David L. ROBINSON
Deputy Director, Chief Federal Reserve Examiner

Alan H. OSTERHOLM, CIA, CISA
Manager, Financial Examinations Section

Paul W. BETTGE
Assistant Director, Division of Reserve Bank Operations

Gregory E. ELLER
Supervisory Financial Analyst, Banking

Gregory L. EVANS
Manager, Financial Accounting

Martha STALLARD
Financial Accounting, Reserve Bank Operations

20th and Constitution, NW
Washington, DC 20551

Federal Reserve Bank of Boston

William McDONOUGH
Executive Vice President

James T. NOLAN
Assistant Vice President

P.O. Box 2076
600 Atlantic Avenue
Boston, MA

Federal Reserve Bank of San Francisco

Nigel R. OGILVIE, CFA
Supervising Financial Analyst
Emerging Issues

101 Market Street
San Francisco, CA

Seattle Branch, Federal Reserve Bank of San Francisco

Jimmy F. KAMADA
Assistant Vice President

Gale P. ANSELL
Assistant Vice President, Business Development

1015, 2nd Avenue
Seattle, WA 98122-3567

Office of the Comptroller of the Currency (OCC)

Bill MORRIS
National Bank Examiner/Policy Analyst,
Core Policy Development Division

Gene GREEN
Deputy Chief Accountant
Office of the Chief Accountant

250 E Street, SW
7th Floor
Washington, DC

Federal Deposit Insurance Corporation (FDIC)

Curtis WONG
Capital Markets, Examination Support

Tanya SMITH
Examination Specialist, International Branch

Doris L. MARSH
Examination Specialist, Policy Branch

550 17th Street, NW
Washington, DC

Office of Thrift Supervision (OTS)

Timothy J. STIER
Chief Accountant

1700 G Street, NW
Washington, DC, 20552

Securities and Exchange Commission, Washington DC

Robert UHL
Professional Accounting Fellow

Pascal DESROCHES
Professional Accounting Fellow

John W. ALBERT
Associate Chief Accountant

Scott BAYLESS
Associate Chief Accountant

Office of the Chief Accountant
Securities and Exchange Commission
450 Fifth Street, NW
Washington, DC, 20549

Securities and Exchange Commission, New York

Robert A. SOLLAZZO
Associate Regional Director

7 World Trade Center
12th Floor
New York, NY 10048

Securities and Exchange Commission, Boston

Edward A. RYAN, Jr
Assistant District Administrator (Regulations)

Boston District Office
73 Tremont Street, 6th Floor
Boston, MA 02108-3912

International Monetary Fund

Alain COUNE
Assistant Director, Office of Internal Audit and Inspection

700 19th Street, NW
Washington DC, 20431

Financial Accounting Standards Board

Halsey G. BULLEN
Project Manager

Jeannot BLANCHET
Project Manager

Teri L. LIST
Practice Fellow

401 Merritt
Norwalk, CN 06856

Henry Kaufman & Company

Dr. Henry KAUFMAN

660 Madison Avenue
New York, NY

Soros Fund Management

George Soros
Chairman

888 Seventh Avenue, Suite 3300
New York, NY 10106

Carnegie Corporation of New York

Armanda FAMIGLIETTI
Associate Corporate Secretary, Director of Grants Management

437 Madison Avenue
New York, NY 10022

Alfred P. Sloan Foundation

Stewart F. CAMPBELL
Financial Vice President and Secretary

630 Fifth Avenue, Suite 2550
New York, NY 10111

Rockefeller Brothers Fund

Benjamin R. SHUTE, Jr
Secretary

437 Madison Avenue
New York, NY 10022-7001

The Foundation Center

79 Fifth Avenue
New York, NY 10003-4230

Citibank

Daniel SCHUTZER
Vice President, Director of Advanced Technology

909 Third Avenue
New York, NY 10022

Prudential-Bache Securities

Bella LOYKHTER
Senior Vice President, Information Technology

Kenneth MUSCO
First Vice President and Director,
Management Internal Control

Neil S. LERNER
Vice President, Management Internal Control

1 New York Plaza
New York, NY

Merrill Lynch

John J. FOSINA
Director, Planning and Analysis

Paul J. FITZSIMMONS
Senior Vice President, District Trust Manager

David E. RADCLIFFE
Senior Vice President, National Manager Philanthropic Consulting

Corporate and Institutional Client Group
World Financial Center, North Tower
New York, NY 10281-1316

HSBC Republic

Susan G. PEARCE
Senior Vice President

Philip A. SALAZAR
Executive Director

452 Fifth Avenue, Tower 6
New York, NY 10018

International Swaps and Derivatives Association (ISDA)

Susan HINKO
Director of Policy

600 Fifth Avenue, 27th Floor, Rockefeller Center
New York, NY 10020-2302

Standard & Poor's

Clifford GRIEP
Managing Director

25 Broadway
New York, NY 10004-1064

Mary PELOQUIN-DODD
Director, Public Finance Ratings

55 Water Street
New York, NY 10041-0003

Moody's Investor Services

Lea CARTY
Director, Corporates

99 Church Street
New York, NY 10022

State Street Bank and Trust

James J. BARR
Executive Vice President, U.S. Financial Assets Services

225 Franklin Street
Boston, MA 02105-1992

MBIA Insurance Corporation

John B. CAOUETTE
Vice Chairman

113 King Street
Armonk, NY 10504

Global Association of Risk Professionals (GARP)

Lev BORODOVSKI
Executive Director, GARP, and
Director of Risk Management, Credit Suisse First Boston (CSFB), New York

Yong LI
Director of Education, GARP, and
Vice President, Lehman Brothers, New York

Dr Frank LEIBER
Research Director, and
Assistant Director of Computational Finance,
Cornell University, Theory Center, New York

Roy NAWAL
Director of Risk Forums, GARP

980 Broadway, Suite 242
Thornwood, NY

Group of Thirty

John WALSH
Director

1990 M Street, NW
Suite 450
Washington, DC, 20036

Broadcom Corporation

Dr Henry SAMUELI
Co-Chairman of the Board, Chief Technical Officer

16215 Alton Parkway
PO Box 57013
Irvine, CA 92619-7013

Edward Jones

Ann FICKEN (Mrs)
Director, Internal Audit

201 Progress Parkway
Maryland Heights, MO 63043-3042

Teachers Insurance and Annuity Association/College Retirement Equities Fund (TIAA/CREF)

John W. SULLIVAN
Senior Institutional trust Consultant

Charles S. DVORKIN
Vice President and Chief Technology Officer

Harry D. PERRIN
Assistant Vice President, Information Technology

730 Third Avenue
New York, NY 10017-3206

Grenzebach Glier & Associates, Inc.

John J. GLIER
President and Chief Executive Officer

55 West Wacker Drive
Suite 1500
Chicago, IL 60601

Massachusetts Institute of Technology

Ms Peggy CARNEY
Administrator, Graduate Office

Michael COEN, PhD Candidate,
ARPA Intelligent Environment Project

Department of Electrical Engineering
and Computer Science
Building 38, Room 444
50 Vassar Street
Cambridge, MA, 02139

Henry Samueli School of Engineering and Applied Science, University of California, Los Angeles

Dean A.R. Frank WAZZAN
School of Engineering and Applied Science

Prof. Stephen E. JACOBSON
Dean of Student Affairs

Dr Les LACKMAN
Mechanical and Aerospace Engineering Department

Prof. Richard MUNTZ
Chair, Computer Science Department

Prof. Dr Leonard KLEINROCK
Telecommunications and Networks

Prof. CHIH-MING HO, PhD
Ben Rich- Lockheed Martin Professor
Mechanical and Aerospace Engineering Department

Dr GANG CHEN
Mechancial and Aerospace Engineering Department

Prof. Harold G. MONBOUQUETTE, PhD
Chemical Engineering Department

Prof. Jack W. JUDY
Electrical Engineering Department

Abeer ALWAN
Bioengineering

Prof. Greg POTTIE
Electrical Engineering Department

Prof. Lieven VANDENBERGHE
Electrical Engineering Department

Anderson Graduate School of Management, University of California, Los Angeles

Prof. John MAMER
Former Dean

Prof. Bruce MILLER

Roundtable Discussion on Engineering and Management Curriculum (2 October 2000)

Dr Henry BORENSTEIN, Honeywell

Dr F. ISSACCI, Honeywell

Dr Ray HAYNES, TRW

Dr Richard CROXALL, TRW

Dr Steven BOULEY, Boeing

Dr Derek CHEUNG, Rockwell

Westwood Village
Los Angeles, CA 90024

University of Maryland

Prof. Howard FRANK
Dean, The Robert H. Smith School of Business

Prof. Lemma W. SENBERT
Chair, Finance Department

Prof. Haluk UNAL
Associate Professor of Finance

Van Munching Hall
College Park, Maryland 20742-1815

Index